Edward Arber

The Shakespeare Anthology, 1592-1616 A.D

Edward Arber

The Shakespeare Anthology, 1592-1616 A.D

ISBN/EAN: 9783337055813

Printed in Europe, USA, Canada, Australia, Japan

Cover: Foto ©Thomas Meinert / pixelio.de

More available books at **www.hansebooks.com**

THE SHAKESPEARE ANTHOLOGY.

1592–1616 A.D.

EDITED BY

Professor EDWARD ARBER, F.S.A.,
FELLOW OF KING'S COLLEGE, LONDON, ETC.

'A thing of beauty is a joy for ever;
Its loveliness increases.'
KEATS.

LONDON:
HENRY FROWDE,
OXFORD UNIVERSITY PRESS WAREHOUSE, AMEN CORNER, E.C.
NEW YORK: 91 & 93 FIFTH AVENUE.
1899.

CONTENTS.

	PAGE
Anonymous Poems . . 24-26, 45-47, 81, 82, 102, 130-132, 162, 163, 179, 180, 192-195, 223-225, 252, 265, 286, 287	
ARMSTRONG (hanged, for the murder of Sir JOHN CARMICHAEL, in November 1600); THOMAS	188
BARNES (1569-1609); BARNABY	66-69
BARNFIELD (1574-1627); RICHARD	18-23
BEAUMONT (1584-1616); FRANCIS	196-208
BEAUMONT, and JOHN FLETCHER; FRANCIS . . .	205-208
BRETON (1545-1626); NICHOLAS	70-80
BROWNE (1591-1643); WILLIAM	276-282
CAMPION, M.D. (? -1619); THOMAS	229-251
CHALKHILL (c. 1600); JOHN	266, 267
CONSTABLE (1562-1613); HENRY	111-120
DANIEL (1562-1619); SAMUEL	95-101
DAVIES (1569-1626); Sir JOHN	27-38
DAVISON (c. 1602); FRANCIS	121-127
DAVISON (c. 1602); WALTER	128, 129
DECKER (1570-1641); THOMAS	189, 190
[? DELONEY (1543-1600); THOMAS]	108-110
DEVEREUX, Earl of ESSEX (1567-1601); ROBERT . .	84, 85
DRAYTON (1563-1631); MICHAEL	253-264
DRUMMOND, of Hawthornden (1585-1649); WILLIAM .	288-290
FLETCHER the Elder, LL.D. (1549-1611); GILES . .	39-41
FLETCHER the Younger, B.D. (1588-1623); GILES . .	291-294

Contents.

	PAGE
FLETCHER (1579-1625); JOHN	16, 205-213
HEYWOOD (? -1650); THOMAS	295-297
Ignoto.	135-146
JAMES I. (1566-1625); King	191
JONSON (1573-1637); BEN	214-222
LODGE, M.D. (1558-1625); THOMAS	86-92
MARLOW (1564-1593); CHRISTOPHER	133, 134
MURRAY (1567-1629); Sir DAVID.	226-228
RALEGH (1552-1618); Sir WALTER	147-161
ROWLANDS (1570-1630); SAMUEL	283-285
SHAKESPEARE (1564-1616); WILLIAM	1-17
Shepherd Tony [It has been thought that this is the pseudonym of some Poet; whose Christian name was ANTHONY.]	181-187
SMITH (c. 1596); WILLIAM	83
SOUTHWELL, S.J. (1561-1595); Rev. ROBERT	51-65
SPENSER (1552-1599); EDMUND	42-44
SUCKLING (1609-1642); Sir JOHN	17
SYLVESTER (1563-1618); JOSHUA	268-271
TOFTE (? -1620); ROBERT	93, 94
VERE, Earl of OXFORD (1540-1604); EDWARD DE	48-50
VERSTEGAN (? -1635); RICHARD	103-107
W.; A. (c. 1600)	168-178
WEBSTER (c. 1600-1630); JOHN	275
WITHER (1588-1667); GEORGE	272-275
WOOTTON (c. 1600); JOHN	164-167
WOTTON (1568-1639); Sir HENRY	298-300
FIRST LINES AND NOTES	301
GLOSSARY AND INDEX	307

THE SHAKESPEARE ANTHOLOGY.

1592–1616 A.D.

ARIEL'S SONG.

FULL fathom five thy father lies!
Of his bones are coral made;
Those are pearls, that were his eyes!
Nothing of him that doth fade;
But doth suffer a sea-change
Into something rich and strange!

Sea Nymphs hourly ring his knell!

BURTHEN.

Ding, dong!
Hark! now I hear them! Ding, dong, bell!

THE SPRING'S SONG.

When daisies pied, and violets blue,
   And lady-smocks all silver white,
And cuckoo-buds of yellow hue,
   Do paint the meadows with delight;
The Cuckoo then, on every tree,
Mocks married men: for thus sings he,
    'Cuckoo!
Cuckoo! Cuckoo!' O, word of fear!
Unpleasing to a married ear!

When Shepherds pipe on oaten straws,
   And merry larks are Ploughmen's clocks;
When turtles tread, and rooks, and daws;
   And maidens bleach their summer smocks:
The Cuckoo then, on every tree, &c.

THE WINTER'S SONG.

When icicles hang by the wall,
   And Dick the Shepherd blows his nail,
And Tom bears logs into the hall,
   And milk comes frozen home in pail;
When blood is nipped, and ways be foul;
Then nightly sings the staring Owl,
    'To-whit! To-who!'
    A merry note,
While greasy Joan doth keel the pot.

When all aloud the wind doth blow,
  And coughing drowns the Parson's saw;
And birds sit brooding in the snow,
  And MARIAN's nose looks red and raw;
When roasted crabs hiss in the bowl:
Then nightly sings the staring Owl, &c.

TELL me, Where is Fancy bred?
Or in the heart, or in the head?
How begot? How nourishèd?
    Reply! Reply!
It is engendered in the eye[s];
With gazing fed; and Fancy dies
In the cradle where it lies.

Let us all ring Fancy's knell!
I'll begin it!
        Ding, dong, bell!

ALL.   Ding, dong, bell!

WHERE the bee sucks, there suck I!
In a cowslip's bell I lie!
There I couch, when owls do cry!
On the bat's back, I do fly,
After summer, merrily!
Merrily, merrily, shall I live now,
Under the blossom that hangs on the bough!

William Shakespeare.

Let me not, to the marriage of true minds,
  Admit impediments! Love is not love,
Which alters, when it alteration finds;
  Or bends, with the remover to remove!
O, no! It is an ever fixèd mark,
  That looks on tempests, and is never shaken.
It is the star to every wand'ring bark;   [taken.
  Whose worth 's unknown, although his height be
Love 's not Time's fool! though rosy lips and cheeks
  Within his bending sickle's compass come.
Love alters not, with his brief hours and weeks;
  But bears it out, even to the edge of Doom!
    If this be error, and upon me proved;
    I never writ, nor no man ever loved!

Betwixt mine Eye and Heart, a league is took;
  And each doth good turns now unto the other.
When that mine Eye is famished for a look;
  Or Heart in love, with sighs himself doth smother:
With my Love's picture, then my Eye doth feast;
  And to the painted banquet bids my Heart.
Another time mine Eye is my Heart's guest;
  And in his thoughts of love doth share a part.
So, either by thy picture, or my love,
  Thyself, away, art present still with me!
For thou, nor farther than my thoughts canst move:
  And I am still with them; and they, with thee!
    Or if they sleep, thy picture in my sight
    Awakes my Heart! to Heart's and Eye's delight.

William Shakespeare.

THE THREE CASKETS.
[' The Merchant of Venice.']

The Gold Casket.

The Inscription outside.

Who chooseth me, shall gain what many men desire.

The Scroll inside.

All that glisters is not gold,
Often have you heard that told!
Many a man, his life hath sold
But my outside to behold!
Gilded timber do worms infold!
 Had you been as wise as bold,
Young in limbs, in judgement old;
Your answer had not been inscrolled,
Fare you well! Your suit is cold!

The Silver Casket.

The Inscription outside.

Who chooseth me, shall get as much as he deserves.

The Scroll inside.

The fire seven times tried this!
Seven times tried, that judgement is,

That did never choose amiss!
Some there be that shadows kiss;
Such have but a shadow's bliss!
There be fools alive iwis,
Silvered o'er; and so was this!
   Take what wife you will, to bed;
I will ever be your head!
So begone! You are sped!

The Lead Casket.

The Inscription outside.

Who chooseth me, must give and hazard all he

The Scroll inside.

You that choose not by the view,
Chance as fair, and choose as true!
Since this fortune falls to you;
Be content, and seek no new!
   If you be well pleased with this,
And hold your fortune for your bliss;
*Turn you, where your Lady is;
And claim her, with a loving kiss!*

GUIDERIUS. Fear no more the heat o' th' sun;
  Nor the furious winter's rages!
Thou, thy worldly task hast done;
  Home art gone, and ta'en thy wages!
    Golden Lads and Girls, all must,
    As Chimney-sweepers, come to dust!

ARVIRAGUS. Fear no more the frown o' th' Great!
  Thou art past the tyrant's stroke!
Care no more to clothe and eat!
  To thee, the reed is as the oak!
    The Sceptre, Learning, Physic must
    All follow this; and come to dust!

GUID. Fear no more the lightning flash!
ARVI.   Nor th' all-dreadèd thunderstone!
GUID. Fear not slander, censure rash!
ARVI.   Thou hast finished joy and moan!
BOTH.   All Lovers young, all Lovers must
    Consign to thee; and come to dust!

GUID.   No exorciser harm thee!
ARVI.   Nor no witchcraft charm thee!
GUID.   Ghost unlaid, forbear thee!
ARVI.   Nothing ill come near thee!
BOTH.   Quiet consummation have;
    And renownèd be thy grave!

William Shakespeare.

My love is strengthened, though more weak in seeming.
 I love not less; though less the show appear.
That love is merchandised! whose rich esteeming,
 The owner's tongue doth publish everywhere.
Our love was new, and then but in the Spring;
 When I was wont to greet it with my Lays:
As Philomel, in summer's front doth sing;
 And stops her pipe, in growth of riper days.
Not that the summer is less pleasant now,
 Than when her mournful hymns did hush the night:
But that wild music burthens every bough;
 And sweets grown common, lose their dear delight.
  Therefore, like her, I some time hold my tongue;
  Because I would not dull you with my Song!

The forward Violet thus did I chide,   [smells,
 'Sweet thief! whence didst thou steal thy sweet that
If not from my Love's breath? The purple pride
 Which on thy soft cheek for complexion dwells,
In my Love's veins, thou hast too grossly dyed!'
 The Lily, I condemnèd for thy hand;
And buds of Marjoram had stolen thy hair!
 The Roses fearfully on thorns did stand;
One blushing shame; another, white despair!
 A third, nor red, nor white, had stolen of both;
And to his robb'ry had annexed thy breath!
 But for his theft, in pride of all his growth,
A vengeful canker eat him up to death!
  More flowers I noted; yet I none could see,
  But, sweet, or colour, it had stolen from thee!

William Shakespeare.

Hark! Hark! The lark at heaven's gate sings!
    And Phœbus 'gins arise,
His steeds to water at those springs;
    On chaliced flowers that lies.
And winking mary-buds begin to ope their golden eyes;
With every thing that pretty is! My Lady sweet, arise!
    Arise! arise!

    How should I, your True Love know
        From another one?
    By his cockle hat and staff;
        And his sendall shoen.

He is dead and gone, Lady!
    He is dead and gone!
At his head, a grass-green turf;
    At his heels, a stone.

White his shroud as the mountain snow,
    Larded with all sweet flowers;
Which bewept, to the ground did not go
    With[out] true-love showers.

    Jog on! jog on the foot-path way;
        And merrily hent the stile a!
    A merry heart goes all the day;
        Your sad, tires in a mile a!

Who is S*ilvia*? *What is she,*
  That all our Swains commend her?
Holy, fair, and wise is she!
  The heaven, such grace did lend her;
That she might admirèd be.

Is she kind, as she is fair?
  For beauty lives with kindness!
Love doth to her eyes repair,
  To help him of his blindness;
And, being helped, inhabits there!

Then to Silvia, let us sing,
  'That Silvia is excelling!'
She excels each mortal thing,
  Upon the dull earth dwelling!
To her, let us garlands bring!

THE FAIRIES' SONG.

You spotted snakes with double tongue,
  Thorny hedgehogs, be not seen!
Newts, and blind-worms, do no wrong!
  Come not near our Fairy Queen!
    Philomel, with melody,
    Sing, in [y]our sweet lullaby,
' Lulla, lulla, lullaby! Lulla, lulla, lullaby!
    Never harm,
    Nor spell, nor charm,
  Come our lovely Lady nigh!
  So, good night! with lullaby.'

William Shakespeare.

1st Fairy. Weaving spiders, come not here!
    Hence, you long-legged spinners, hence!
    Beetles black, approach not near!
    Worm, nor snail, do no offence!
    Philomel, with melody, &c.

2nd Fairy. Hence, away! Now, all is well!
    One aloof, stand sentinel!

    Sigh no more, Ladies! sigh no more!
      Men were deceivers ever!
    One foot in sea, and one on shore;
      To one thing constant never!
        Then, sigh not so!
        But let them go;
    And be you blithe and bonny!
    Converting all your sounds of woe
      Into 'Hey nonny, nonny!'

    Sing no more Ditties! Sing no mo,
      Of dumps so dull and heavy!
    The fraud of men was ever so,
      Since summer first was leavy!
        Then, sigh not so! &c.

William Shakespeare.

That time of year, thou mayst in me behold,
  When yellow leaves, or none, or few, do hang
Upon those boughs, which shake against the cold;
  Bare ruined Quires! where, late, the sweet birds sang.
In me, thou seest the twilight of such day
  As, after sunset, fadeth in the West;
Which, by-and-by, black Night doth take away;
  Death's second self, that seals up all in rest!
In me, thou seest the glowing of such fire,
  That on the ashes of his youth doth lie,
As the death-bed whereon it must expire;
  Consumed with that, which it was nourished by.
    This, thou perceiv'st! which makes thy love more strong
    To love that well, which thou must leave ere long.

Not marble, nor the gilded monument
  Of Princes, shall outlive this powerful rhyme!
But you shall shine more bright in these contents,
  Than unswept stone, besmeared with sluttish Time.
When wasteful war shall statues overturn;
  And broils root out the work of masonry;
Nor Mars his sword, nor war's quick fire, shall burn
  The living record of your memory!
'Gainst death, and all oblivious enmity;
  Shall you pace forth! Your praise shall still find room!
Even in the eyes of all posterity
  That wear this world out, to the ending Doom.
    So till the Judgement that yourself arise,
    You live in this; and dwell in Lovers' eyes!

William Shakespeare.

Come unto these yellow sands;
  And then take hands!
Courtesied when you have, and kist
  The wild waves whist;
Foot it featly here and there;
  And, sweet Sprites, hear
    The Burthen.

Burthen, dispersedly.

Hark! Hark! bow-wow!
The watch-dogs bark! bow-wow!

Hark! Hark! I hear
The strain of strutting Chanticleer
Cry, 'Cock-a-doodle do!'

O, Mistress mine, where are you roaming?
O, stay, and hear! Your True Love's coming;
  That can sing both high and low.
    Trip no further, pretty Sweeting!
    Journeys end in Lovers' meeting,
  Every wise man's son doth know!

What is Love? 'Tis not hereafter!
Present mirth hath present laughter;
  What's to come is still unsure!
    In delay, there lies no plenty!
    Then come, kiss me, sweet and twenty!
  Youth's a stuff will not endure!

UNDER the greenwood tree,
Who loves to lie with me;
And turn his merry note
Unto the sweet bird's throat;
Come hither! Come hither! Come hither!
  Here shall he see
  No enemy
But winter and rough weather!

Who doth ambition shun,
And loves to live i' th' sun;
Seeking the food he eats,
And pleased with what he gets;
Come hither! Come hither! Come hither! &c.

ORPHEUS, with his lute, made trees,
And the mountain tops that freeze,
 Bow themselves, when he did sing!
  To his music, plants and flowers
  Ever sprang! as sun and showers
There had made a lasting Spring.

Every thing that heard him play,
Even the billows of the sea,
 Hung their heads; and then lay by!
  In sweet Music is such art,
  Killing care and grief of heart.
 Fall asleep! or, hearing, die!

William Shakespeare.

      Blow, blow, thou winter wind!
      Thou art not so unkind
      As Man's ingratitude!
        Thy tooth is not so keen;
        Because thou art not seen,
      Although thy breath be rude.
Heigh ho! Sing, Heigh ho! unto the green holly!
Most friendship is feigning! most loving, mere folly!
      The[n], Heigh ho! the holly!
      This life is most jolly!

      Freeze, freeze, thou bitter sky!
      That dost not bite so nigh
      As benefits forgot!
        Though thou the waters warp;
        Thy sting is not so sharp
      As friend remembered not!
Heigh ho! Sing, Heigh ho! unto the green holly! &c.

      Come away, come away, death!
        And in sad cypress let me be laid.
      Fly away, fly away, breath!
        I am slain by a fair cruel Maid.
      My shroud of white, stuck all with yew,
          O, prepare it!
      My part of death, no one so true
          Did share it!

Not a flower, not a flower sweet
  On my black coffin, let there be strown!
Not a friend, not a friend greet
  My poor corse! where my bones shall be thrown.
A thousand thousand sighs to save,
      Lay me, O, where
Sad True Lover never find my grave,
      To weep there!

Take, O, take those lips away,
  That so sweetly were forsworn!
And those eyes, the break of day;
  Lights that do mislead the Morn!
    But my kisses bring again! bring again!
    Seals of love; but sealed in vain! sealed in vain!

JOHN FLETCHER.

[He inserted the above stanza in *The Bloody Brother*; and then added the following one. Both are thought to be translations from the Latin of CAIUS CORNELIUS GALLUS.—E. A.]

  Hide, O, hide those hills of snow;
    Which thy frozen bosom bears!
  On whose tops, the pinks that grow,
    Are of those that April wears.
      But first set my poor heart free!
      Bound in those icy chains by thee.

Shakespeare and Suckling.

VERSES BY SHAKESPEARE, COMPLETED BY SUCKLING.

ONE of her hands one of her cheeks lay under,
 Cozening the pillow of a lawful kiss :
Which therefore swelled, and seemed to part asunder;
 As angry to be robbed of such a bliss.
  The one looked pale, and for revenge did long;
  While t'other blushed, 'cause it had done the wrong.

Out of the bed, the other fair hand was
 On a green satin quilt : whose perfect white
Looked like a daisy in a field of grass;
 And shewed like unmelt snow unto the sight*.
There lay this pretty perdue, safe to keep   **Thus far SHAKESPEARE.*
The rest o' th' body, that lay fast asleep.

Her eyes (and therefore it was night!) close laid,
 Strove to imprison Beauty till the morn :
But yet the doors were of such fine stuff made,
 That it broke through, and shewed itself in scorn;
  Throwing a kind of light about the place,
  Which turned to smiles still as 't came near her face.

Her beams (which some dull men called hair!) divided;
 Part with her cheeks, part with her lips, did sport :
But these, as rude, her breath put by still. Some
 Wiselier downwards sought : but falling short,
  Curled back in rings; and seemed to turn again
  To bite the part so unkindly held them in.

THE UNKNOWN SHEPHERD'S COMPLAINT.

My flocks feed not! My ewes breed not!
  My rams speed not! All is amiss!
Love is denying! Faith is defying!
  Hearts renying, causer of this!
All my merry jigs are quite forgot!
All my Lady's love is lost, God wot!
Where her faith was firmly fixed in love;
There a 'Nay!' is placed, without remove.
    One silly cross wrought all my loss!
      O, frowning FORTUNE! cursèd fickle Dame!
    For now I see, inconstancy
      More in women than in men remain!

In black, mourn I! All fears scorn I!
  Love hath forlorn me, living in thrall!
Heart is bleeding, all help needing!
  O, cruel speeding, fraughted with gall!
My shepherd's pipe can sound no deal!
My wether's bell rings doleful knell!
My curtail dog, that wont to have played
Plays not at all! but seems afraid.
    With sighs so deep, procures to weep
      In howling wise, to see my doleful plight.
    How sighs resound, through heartless ground,
      Like a thousand vanquished men in bloody fight.

Clear wells spring not! Sweet birds sing not!
  Green plants bring not forth their dye!
Herds stand weeping! Flocks all sleeping!
  Nymphs back peeping fearfully!
All our pleasure known to us poor Swains,
All our merry meeting on the plains,
All our evening sports, from us are fled!
All our love is lost; for love is dead!
    Farewell, sweet Love! thy like ne'er was
      For sweet content! the cause of all my moan.
    Poor CORIDON must live alone!
      Other help for him, I see that there is none!

      As it feil upon a day
  In the merry month of May,
  Sitting in a pleasant shade,
  Which a grove of myrtles made,
  Beasts did leap, and birds did sing;
  Trees did grow, and plants did spring.
  Every thing did banish moan,
  Save the nightingale alone.

      She, poor bird, as all forlorn,
  Leaned her breast up-till a thorn,
  And there sung the dolefull'st Ditty,
  That to hear, it was great pity!
  'Fie! Fie! Fie!' now would she cry,
  'Teru! Teru!' by-and-by.
  That to hear her so complain,

Scarce I could from tears refrain:
For her griefs, so lively shown,
Made me think upon my own.

   'Ah,' thought I, 'thou mourn'st in vain!
None takes pity on thy pain!
Senseless trees, they cannot hear thee!
Ruthless bears, they will not cheer thee!
King PANDION, he is dead!
All thy friends are lapped in lead!
All thy fellow birds do sing,
Careless of thy sorrowing!
Whilst, as fickle FORTUNE smiled,
Thou and I were both beguiled.
   'Every one that flatters thee,
Is no friend in misery.
Words are easy, like the wind:
Faithful friends are hard to find!
Every man will be thy friend,
Whilst thou hast wherewith to spend;
But if store of crowns be scant,
No man will supply thy want!

   'If that one be prodigal,
"Bountiful!" they will him call;
And with suchlike flattering,
"Pity but he were a King!"
If he be addict to vice;
Quickly him they will intice!
If to women he be bent;

They have, at commandment!
But if FORTUNE once do frown,
Then, farewell, his great renown!
They that fawned on him before,
Use his company no more!

'He that is thy friend indeed,
He will help thee in thy need!
If thou sorrow, he will weep!
If thou wake, he cannot sleep!
Thus, of every grief in heart,
He, with thee, doth bear a part!

'These are certain signs, to know
Faithful friend from flatt'ring foe.'

IN PRAISE OF MUSIC AND POETRY.

IF Music and sweet Poetry agree,
    As they must needs, the Sister and the Brother!
Then must the love be great 'twixt thee and me,
    Because thou lov'st the one; and I, the other.
DOWLAND to thee is dear! whose heavenly touch
    Upon the lute doth ravish human sense;
SPENSER, to me! whose deep conceit is such
    As, passing all conceit, needs no defence.
Thou lov'st to hear the sweet melodious sound
    That PHŒBUS' lute, the Queen of Music, makes!
And I, in deep delight am chiefly drowned,
    When as himself, to singing he betakes!
One God is God of both, as Poets feign:
One Knight loves both; and both in thee remain!

Richard Barnfield.

AGAINST THE DISPRAISERS
OF POETRY.

CHAUCER is dead; and GOWER lies in grave!
  The Earl of SURREY, long ago, is gone!
Sir PHILIP SIDNEY's soul, the heavens have!
  GEORGE GASCOIGNE, him beforne, was tombed in stone!
Yet though their bodies lie full low in ground,
  As every thing must die, that erst was born;
Their living fame, no fortune can confound!
  Nor ever shall their labours be forlorn!
And you, that discommend sweet Poetry,
  So that the subject of the same be good,
Here, may you see your fond simplicity!
  Sith Kings have favoured it, of royal blood.
The King of Scots, now living, is a Poet;
As his *Lepanto* and his *Furies* show it!

Richard Barnfield.

A REMEMBRANCE OF SOME ENGLISH POETS.

LIVE, SPENSER, ever in thy *Fairy Queen*;
Whose like, for deep conceit, was never seen!
Crowned mayst thou be, unto thy more renown,
As King of Poets, with a laurel crown!

And DANIEL, praisèd for thy sweet-chaste Verse,
Whose fame is graved on *ROSAMOND*'s black hearse,
Still mayst thou live! and still be honourèd
For that rare Work, *The White Rose and the Red.*

And DRAYTON, whose well-written Tragedies
And sweet *Epistles* soar thy fame to skies!
Thy learnèd name is equal with the rest;
Whose stately Numbers are so well addrest.

And SHAKESPEARE, thou, whose honey-flowing vein,
Pleasing the World, thy praises doth obtain;
Whose *VENUS*, and whose *LUCRECE* sweet and chaste,
Thy name in Fame's immortal book have placed.
   Live ever you! at least, in fame live ever!
   Well may the body die; but fame dies never!

Anonymous.

'SIR PAINTER! Are thy colours ready set?
  My Mistress cannot be with thee to-day;
  She's gone into the field, to gather May,
The timely Primrose, and the Violet!
    Yet, that thou mayst not disappointed be;
    Come, draw her picture by my fantasy!

'And well for thee! to paint her by thine ear:
  For should thine eye unto that office serve,
  Thine eye and hand, thy art and heart, would swerve!
Such majesty her countenance doth bear.
    And where thou wert APELLES thought before;
    For failing so, thou shouldst be praised no more!

'Draw first her Front! a perfect ivory white,
  High, spacious, round, and smooth; on either side,
  Her Temples, branched with veins blue, opening wide,
As in the map, Danubius runs in sight.
    Colour her semicircled Brows with jet!
    The throne where LOVE triumphantly doth sit.

'Regard her Eye! Her Eye, a wondrous part!
  It woundeth deep; and cureth by-and-by!
  It drives away; and draweth courteously!
It breeds, and calms, the tempest of the heart!
    And what to lightning JOVE belongeth to;
    The same, her looks, with more effect can do!

'Her Cheek resembleth, every kind of way,
   The lily stained with sweet Adonis' blood,
   As wounded, he strayed up and down the wood:
For whom fair Venus languished many a day!
   Or, plainly, more to answer your demand,
   Her Cheeks are roses overcast with lawn!

'Her lovely Lip doth others' all excel!
   On whom it please (ay me!) a kiss bestow;
   He never tasteth afterward of woe!
Such special virtue in the touch doth dwell.
   The colour, tempered of the morning red,
   Wherewith Aurora doth adorn her head.

'Her ample Chest, a heavenly plot of ground!
   The space between, a Paradise at least!
   Parnassus-like, her twifold mounting breast!
Her heavenly graces heapingly abound!
   Love spreads his conquering Colours in this Field;
   Whereto the race of Gods and men do yield....

'Before her Feet, upon a marble stone,
   Inflamèd with the sunbeams of her eye,
   Depaint my heart, that burneth passionately!
And if thy pencil can set down such moan
   Thy picture's self will feeling semblance make
   Of ruth and pity, for my torments' sake.

Anonymous.

'How now, APELLES! Are thy senses ta'en?
　Hast drawn a picture; or drawn out thy heart?
　Wilt thou be held a Master of thine art;
And temper colours tending to thy bane?
　　Happy my heart! that in her sunshine fries,
　　Above thy hap; that in her shadow dies!'

My Thoughts are winged with Hopes; my Hopes,
　　with Love!
　Mount, Love, unto the moon, in clearest night!
And say, 'As she doth in the heavens move,
　On earth so wanes, and waxeth, my delight!'
　　And whisper this, but softly, in her ears,
　　'Hope oft doth hang the head; and Trust, shed
　　　tears!'

And you, my Thoughts, that some mistrust do carry,
　If, for mistrust, my Mistress do you blame;
Say, 'Though you alter; yet you do not vary!
　As She doth change, and yet remain the same.
　　Distrust doth enter hearts, but not infect;
　　And love is sweetest, seasoned with suspect!'

If She, for this, with clouds do mask her eyes;
　And make the heavens dark with her disdain:
With windy sighs, disperse them in the skies!
　Or with thy tears, dissolve them into rain!
　　Thoughts, Hopes, and Love, return to me no more!
　　Till CYNTHIA shine, as she hath done before.

Sir John Davies.

A CONTENTION BETWIXT A WIFE, A WIDOW, AND A MAID.

WIFE. WIDOW, well met! Whither go you, to-day?
    Will you not to this solemn offering go?
You know it is ASTREA's Holy Day!
    The Saint to whom all hearts devotion owe.

WIDOW. Marry, what else! I purposed so to do.
    Do you not mark, how all the Wives are fine!
And how they have sent presents ready too,
    To make their offering at ASTREA's shrine!

See, then, the shrine; and tapers burning bright!
    Come, friend! and let us first ourselves advance!
We know our place! and (if we have our right)
    To all the parish we must lead the dance!

But, soft! what means this bold presumptuous Maid
    To go before! without respect of us!
Your forwardness, proud Maid! must now be stayed!
    Where learned you to neglect your betters thus?

MAID. Elder you are; but not my betters here!
    This place, to Maids a privilege must give!
The Goddess, being a Maid, holds Maidens dear;
    And grants to them her own prerogative.

Besides, on all true Virgins, at their birth,
    Nature hath sent a crown of excellence;
That all the Wives and Widows of the earth
    Should give them place, and do them reverence!

Sir John Davies.

Wife. If to be born a Maid be such a grace,
    So was I born, and graced by Nature too!
But seeking more perfection to embrace,
    I did become a Wife! as others do.

Widow. And if the Maid and Wife such honour have,
    I have been both, and hold a third degree!
Most Maids are Wards; and every Wife, a slave!
    I have my 'livery sued'; and I am free!

Maid. That is the fault! That you have Maidens been;
    And were not constant to continue so!
The fall of Angels did increase their sin,
    In that they did so pure a state forego.

But, Wife! and Widow! if your wits can make
    Your state and persons of more worth than mine;
Advantage to this place I will not take!
    I will both place and privilege resign!

Wife.   Why, Marriage is an honourable state!
Widow.   And Widowhood is a reverend degree!
Maid.   But Maidenhead, that will admit no mate,
    Like Majesty itself, must sacred be!

Wife.   The Wife is mistress of her family
Widow.   Much more the Widow! for she rules alone.
Maid.   But mistress of mine own desires am I!
    When you rule others' wills, and not your own!

Wife.   Only the Wife enjoys the virtuous pleasure!
Widow.   The Widow can abstain from pleasures known!
Maid.   But th' uncorrupted Maid preserves such measure,
    As, being by pleasures wooed, she cares for none!

Sir John Davies.

WIFE. The Wife is like a fair supported vine!
WIDOW. So was the Widow; but now stands alone:
    For, being grown strong, she needs not to incline!
MAID. Maids, like the Earth, supported are of none!

WIFE. The Wife is as a diamond richly set!
MAID. The Maid, unset, doth yet more rich appear!
WIDOW. The Widow, a jewel in the cabinet!
    Which, though not worn, is still esteemed as dear.

WIFE. The Wife doth love; and is beloved again!
WIDOW. The Widow is awaked out of that dream!
MAID. The Maid's white mind had never such a stain!
    No Passion troubles her clear virtues' stream.

    Yet if I would be loved; loved would I be
    Like her, whose virtue in the bay is seen!
    Love to Wife fades with satiety;
    Where love, never enjoyed, is ever green!

WIDOW. Then what's a Virgin, but a fruitless bay!
MAID. And what's a Widow, but a rose-less briar!
    And what are Wives, but woodbinds! which decay
    The stately oaks, by which themselves aspire!

    And what is Marriage, but a tedious yoke!
WIDOW. And what Virginity, but sweet self-love!
WIFE. And what's a Widow, but an axle broke;
    Whose one part failing, neither part can move!

WIDOW. Wives are as birds, in golden cages kept!
WIFE. Yet in those cages cheerfully they sing!
WIDOW. Widows are birds, out of those cages leapt,
    Whose joyful notes make all the forest ring.

Sir John Davies.

Maid. But Maids are birds, amidst the woods secure!
   Which never hand could touch; nor net could take;
   Nor whistle could deceive; nor bait allure:
   But free, unto themselves do music make!

Wife. The Wife is as the turtle with her mate!
Widow. The Widow, as the widow dove alone;
   Whose truth shines most in her forsaken state!
Maid. The Maid, a Phœnix; and is still but one!

Wife. The Wife's a soul, unto her body tied!
Widow. The Widow, a soul departed into bliss!
Maid. The Maid, an Angel, which was stellified;
   And now t' as fair a House descended is!

Wife. Wives are fair Houses, kept and furnished well!
Widow. Widows, old Castles, void, but full of State!
Maid. But Maids are Temples, where the Gods do dwell!
   To whom alone, themselves they dedicate.

   But marriage is a Prison during life;
   Where one way out, but many entries be!
Wife. The Nun is kept in cloister; not the Wife!
   Wedlock alone doth make the Virgin free!

Maid. The Maid is ever fresh, like Morn in May!
Wife. The Wife, with all her beams is beautified,
   Like to high Noon, the glory of the day!
Widow. The Widow, like a mild sweet Eventide!

Wife. An Office well supplied is like the Wife!
Widow. The Widow, like a gainful Office void!
Maid. But Maids are like contentment in this life;
   Which all the World have sought, but none enjoyed!

Sir John Davies.

	Go, Wife! to Dunmow; and demand your Flitch!
WIDOW.	Go, gentle Maid! go, lead thee apes in hell!
WIFE.	Go, Widow! make some younger brother rich;
	And then take thought, and die: and all is well!

	Alas, poor Maid! that hast no help, nor stay!
WIDOW.	Alas, poor Wife! that nothing dost possess!
MAID.	Alas, poor Widow! Charity doth say,
	'Pity the Widow and the fatherless!'

WIDOW.	But happy Widows have the World at will!
WIFE.	But happier Wives! whose joys are ever double!
MAID.	But happiest Maids! whose hearts are calm and still;
	Whom fear, nor hope, nor love, nor hate, doth trouble!

WIFE.	Every true Wife hath an indented heart,
	Wherein the Covenants of Love are writ;
	Whereof her husband keeps the Counterpart,
	And reads his comforts and his joys in it.

WIDOW.	But every Widow's heart is like a Book;
	Where her joys past, imprinted do remain:
	But when her judgement's eye therein doth look,
	She doth not wish they were to come again!

MAID.	But the Maid's heart, a fair white Table is,
	Spotless and pure; where no impressions be
	But the immortal characters of bliss;
	Which only GOD doth write, and Angels see.

WIFE.	But Wives have children. What a joy is this!
WIDOW.	Widows have children too! But Maids have none!
MAID.	No more have Angels! Yet they have more bliss
	Than ever yet to mortal man was known!

Sir John Davies.

WIFE. The Wife is like a fair manurèd field!
WIDOW. The Widow once was such; but now doth rest!
MAID. The Maid, like Paradise, undressed, untilled,
        Bears crops of native virtue in her breast!

WIFE. Who would not die a Wife, as LUCRECE died!
WIDOW. Or live a Widow, as PENELOPE!
MAID. Or be a Maid, and so be stellified;
        As all the Virtues, and the Graces, be!

WIFE. Wives are warm climates well inhabited:
        But Maids are frozen zones, where none may dwell!
MAID. But fairest people in the North are bred;
        Where Africa breeds monsters black as hell!

WIFE. I have my husband's honour and his place!
WIDOW. My husband's fortunes all survive to me!
MAID. The moon doth borrow light! You borrow grace;
        When Maids, by their own virtues gracèd be!

        White is my colour! and no hue but this
        It will receive. No tincture can it stain!
WIFE. My white hath took one colour; but it is
        An honourable purple dyed in grain.

WIDOW. But it hath been my fortune to renew
        My colour twice, from that it was before:
        But now my black will take no other hue;
        And therefore now I mean to change no more!

WIFE. Wives are fair apples, served in golden dishes!
WIDOW. Widows, good wine! which time makes better much.
MAID. But Maids are grapes, desired by many wishes!
        But that they grow so high as none can touch.

Sir John Davies.

Wife. I have a daughter equals you, my Girl!
Maid. The daughter doth excel the mother, then,
   As pearls are better than the mother of pearl!
   Maids lose their value, when they match with men!

Widow. The man with whom I matched, his worth was such,
   As now I scorn a Maid should be my peer!
Maid. But I will scorn the man you praise so much!
   For Maids are matchless! and no mate can bear.

   Hence is it that the Virgin never loves;
   Because her like, she finds not anywhere!
   For likeness evermore affection moves:
   Therefore the Maid hath neither Love, nor peer!

Wife. Yet many Virgins, married Wives would be!
Widow. And many a Wife would, be a Widow fain!
Maid. There is no Widow but desires to see
   (If so she might!) her maiden days again!

Widow. There never was a Wife that liked her lot!
Wife. Nor Widow, but was clad in mourning weeds!
Maid. Do what you will! marry, or marry not!
   Both this estate, and that, repentance breeds!

Wife. But she that this estate, and that, hath seen,
   Doth find great odds between the Wife and Girl!
Maid. Indeed she doth! as much as is between
   The melting hailstone and the solid pearl!

Wife. If I were Widow, my merry days were past!
Widow. Nay! then you first become sweet Pleasure's guest!
   For Maidenhead is a continual fast!
Wife. And Marriage is a continual feast!

MAID. Wedlock indeed hath oft comparèd been
         To Public Feasts, where meet a public rout:
       Where they that are without, would fain go in;
         And they that are within, would fain go out!

       Or to the jewel, which this virtue had:
         That men were mad till they might it obtain;
       But when they had it, they were twice as mad,
         Till they were dispossessed of it again!

WIFE. Maids cannot judge! because they cannot tell
         What comforts and what joys in marriage be!
MAID. Yes! Yes! Though blessed Saints in Heaven do dwell;
         They do the souls in Purgatory see!

WIFE. If every Wife do live in Purgatory,
         Then sure it is that Widows live in bliss;
       And are translated to a state of glory!
         But Maids, as yet, have not attained to this!

MAID. Not Maids! To spotless Maids this gift is given,
         To live in incorruption from their birth;
       And what is that, but to inherit Heaven!
         Even while they dwell upon the spotted Earth:

       The perfectest of all created things;
         The purest gold, that suffers no allay;
       The sweetest flower that on th' earth's bosom springs;
         The pearl unbored, whose price no price can pay;

       The crystal glass, that will no venom hold;
         The mirror, wherein Angels love to look;
       DIANA's bathing fountain, clear and cold;
         Beauty's fresh rose; and Virtue's living book.

Sir John Davies.

Of Love and Fortune both, the Mistress born;
    The sovereign spirit, that will thrall to none;
The spotless garment, that was never worn;
    The princely eagle, that still flies alone.

She sees the World; yet her clear thought doth take
    No such deep print as to be changed thereby:
As when we see the burning fire doth make
    No such impression as doth burn the eye.

Wife.   No more, sweet Maid! Our strife is at an end!
    Cease now! I fear we shall transformèd be
To chattering pies! as they that did contend
    To match the Muses in their harmony!

Widow.   Then let us yield the honour, and the place;
    And let us both be suitors to the Maid!
That, since the Goddess gives her special grace,
    By her clear hands the off'ring be conveyed!

Maid.   Your speech, I doubt, hath some displeasure moved;
    Yet let me have the offering, I will see!
I know She hath both Wives and Widows loved;
    Though She would neither Wife nor Widow be!

Sir John Davies.

YET OTHER TWELVE WONDERS OF THE WORLD.

I. THE COURTIER.

LONG have I lived in Court: yet learned not, all this while,
To sell poor Suitors smoke! nor where I hate, to smile!
Superiors to adore; Inferiors to despise!
To fly from such as fall; to follow such as rise!
To cloak a poor desire under a rich array!
Not to aspire by vice! though 'twere the quicker way.

II. THE DIVINE.

My Calling is divine; and I from GOD am sent.
I will no chop-church be; nor pay my Patron rent!
Nor yield to sacrilege! but, like the kind true mother,
Rather will lose all the child, than part it with another!
Much wealth I will not seek! nor worldly masters serve;
So to grow rich and fat, while my poor flock doth starve.

III. THE SOLDIER.

My Occupation is the noble trade of Kings!
The trial that decides the highest right of things!
Though MARS my master be, I do not VENUS love;
Nor honour BACCHUS oft; nor often swear by JOVE!
Of speaking of myself, I all occasion shun;
And rather love to do, than boast what I have done.

IV. THE LAWYER.

The Law my Calling is! My robe, my tongue, my pen,
Wealth and Opinion gain; and make me judge of men.
The known dishonest Cause, I never did defend!
Nor span out Suits in length: but wished and sought an end.

Nor counsel did bewray; nor of both parties take;
Nor ever took I fee, for which I never spake.

V. THE PHYSICIAN.

I study to uphold the slippery state of Man;
Who dies, when we have done the best, and all, we can!
From practice, and from books, I draw my learnèd skill;
Not from the known receipt of 'Pothecary's bill.
The earth, my faults doth hide! The World, my cures doth see!
What Youth and Time effect is oft ascribed to me.

VI. THE MERCHANT.

My trade doth every thing to every land supply,
Discover unknown coasts, strange countries doth ally.
I never did forestall! I never did ingross!
Nor custom did withdraw; though I returned with loss!
I thrive by fair exchange, by selling and by buying;
And not by Jewish use, reprisal, fraud, or lying!

VII. THE COUNTRY GENTLEMAN.

Though strange outlandish spirits praise towns, and country scorn,
The country is my home! I dwell where I was born!
There profit and command, with pleasure I partake;
Yet do not hawks and dogs, my sole companions make!
I rule; but not oppress! end quarrels; not maintain!
See towns; but dwell not there, t' abridge my charge, or train!

VIII. THE BACHELOR.

How many things, as yet, are dear alike to me!
The field! the horse! the dog! love! arms! or liberty!
I have no wife, as yet; whom I may call mine own!
I have no children yet; that by my name are known!
Yet, if I married were, I would not wish to thrive,
If that I could not tame the veriest shrew alive!

IX. THE MARRIED MAN.

I only am the man, among all married men,
That does not wish the Priest, to be unlinked again!
And though my shoe did wring, I would not make my moan,
Nor think my neighbour's chance more happy than mine own
Yet court I not my Wife! but yield observance due;
Being neither fond! nor cross! nor jealous! nor untrue!

X. THE WIFE.

The first of all our sex came from the side of Man;
I thither am returned, from whence our sex began.
I do not visit oft; nor many, when I do!
I tell my mind to few; and that in counsel too!
I seem not sick, in health; nor sullen, but in sorrow!
I care for somewhat else, than what to wear to-morrow.

XI. THE WIDOW.

My husband knew, how much his death would grieve me;
And therefore left me wealth, to comfort and relieve me.
Though I no more will have; I must not love disdain!
PENELOPE herself did suitors entertain!
And yet, to draw on such as are of best esteem,
Nor younger than I am, nor richer, will I seem!

XII. THE MAID.

I, marriage would forswear; but that I hear men tell,
That she that dies a Maid must lead an ape in hell.
Therefore, if Fortune come, I will not mock and play;
Nor drive the bargain on, till it be driven away!
Titles and Lands I like: yet rather fancy can
A man that wanteth gold; than gold that wants a man!

Giles Fletcher the Elder, LL.D.

SAD, all alone, not long I musing sat,
  But that my thoughts compelled me to aspire!
A laurel garland in my hand I gat;
  So the Muses I approached the nigher.
My suit was this, A Poet to become!
  To drink with them; and from the heavens be fed!
PHŒBUS denied; and sware, 'There was no room,
  Such to be Poets as fond Fancy led!'
With that, I mourned; and sat me down to weep.
  VENUS, she smiled; and, smiling, to me said:
'Come, drink with me; and sit thee still and sleep!'
  This voice I heard; and VENUS I obeyed.
That poison, Sweet! hath done me all this wrong;
For now of Love must needs be all my Song!

LIKE MEMNON's rock, touched with the rising sun,
  Which yields a sound, and echoes forth a voice:
But, when it's drowned in western seas, is dumb;
  And, drowsy-like, leaves off to make a noise.
So I, my Love! enlightened with your shine,
  A Poet's skill within my soul I shroud!
Not rude, like that which finer Wits decline;
  But such as Muses to the best allowed!
But when your figure and your shape is gone;
  I speechless am! like as I was before:
Or if I write, my Verse is filled with moan;
  And blurred with tears, by falling in such store.
Then, muse not, LICIA! if my Muse be slack;
For when I wrote, I did thy beauty lack!

DISTANCE of place, my Love and me did part;
  Yet both did swear, We never would remove!
In sign thereof, I bade her take my heart!
  Which did, and doth, and cannot chose but, love.
Thus did we part, in hope to meet again;
Where both did vow, most constant to remain!

A she there was, that passed betwixt us both;
  By whom, each knew, how other's cause did fare;
For men, to trust men in their love are loth!
  Thus had we both, of love a Lover's care.
Haply he seeks his sorrows to renew,
That for his Love doth make another sue!

By her, a kiss, a kiss to me, She sent;
  A kiss, for price, more worth than purest gold!
She gave it her! To me, the kiss was meant!
  A she to kiss! what harm, if she were bold.
Happy those lips, that had so sweet a kiss!
For Heaven itself scarce yields so sweet a bliss.

This modest she, blushing for shame of this,
  Or loth to part from that she liked so well,
Did play false play; and gave me not the kiss!
  Yet my Love's kindness could not choose but tell.
Then blame me not! That, kissing, sighed, and swore,
'I kissed but her; whom you had kissed before!'

'Sweet! love me more! and blame not me, sweet Love!
  I kissed those lips; yet harmless, I do vow!
Scarce would my lips, from off those lips remove;
  For still methought, sweet Fair! I kissèd you!
And thus, kind Love, the sum of all my bliss
Was both begun, and ended, in a kiss.

'Then send me more; but send them by your friend!
  Kiss none but her; nor her, nor none at all!
Beware by whom such treasures you do send!
  I must them lose; except I for them call!
And love me, Dear! and still, still, kissing be!
Both like and love; but none, sweet Love! but me!'

My Love lay sleeping, where birds music made;
  Shutting her eyes, disdainful of the light.
The heat was great; but greater was the shade,
  Which her defended from his burning sight.
This CUPID saw, and came a kiss to take;
  Sucking sweet nectar from her sugared breath.
She felt the touch, and blushed, and did awake!
  Seeing 'twas LOVE, which She did think was DEATH,
She cut his wings, and causèd him to stay:
  Making a vow, He should not thence depart;
Unless to her, the wanton Boy should pay
  The truest, kindest, and most loving heart!
His feathers still She usèd for a fan;
Till, by exchange, my heart his feathers wan!

Edmund Spenser.

LIKE as a huntsman, after weary chase,
  Seeing the game from him escaped away,
Sits down to rest him, in some shady place,
  With panting hounds beguilèd of their prey—
So, after long pursuit and vain assay,
  When I, all weary, had the chase forsook,
The gentle Dear returned the selfsame way,
  Thinking to quench her thirst at the next brook.
There She, beholding me with milder look,
  Sought not to fly, but fearless still did bide,
Till I in hand, her yet half trembling took;
  And, with her own good will, her firmly tied.
Strange thing, meseemed, to see a beast so wild,
So goodly won, with her own will beguiled!

ONE day, I wrote her name upon the strand;
  But came the waves, and washèd it away!
Again I wrote it, with a second hand;
  But came the tide, and made my pains his prey!
'Vain man,' said She, 'that dost in vain assay,
  A mortal thing so to immortalize!
For I myself shall, like to this, decay;
  And eke my name be wipèd out likewise!'
'Not so,' quod I: 'let baser things devise
  To die in dust; but you shall live by fame!
My Verse, your virtues rare shall eternize;
  And in the heavens write your glorious name!
Where, when as death shall all the World subdue,
Our love shall live, and later life renew!'

Edmund Spenser.

IN youth, before I waxèd old,
　The blind boy, VENUS' baby,
For want of cunning, made me bold
　In bitter hive to grope for honey:
　　　But when he saw me stung, and cry;
　　　He took his wings, and away did fly!

　As DIANE hunted on a day,
　She chanced to come where CUPID lay,
　　　His quiver by his head;
　One of his shafts, she stole away;
　And one of hers did close convey
　　　Into the other's stead.
With that, LOVE wounded my Love's heart;
But DIANE, beasts with CUPID's dart!

　I SAW, in secret, to my Dame,
　How little CUPID humbly came,
And said to her, 'All hail! my mother!'
　　But when he saw me laugh; for shame,
　　His face with bashful blood did flame;
Not knowing VENUS from the other.
　　'Then never blush, CUPID!' quoth I,
　　'For many have erred in this Beauty!'

Edmund Spenser.

MARK, when She smiles with amiable cheer!
  And tell me, Whereto can ye liken it?
When on each eyelid sweetly do appear
  A hundred Graces, as in shade to sit.
Likest, it seemeth, in my simple wit,
  Unto the fair sunshine, in summer's day,
That, when a dreadful storm away is flit,
  Through the broad world doth spread his goodly ray.
At sight whereof, each bird that sits on spray,
  And every beast that to his den was fled,
Comes forth afresh out of their late dismay;
  And to the light lift up their drooping head.
So my storm-beaten heart likewise is cheered
With that sunshine, when cloudy looks are cleared.

SWEET Smile, the Daughter of the Queen of Love,
  Expressing all thy mother's powerful art!
With which she wonts to temper angry JOVE;
  When all the Gods he threats with thund'ring dart.
Sweet is thy virtue, as thyself sweet art!
  For when on me thou shinedst late, in sadness,
A melting pleasance ran through every part;
  And me revived with heart-[th]robbing gladness.
Whilst wrapt with joy resembling heavenly madness,
  My soul was ravished quite, as in a trance;
And feeling thence no more her sorrow's sadness,
  Fed on the fullness of that cheerful glance.
More sweet than Nectar, or ambrosial meat,
Seemed every bit, which thenceforth I did eat.

Anonymous.

'I PRAY thee, LOVE! say, Whither is this posting?
  Since with thy deity first I was acquainted,
I never saw thee, thus distracted, coasting,
            With countenance tainted,

'Thy conquering arrows broken in thy quiver,
  Thy brands, that wont the inward marrow sunder,
Fireless and forceless, all-a-pieces shiver,
            With mickle wonder.

'That maketh, next, my stayless thoughts to hover;
  I cannot sound this uncouth cause of being!
The veil is torn, that did thy visage cover;
            And thou art seeing!'

'A stranger, one,' quoth LOVE, 'of good demerit,
  Did suit and service to his Sovereign proffer.
In any case, She would not seem to hear it;
            But scorned the offer!

'And, very now, upon this Maying morrow,
  By break of day, he found me at my harbour.
I went with him, to understand his sorrow,
            Unto her arbour;

'Where he, love torments dolefully unfolded,
  With words that might a tiger's heart have charmed!
His sighs and tears, the mountain, yea, had moulted;
            And She not warmed!

Anonymous.

'Her great disdain against her Lover proved,
  Kindled my brand, that to her breast I seated;
The flames, between her paps them often moved;
            Nor burnt! nor heated!

'My arrows keen I afterward assayed!
  Which from her breast, without effect rebounded;
And, as a ball, on marble floor they played;
            With force confounded.

'The brand that burnt old PRIAM's town to ashes;
  Now first his operation wants it then:
The dart that emerald skies in pieces dashes,
            Scorned by a woman!

'Thus, while I said, She toward me arrived,
  And with a touch of triumph, never doubted
To tear the veil, that use of sight bereaved.
            So LOVE was louted!

'The veil of error from mine eyes bereaved;
  I saw Heaven's Hope! and Earth her Treasury!
"Well mayst thou err!" said I, "I am deceived!
            Bent to pleasure thee.

'"Cease, hapless man! my succours to importune!
  She only, She, my stratagems repelleth!
Vainly endeavour I to tempt her fortune,
            That so excelleth!

Anonymous.

'" Content thee, man ! that thou didst see and suffer !
And be content to suffer, see, and die !
And die content; thou once didst move her !
    She displeased thereby."
' And herewithal, I left the man adying;
 For, by his Passions, I perceived none other.
I hie me, thus ashamed, with speedy flying,
    To tell my mother ! '

 WEEP you no more, sad fountains !
  What need you flow so fast !
 Look, how the snowy mountains
  Heaven's sun doth gently waste !
 But my Sun's heavenly eyes
   View not your weeping !
  That now lies sleeping
Softly; now softly lies
  Sleeping.

 Sleep is a reconciling;
  A rest that peace begets !
 Doth not the sun rise smiling,
  When fair at e'en he sets !
 Rest you; then, rest, sad eyes !
   Melt not in weeping;
  While She lies sleeping
Softly; now softly lies
  Sleeping.

Edward de Vere, Earl of Oxford.

Who taught thee first to sigh, 'Alas!' my heart?   Love.
Who taught thy tongue the woeful words of plaint?   Love.
Who filled your eyes with tears of bitter smart?   Love.
Who gave thee grief, and made thy joys so faint?   Love.
Who first did paint with colours pale thy face?   Love.
Who first did break thy sleeps of quiet rest?   Love.
Above the rest in Court, who gave thee grace?   Love.
Who made thee strive in honour to be best?   Love.
In constant troth, to bide so firm and pure?   Love.
To scorn the World, regarding but thy friends?   Love.
With patient mind, each Passion to endure?   Love.
In one desire to settle to the end?   Love.
Love then thy choice! wherein such choice thou bind;
As nought but death may ever change thy mind.

THE SHEPHERD'S COMMENDATION OF HIS NYMPH.

What Shepherd can express
The favour of her face!
To whom, in this distress,
I do appeal for grace.
A thousand Cupids fly
About her gentle eye:

Edward de Vere, Earl of Oxford.

From which, each throws a dart,
  That kindleth soft sweet fire
Within my sighing heart;
  Possessèd by desire.
    No sweeter love I try
    Than in her love to die.

The lily in the field,
  That glories in his white,
For pureness, now must yield
  And render up his right!
    Heaven, pictured in her face,
    Doth promise joy and grace!

Fair CYNTHIA's silver light,
  That beats on running streams,
Compares not with her white;
  Whose hairs are all sunbeams.
    So bright my Nymph doth shine,
    As day unto mine eyne!

With this, there is a red
  Exceeds the damask rose;
Which in her cheeks is spread,
  Whence every favour grows.
    In sky, there is no star,
    That She surmounts not far!

Edward de Vere, Earl of Oxford

When Phœbus, from the bed
  Of Thetis doth arise,
The morning, blushing red,
  In fair carnation wise,
    He shews in my Nymph's face,
    As Queen of every grace!

This pleasant lily white,
  This taint of roseate red,
This Cynthia's silver light,
  This sweet fair Dea spread,
    These sunbeams in mine eye,
    These beauties make me die!

Rev. Robert Southwell, S.J.

TIMES GO BY TURNS.

The loppèd tree, in time, may grow again!
Most naked plants renew both fruit and flower!
The sorriest wight may find release of pain!
  The driest soil suck in some moist'ning shower!
    Times go by turns! and chances change, by course,
    From foul to fair; from better hap, to worse!

The sea of Fortune doth not ever flow!
  She draws her favours to the lowest ebb;
Her tides hath equal times to come and go;
  Her loom doth weave the fine and coarsest web!
    No joy so great; but runneth to an end!
    No hap so hard; but may, in fine, amend!

Not always Fall of Leaf; nor ever Spring!
  No endless night; yet not eternal day!
The saddest birds a season find to sing!
  The roughest storm, a calm may soon allay!
    Thus, with succeeding turns, GOD tempereth all!
    That Man may hope to rise; yet fear to fall.

A chance may win, that by mischance was lost!
  The net that holds no great, takes little, fish!
In some things, all! in all things, none, are crossed!
  Few, all they need; but none have all they wish!
    Unmeddled joys here to no man befall!
    Who least, hath some! who most, hath never all!

LOVE'S SERVILE LOT.

Love, Mistress is of many minds;
    Yet few know whom they serve!
They reckon least, how little Love
    Their service doth deserve!

The Will She robbeth from the Wit,
    The Sense from Reason's lore;
She is delightful in the rind,
    Corrupted in the core.

She shroudeth Vice in Virtue's veil;
    Pretending good in ill!
She off'reth joy, affordeth grief!
    A kiss, where she doth kill!

A honey-shower rains from her lips!
    Sweet lights shine in her face!
She hath the blush of virgin mind;
    The mind of viper's race!

She makes thee seek; yet fear to find!
    To find; but not enjoy!
In many frowns, some gliding smiles
    She yields; to more annoy!

She woos thee to come near her fire;
　Yet does She draw it from thee!
Far off She makes thy heart to fry;
　And yet to freeze within thee!

She letteth fall some luring baits,
　For fools to gather up!
Too sweet, too sour, to every taste
　She tempereth her cup!

Soft souls, She binds in tender twist;
　Small flies, in spinner's web!
She sets afloat some luring streams;
　But makes them soon to ebb!

Her wat'ry eyes have burning force;
　Her floods and flames conspire!
Tears kindle sparks! sobs, fuel are!
　And sighs do blow her fire!

May never was the Month of Love;
　For May is full of flowers!
But rather April, wet by kind;
　For Love is full of showers!

Like Tyrant, cruel wounds She gives;
　Like Surgeon, salve She lends:
But salve and sore have equal force,
　For death is both their ends!

With soothing words, inthrallèd souls
    She chains in servile bands!
Her eye, in silence, hath a speech;
    Which eye best understands!

Her little sweet hath many sours;
    Short hap, immortal harms!
Her loving looks are murd'ring darts;
    Her songs, bewitching charms!

Like winter rose, and summer ice,
    Her joys are still untimely!
Before her, Hope! behind, Remorse!
    Fair first; in fine, unseemly!

Moods, Passions, Fancies, Jealous Fits,
    Attend upon her train!
She yieldeth rest without repose;
    A heaven, in hellish pain!

Her house is Sloth; her door, Deceit;
    And slippery Hope, her stairs
Unbashful Boldness bids her guests;
    And every Vice repairs!

Her diet is of such delight[s]
    As please, till they be past;
But, then, the poison kills the heart,
    That did entice the taste.

Her sleep in sin doth end in wrath!
    Remorse rings her awake!
Death calls her up! Shame drives her out!
    Despairs, her upshot make!

Plough not the seas! Sow not the sands!
    Leave off your idle pain!
Seek other Mistress for your minds!
    Love's service is in vain!

I DIE ALIVE.

O, LIFE! what lets thee from a quick decease?
    O, Death! what draws thee from a present prey?
My feast is done! My soul would be at ease!
    My Grace is said! O, Death, come, take away!

I live; but such a life as ever dies!
    I die; but such a death as never ends!
My death, to end my dying life denies;
    And life, my living death no whit amends!

Thus still I die; yet still I do revive!
    My living death, by dying life is fed!
Grace, more than Nature, keeps my heart alive;
    Whose idle hopes and vain desires are dead.

Not where I breathe; but where I love, I live!
    Not where I love; but where I am, I die!
The life I wish, must future glory give!
    The deaths I feel, in present dangers lie!

CONTENT AND RICH.

I DWELL in Grace's Court,
  Enriched with Virtue's rights:
Faith guides my wit! Love leads my will!
  Hope, all my mind delights!

In lowly vales, I mount
  To Pleasure's highest pitch!
My silly shroud true Honour brings!
  My poor estate is rich!

My Conscience is my crown!
  Contented thoughts, my rest!
My heart is happy in itself;
  My bliss is in my breast!

Enough, I reckon wealth!
  A Mean, the surest lot:
That lies too high for base contempt;
  Too low for envy's shot.

My wishes are but few;
  All easy to fulfil!
I make the limits of my power
  The bo[u]nds unto my will!

Rev. Robert Southwell, S.J.

I have no hopes but one,
    Which is of heavenly reign!
Effects attained, or not desired,
    All lower hopes refrain!

I feel no care of coin;
    Well-doing is my wealth!
My mind to me an empire is;
    While grace affordeth health.

I clip high-climbing thoughts,
    The wings of swelling pride!
Their fall is worst, that from the height
    Of greatest honour slide!

Sith sails of largest size,
    The storm doth soonest tear;
I bear so low and small a sail
    As freeth me from fear!

I wrestle not with rage,
    While fury's flame doth burn;
It is in vain to stop the stream,
    Until the tide doth turn:

But when the flame is out,
    And ebbing wrath doth end;
I turn a late enragèd foe
    Into a quiet friend!

And, taught with often proof,
    A tempered calm I find
To be most solace to itself;
    Best cure for angry mind!

Spare diet is my fare;
    My clothes, more fit than fine!
I know I feed and clothe a foe;
    That, pampered, would repine!

I envy not their hap,
    Whom favour doth advance!
I take no pleasure in their pain,
    That have less happy chance!

To rise by others' fall,
    I deem a losing gain!
All states, with others' ruin built,
    To ruin run amain!

No change of Fortune's calms
    Can cast my comforts down!
When Fortune smiles, I smile to think
    How quickly she will frown!

And when, in froward mood,
    She proves an angry foe,
Small gain I found to let her come;
    Less loss to let her go!

Rev. Robert Southwell, S.J.

LOSS IN DELAYS.

SHUN delays! They breed remorse!
Take thy time, while time doth serve thee!
Creeping snails have weakest force:
Fly their fault, lest thou repent thee!
    Good is best when soonest wrought!
    Ling'ring labours come to nought!

Hoist up sail, while gale doth last;
    Tide and wind stay no man's pleasure!
Seek not time, when time is past;
    Sober speed is wisdom's leisure!
    After-wits are dearly bought;
    Let thy fore-wit guide thy thought!

Time wears all his locks before;
    Take thou hold upon his forehead!
When he flies, he turns no more;
    And, behind, his scalp is naked!
    Works adjourned have many stays!
    Long demurs breed new delays!

Seek thy salve, while sore is green;
    Festered wounds ask deeper lancing!
After-cures are seldom seen;
    Often sought, scarce ever chancing!
    Time and place give best advice!
    Out of season, out of price!

Crush the serpent in the head!
Break ill eggs ere they be hatched!
Kill bad chickens in the tread;
Fligg, they hardly can be catched!
In the rising, stifle ill!
Lest it grow against thy will.

Drops do pierce the stubborn flint;
Not by force, but often falling!
Custom kills, with feeble dint;
More by use, than strength, prevailing!
Single sands have little weight;
Many make a drowning freight!

Tender twigs are bent with ease;
Agèd trees do break with bending!
Young desires make little press;
Growth doth make them past amending!
Happy man! that soon 'doth knock
Babel's babes against the rock'![1]

UPON THE IMAGE OF DEATH.

BEFORE my face the picture hangs,
That daily should put me in mind
Of those cold names and bitter pangs
That shortly I am like to find.
But yet, alas, full little I
Do think hereon, that I must die!

[1] Ps. cxxxvii. 8, 9.

Rev. Robert Southwell, S.J.

I often look upon a face
   Most ugly, grisly, bare, and thin!
I often view the hollow place,
   Where eyes and nose had sometime been!
      I see the bones, across that lie;
      Yet little think that I must die!

I read the label underneath,
   That telleth me whereto I must!
I see the sentence eke that saith,
   Remember, Man, that thou art dust!
      But yet, alas, but seldom I
      Do think, indeed, that I must die!

Continually at my bed's head
   A hearse doth hang, which doth me tell
That I, ere morning, may be dead;
   Though now I feel myself full well:
      But yet, alas, for all this I
      Have little mind that I must die!

The gown which I do use to wear;
   The knife wherewith I cut my meat;
And eke that old and ancient chair,
   Which is my only usual seat:
      All those do tell me I must die;
      And yet my life amend not I!

My ancestors are turned to clay,
  And many of my mates are gone;
My youngers daily drop away;
  And can I think to 'scape alone?
    No! No! I know that I must die;
    And yet my life amend not I!

Not SOLOMON, for all his wit;
  Nor SAMSON, though he were so strong;
No King, nor person, ever yet
  Could 'scape; but death laid him along!
    Wherefore I know that I must die;
    And yet my life amend not I!

Though all the East did quake to hear
  Of ALEXANDER's dreadful name;
And all the West did likewise fear
  To hear of JULIUS CÆSAR's fame:
    Yet both, by death, in dust now lie;
    Who, then, can 'scape, but he must die?

If none can 'scape Death's dreadful dart;
  If rich and poor his beck obey;
If strong, if wise, if all, do smart;
  Then I to 'scape shall have no way!
    O, grant me grace, O GOD! that I
    My life may mend; sith I must die!

Rev. Robert Southwell, S.J.

SCORN NOT THE LEAST!

WHERE wards are weak, and foes encount'ring strong;
  Where mightier do assault than do defend:
The feebler part puts up enforcèd wrong;
  And silent sees, that speech could not amend!
    Yet Higher Powers must think, (though they repine,)
    When sun is set, the little stars will shine!

When pike doth range, the silly tench doth fly,
  And crouch in privy creeks with smaller fish!
Yet pike are caught; when little fish go by!
  These fleet afloat; while those do fill the dish!
    There is a time even for worms to creep,
    And suck the dew; while all their foes do sleep!

The merlin cannot ever soar on high;
  Nor greedy greyhound still pursue the chase!
The tender lark will find a time to fly;
  And fearful hare, to run a quiet race!
    He that high growth on cedars did bestow,
    Gave also lowly mushrumpts leave to grow!

In AMAN's pomp, poor MARDOCHEUS wept:
  Yet GOD did turn his fate upon his foe!
The Lazar pined, while DIVES' feast was kept:
  Yet he, to heaven; to hell did DIVES go!
    We trample grass, and prize the flowers of May;
    Yet grass is green, when flowers do fade away!

NEW PRINCE, NEW POMP.

BEHOLD, a silly tender Babe,
    In freezing winter night,
In homely manger, trembling lies!
    Alas, a piteous sight!

The inns are full. No man will yield
    This little Pilgrim bed!
But forced he is, with silly beasts,
    In crib to shroud his head.

Despise him not for lying there;
    First, What he is inquire!
An orient pearl is often found
    In depth of dirty mire.

Weigh not his crib, his wooden dish;
    Nor beasts that by him feed!
Weigh not his mother's poor attire;
    Nor JOSEPH's simple weed!

This stable is a Prince's Court;
    The crib, his Chair of State;
The beasts are parcel of his pomp;
    The wooden dish, his plate.

The persons in that poor attire,
  His royal liveries wear.
The Prince himself is com'n from Heaven.
  This pomp is prizèd there!
With joy approach, O, Christian wight!
  Do homage to thy King!
And highly praise his humble pomp;
  Which he from Heaven doth bring.

THE BURNING BABE.

As I, in hoary winter's night, stood shivering in the snow;
Surprised I was with sudden heat, which made my heart to glow:
And lifting up a fearful eye, to view what fire was near,
A pretty Babe, all burning bright, did in the air appear;
Who, scorchèd with exceeding heat, such floods of tears did shed,
As though his floods should quench his flames, which with
    his tears were bred:
'Alas!' quoth he, 'but newly born, in fiery heats I fry;
Yet none approach to warm their hearts, or feel my fire but I!
My faultless Breast, the furnace is; the fuel, wounding Thorns;
Love is the fire, and Sighs, the smoke; the ashes, Shames and
    Scorns.
The fuel Justice layeth on; and Mercy blows the coals:
The metal in this furnace wrought, are men's defilèd Souls.
For which, as now, on fire I am, to work them to their good;
So will I melt into a bath! to wash them in my blood!'
With this, he vanished out of sight, and swiftly shrank away;
And straight I callèd unto mind, that it was Christmas Day.

Lovely Maya, Hermes' mother,
  Of fair Flora much befriended!
  To whom this sweet month is commended.
This month more sweet than any other!
  By thy sovereignty defended.

Daisies, cowslips, and primroses,
  Fragrant violets, and sweet minthe,
  Match with purple hyacinth!
Of these, each where, Nymphs make trim posies;
  Praising their mother, Berycinth.

Behold, a herd of jolly Swains
  Go flocking up and down the mead!
  A troop of lovely Nymphs do tread;
And dearnly dancing on yon plains,
  Each doth, in course, her Hornpipe lead!

Before the Grooms, plays Peers the Piper!
  They bring in hawthorn and sweet-briar!
  And damask roses they would bear;
But them they leave, till they be riper!
  The rest, round Morrises dance there.

With frisking gambols and such glee,
  Unto the lovely Nymphs they haste!
  Who, there in decent order placed,
Expect who shall Queen Flora be;
  And with the May Crown chiefly graced!

Barnaby Barnes.

The Shepherds poopen in their pipe!
   One leads his wench a Country Round;
   Another sits upon the ground,
And doth his beard from drivel wipe;
   Because he would be handsome found.

To see the frisking, and the scouping!
   To hear the Herdgroom's wooing speeches!
   Whiles one, to dance his girl beseeches,
The lead-heeled lazy luskings louping
   Fling out, in their new motley breeches!

This done, with jolly cheer and game,
   The bach'lor Swains and young Nymphs met,
   Where in an arbour they were set.
Thither, to choose a Queen they came;
   And soon concluded her to fet.

There, with a garland, they did crown
   PARTHENOPE, my true sweet Love!
   Whose beauty, all the Nymphs above,
Did put the lovely Graces down.
   The Swains, with shouts, rocks' echoes move!

To see the Rounds, the Morris Dances,
   The leaden Galliards, for her sake!
   To hear those Songs, the Shepherds make!
One with his hobby-horse still prances;
   While some, with flowers, a highway make!

There, in a mantle of light green,
(Reserved, by custom, for that day)
PARTHENOPE, they did array!
And did create her, Summer's Queen;
And Ruler of their merry May!

ONE night, I did attend my sheep;
Which I, with watchful ward, did keep
    For fear of wolves' assaulting.
For, many times, they broke my sleep;
And would into the cottage creep,
    Till I sent them out halting!

At length, methought, about midnight,
(What time clear CYNTHIA shineth bright)
    Beneath, I heard a rumbling.
At first, the noise did me affright:
But nought appearèd in my sight;
    Yet still heard something tumbling.

At length, good heart I took to rise,
And then myself crossed three times thrice;
    Hence, a sharp sheephook raught!
I feared the wolf had got a prize;
Yet how he might, could not devise!
    I, for his entrance sought.

Barnaby Barnes.

At length, by moonlight, could I espy
A little boy did naked lie
   Frettished, amongst the flock.
I, him approachèd somewhat nigh.
He groaned as he were like to die;
   But falsely did me mock.

For pity, he cried, 'Well-a-day!
Good master, help me! if you may;
   For I am almost starved!'
I pitied him, when he did pray,
And brought him to my couch of hay:
   But guess as I was served!

He bare about him a long dart,
Well gilded with fine painter's art,
   And had a pile of steel.
On it I lookèd every part.
Said I, 'Will this pile wound a heart?'
   'Touch it!' quoth he, 'and feel!'

With that, I touched the javelin's point.
Eftsoons it piercèd to the joint!
   And rageth now so fierce,
That all the balms which it anoint,
Cannot prevail with it, a point!
   But it mine heart will pierce.

PHILLIDA AND CORIDON.

In the merry month of May,
In a morn, by break of day,
Forth I walked by the wood-side,
When as May was in his pride.

There I spièd all alone
PHILLIDA and CORIDON.
Much ado there was, God wot!
He would love; and she would not.
She said, 'Never man was true!'
He said, 'None was false to you!'
He said, 'He had loved her long!'
She said, 'Love should have no wrong!'
CORIDON would kiss her then.
She said, 'Maids must kiss no men,
Till they did for good and all!'

Then she made the Shepherd call
All the heavens, to witness truth!
Never loved a truer youth!

Thus, with many a pretty oath,
'Yea!' and 'Nay!' 'faith' and 'troth,'
Such as silly Shepherds use,
When they will not love abuse;
Love, which had been long deluded,
Was, with sweet kisses, concluded:
And PHILLIDA, with garlands gay,
Was made the Lady of the May.

Nicholas Breton.

PRETTY twinkling starry eyes!
How did Nature first devise
Such a sparkling in your sight
As to give LOVE such delight!
As to make him, like a fly,
Play with looks, until he die!

Sure, ye were not made at first,
For such mischief to be curst,
As to kill Affection's care,
That doth only truth declare.
Where Worth's wonders never wither;
LOVE and Beauty live together!

Blessed eyes! then, give your blessing!
That, in Passion's best expressing,
LOVE (that only lives to grace ye!)
May not suffer Pride deface ye;
But, in gentle thoughts' directions,
Show the praise of your perfections!

Nicholas Breton.

WHO can live in heart so glad
As the merry Country Lad!
Who, upon a fair green balk,
May, at pleasure, sit and walk;
And, amid the azure skies,
See the morning sun arise!
While he hears, in every Spring,
How the birds do chirp and sing;
Or, before the hounds in cry,
See the hare go stealing by;
Or, along the shallow brook,
Angling with a baitèd hook,
See the fishes leap and play,
In a blessèd sunny day;
Or to hear the partridge call
Till she have her covey all;
Or to see the subtle fox,
How the villain plies the box!
After feeding on his prey;
How he closely sneaks away
Through the hedge, and down the furrow,
Till he gets into his burrow!
Then the bee to gather honey;
And the little black-haired coney,
On a bank, for sunny place,
With her forefeet wash her face:
Are not these, with thousands moe
Than the Courts of Kings do know,
The true pleasing spirit's sights,
That may breed true love's delights?

Nicholas Breton.

But with all this happiness,
To behold that Shepherdess!
To whose eyes all Shepherds yield;
All the fairest in the field.
Fair AGLAIA! in whose face
Lives the Shepherd's highest grace.
　In whose worthy-wonder praise;
See what her true Shepherd says!
　'She is neither proud nor fine,
But in spirit more divine;
She can neither lower nor leer,
But a sweeter smiling cheer;
She had never painted face,
But a sweeter smiling grace;
She can never love dissemble;
Truth doth so her thoughts assemble,
That, where wisdom guides her will,
She is kind and constant still.
All in sum, she is that creature,
Of that truest comfort's nature,
That doth show (but in exceedings)
How their praises had their breedings!
　'Let, then, Poets feign their pleasure,
In their fictions of Love's treasure;
Proud high spirits seek their graces
In their idol painted faces!
My love's spirit's lowliness,
In affection's humbleness,
Under heaven no happiness
Seeks, but in this Shepherdess!

'For whose sake, I say, and swear
By the Passions that I bear,
Had I got a Kingly grace,
I would leave my Kingly place,
And in heart be truly glad
To become a Country Lad,
Hard to lie, and go full bare,
And to feed on hungry fare;
So I might but live to be,
Where I might but sit to see,
Once a day, or all day long,
The sweet subject of my Song.
'In AGLAIA's only eyes,
All my worldly Paradise!'

A SWEET CONTENTION BETWEEN LOVE, HIS MISTRESS, AND BEAUTY.

LOVE and my Mistress were at strife, Who had the greater power on me?
Betwixt them both, O, what a life! Nay, what a death, is this to be!
She said, She did it with her eye! He said, He did it with his dart!
Betwixt them both (a silly wretch!) 'tis I that have the wounded heart!
She said, She only spake the word that did enchant me, 'pearing sense.
He said, He only gave the sound, that entered heart without defence.
She said, They were her only hairs, on which the dainty Muses wait.
He said, He was the only mean[s] that entered Muses in conceit.
She said, Her beauty was the mark that did amaze the highest mind.
He said, He only made the mist, whereby the senses grew so blind.
She said, That only for her sake, the best would venture life and limb!

He said, She was too much deceived! They honoured her, because
  of him!
Long while, alas, She would not yield; but it was She that ruled
  the roast:
Until, by proof, She did confess. If he were gone; her joy were lost!
And then She cried, 'O dainty LOVE! I now do find it is for thee,
That I am loved and honoured both; and thou hast power to
  conquer me!'

But when I heard her yield to LOVE, O, how my heart did leap for joy!
That now I had some little hope to have an end of mine annoy.
For though that FANCY, Beauty found, a power all too pitiless;
Yet LOVE would never have the heart to leave his Servant comfortless!
But as, too soon, before the Field, the trumpets sound the overthrow;
So, all too soon, I joyed too much! for I awaked; and nothing so!

'ON a hill there grows a flower,
 Fair befall the dainty sweet!
By that flower, there is a bower;
 Where the heavenly Muses meet.

'In that bower, there is a chair,
 Fringèd all about with gold;
Where doth sit the fairest Fair
 That ever eye did yet behold.

'It is PHILLIS fair and bright,
 She that is the Shepherds' joy!
She that, VENUS did despite;
 And did blind her little boy.

'This is she, the wise, the rich,
 That the World desires to see.
This is *ipsa quæ*, the which
 There is none but only she!

'Who would not this face admire!
  Who would not this Saint adore!
Who would not this sight desire;
  Though he thought to see no more!
'O, fair eyes! yet let me see
  One good look; and I am gone!
Look on me! for I am he,
  Thy poor silly CORIDON!
'Thou that art the Shepherds' Queen!
  Look upon thy silly Swain!
By thy comfort have been seen
  Dead men brought to life again!'

RARE NEWS.

NEWS from the heavens! All wars are at an end!
  'Twixt Higher Powers a happy Peace concluded.
Fortune and Faith are sworn each other's friend;
  And Love's desire shall never be deluded!
Time hath set down the compass of his course;
  Nature, her work; and Excellence, her art;
Care, his content; and Cruelty, his curse;
  Labour, his desire; and Honour, his desert.
Words shall be deeds; and Men shall be divine!
  Women, all Saints, or Angels, in degrees!
Clouds shall away! The sun shall ever shine!
  Heavens shall have power to hinder none of these!
These are the Articles of the Conclusion;
  Which, when they fall, then look for a confusion!

Nicholas Breton.

A SWEET PASTORAL.

GOOD Muse! rock me asleep with some sweet harmony!
This weary eye is not to keep thy wary company!
Sweet LOVE, be gone a while! Thou knowest my heaviness!
Beauty is born but to beguile my heart of happiness.
　See, how my little flock, that loved to feed on high,
Do headlong tumble down the rock, and in the valley die.
The bushes and the trees, that were so fresh and green,
Do all their dainty colour leese; and not a leaf is seen!
The blackbird and the thrush, that made the woods to ring,
With all the rest, are now at hush; and not a note they sing!
Sweet PHILOMEL, the bird that hath the heavenly throat,
Doth now, alas, not once afford recording of a note!
The flowers have had a frost! Each herb hath lost her savour;
And PHILLIDA the Fair hath lost the comfort of her favour.
　Now all these careful sights so kill me in conceit,
That now to hope upon delights, it is but mere deceit!
And therefore, my sweet Muse! that know'st what help is best,
Do now thy heavenly cunning use! to set my heart at rest;
And, in a dream, bewray what Fate shall be my friend:
Whether my life shall still decay; or when my sorrow end?

———

SAY, that I should say, 'I love ye!'
　Would you say, ''Tis but a saying!'
But if Love in prayers move ye;
　Will you not be moved with praying?

Think, 'I think that Love should know ye!'
　Will you think, ''Tis but a thinking!'
But if Love, the thought do show ye;
　Will ye loose your eyes with winking?

Nicholas Breton.

Write, that I do write you 'blessèd'!
  Will you write, '"Tis but a writing!'
But if Truth and Love confess it;
  Will ye doubt the true enditing?

No! I say, and think, and write it;
  Write, and think, and say, your pleasure!
Love, and Truth, and I, endite it,
  'You are blessèd out of measure!'

CORIDON'S SUPPLICATION TO PHILLIS.

'Sweet Phillis! if a silly Swain
  May sue to thee for grace;
See not thy loving Shepherd slain,
  With looking on thy face!
But think, what power thou hast got
  Upon my flock and me!
Thou seest, they now regard me not;
  But all do follow thee!

'And if I have so far presumed,
  With prying in thine eyes;
Yet let not comfort be consumed!
  That in thy pity lies:
But as thou art that Phillis fair,
  That Fortune favour gives;
So let not love die in despair!
  That in thy favour lives.

'The deer do browse upon the briar,
  The birds do pick the cherries;
And will not Beauty grant Desire
  One handful of her berries?
If so it be, that thou hast sworn,
  That none shall look on thee;
Yet let me know, thou dost not scorn
  To cast a look on me!

'But if thy beauty make thee proud;
  Think then, what is ordained!
The heavens have never yet allowed
  That LOVE should be disdained!
Then lest the Fates, that favour LOVE,
  Should curse thee for unkind;
Let me report, for thy behoof,
  The honour of thy mind!

'Let CORIDON, with full consent,
  Set down what he hath seen!
That PHILLIDA, with LOVE's content,
  Is sworn the Shepherds' Queen.'

UPON A SCOFFING LAUGHTER GIVEN BY A GENTLEWOMAN.

'LAUGH not too much! Perhaps, you are deceived!
All are not fools, that have but simple faces!
Mists are abroad! Things may be misconceived!
  Frumps and disdains are favours in disgraces!
Now, if you do not know what mean these speeches,
Fools have long coats; and monkeys have no breeches!

'Tihee again! Why, what grace is this?
  Laugh a man out, before he can get in!
Fortune so cross, and Favour so amiss!
  Doomsday at hand, before the world begin!'
    'Marry, Sir! then but if the weather hold,
    Beauty may laugh, and Love be a-cold!'

'Yet leave betimes your laughing too too much;
  Or find the fox, and then begin the chase!
Shut not a rat within a sugar hutch;
  And think you have a squirrel in the place!
    But when you laugh, let this go for a jest—
    Seek not a woodcock in a swallow's nest!'

OF TRUTH, WISDOM, VIRTUE, AND LOVE.

TRUTH shews herself in secret of her trust;
  Wisdom, her grace in honour of her love;
Virtue, her life, where Love is not unjust;
  Love is the sweet that doth no sorrow prove.
Truth hath in hate to hear a feignèd tale;
  Wisdom doth frown, where Folly is in place;
Honour is gone, where Beauty is too small;
  And Virtue lies, where Love is in disgrace.
I leave your truth to your desirèd trust!
  Your wisdom to the wonder of the wise!
Your highest joy to judgement of the just;
  Where Virtue lives, and Virtue never dies!
And He vouchsafe you, that all Truth preserveth,
What Truth of Love, and Love of Truth, deserveth!

Anonymous.

OLD MELIBŒUS' SONG,
COURTING HIS NYMPH.

LOVE's Queen (long waiting for her True Love,
Slain by a boar which he had chased)
Left off her tears, and me embraced.
She kissed me sweet, and called me, 'New Love!'
    With my silver hair she toyèd!
    In my stayèd looks she joyèd!
'Boys,' she said, 'breed Beauty's sorrow;
Old men cheer it, even and morrow!'

My face, she named 'the seat of favour'!
    All my defects her tongue defended!
My shape she praised: but most commended
My breath, more sweet than balm in savour!
    'Be, Old Man! with me delighted!
    Love for love shall be requited!'
With her toys, at last she won me;
Now she coys, that hath undone me!

COME, Shepherd Swains! that wont to hear me sing;
    Now sigh and groan!
Dead is my Love! my hope! my joy! my Spring!
    Dead, dead, and gone!

Oh! She that was your Summer's Queen,
    Your day's delight,
Is gone! and will no more be seen!
    O, cruel spite!

Anonymous.

Break all your pipes! that wont to sound
  With pleasant cheer;
And cast yourselves upon the ground,
  To wail my Dear!

Come, Shepherd Swains! Come, Nymphs! and all arow,
  To help me cry,
'Dead is my Love! and, seeing She is so;
  Lo, now I die!'

When day is gone, and darkness come;
  The toiling tired wight
Doth use to ease his weary bones
  By rest in quiet night.

When storm is stayed, and harbour won;
  The seaman, set on shore,
With comfort doth requite the care
  Of perils past before.

When Love hath won, where it did woo,
  And lights where it delights;
Contented mind thenceforth forgets
  The frown of former spites.

William Smith.

WHEN She was born, whom. I entirely love;
Th' immortal Gods, her birth-rites forth to grace,
Descending from their glorious seat above,
They did on her these several virtues place:
First, SATURN gave to her Sobriety;
JOVE then enduèd her with Comeliness;
And SOL with Wisdom did her beautify.
MERCURY with Wit and Knowledge did her bless;
VENUS with Beauty did all parts bedeck;
LUNA therewith did Modesty combine;
DIANA chaste, all loose desires did check:
And like a lamp in clearness She doth shine!
But MARS, according to his stubborn kind,
No virtue gave; but a disdainful mind!

YOU, that embrace enchanting Poesy,
Be gracious to perplexèd CORIN's lines!
You, that do feel Love's proud authority,
Help me to sing my sighs and sad designs!
CHLORIS, requite not faithful love with scorn;
But, as thou oughtest, have commiseration!
I have enough anatomized and torn
My heart! thereof to make a pure oblation.
Likewise consider, how thy CORIN prizeth
Thy parts, above each absolute perfection!
How he, of every precious thing, deviseth
To make thee Sovereign! Grant me then affection;
Else thus I prize thee—CHLORIS is alone
More hard than gold! or pearl! or precious stone!

Robert Devereux, Earl of Essex.

'CHANGE thy mind! since She doth change.
  Let not Fancy still abuse thee!
Thy untruth can not seem strange;
  When her falsehood doth accuse thee.
    Love is dead; and thou art free!
    She doth live; but dead to thee!

'When She loved thee best a while;
  See how still She did delay thee!
Using shows for to beguile
  Those vain hopes which have betrayed thee.
    Now thou seest, but all too late,
    Love loves truth; which Women hate!'

Love, farewell! more dear to me
  Than my life which thou preservedst!
Life, thy joy is gone from thee!
  Others have what thou deservedst.
    They enjoy what's not their own!
    Happier life to live alone!

Yet, thus much, to ease my mind,
  Let her know what She hath gotten!
She, whom time hath proved unkind,
  Having changed, is quite forgotten!
    FORTUNE now hath done her worst;
    Would she had done so at first

Robert Devereux, Earl of Essex.

'Love no more! since She is gone.
She is gone, and loves another.
Having been deceived by one,
    Leave to love; and love no other!
      She was false; bid her adieu!
      She was best; but yet untrue!'

THERE is none, O, none but you!
    Who from me estrange the sight;
Whom mine eyes affect to view,
    And chained ears hear with delight.

Others' beauties, others move;
    In you, I all the graces find!
Such are the effects of love,
    To make them happy that are kind.

Women in frail beauty trust;
    Only seem you kind to me!
Still be truly kind and just;
    For that can't dissembled be!

Dear! afford me then your sight!
    That, surveying all your looks,
Endless volumes I may write,
    And fill the world with envied books:

Which, when after Ages view,
    All shall wonder and despair;
Women, to find a man so true!
    And men, a woman half so fair!

Thomas Lodge, M.D.

THE BARGINET OF ANTIMACHUS.

IN pride of youth, in midst of May,
When birds, with many a merry lay,
    Salute the sun's uprising;
I sat me down fast by a spring,
And, while these merry chanters sing,
    I fell upon surmising.

Amidst my doubt and mind's debate,
Of change of time, of world's estate,
    I spied a boy attirèd
In silver plumes, yet naked quite;
Some pretty feathers fit for flight,
    Wherewith he still aspirèd.

A bow he bare, to work men's wrack;
A little quiver at his back,
    With many arrows fillèd:
And, in his soft and pretty hand,
He held a lively burning brand,
    Wherewith he Lovers killèd.

Fast by his side, in rich array,
There sat a lovely Lady gay,
    His mother, as I guessèd:
That set the lad upon her knee,
And trimmed his bow, and taught him flee,
    And mickle love professèd.

Oft from her lap, at sundry stours,
He leaped, and gathered summer flowers,
  Both violets and roses.
But see the chance! that followed fast,
As he the pomp of prime doth waste,
  Before that he supposes.

A bee, that harboured hard thereby,
Did sting his hand, and made him cry,
  'O, mother, I am wounded!'
Fair VENUS, that beheld her son,
Cried out, 'Alas, I am undone!'
  And thereupon she swounded.

'My little lad!' the Goddess said,
'Who hath my CUPID so dismayed?'
  He answered, 'Gentle mother!
The honeyworker in the hive,
My grief and mischief doth contrive.
  Alas, it is none other!'

She kissed the lad. Now, mark the chance!
And straight she fell into a trance,
  And, crying, thus concluded:
'Ah! wanton boy! like to the bee,
Thou, with a kiss, hast wounded me;
  And hapless love included!'

Thomas Lodge, M.D.

'A little bee doth thee affright!
But, ah! my wounds are full of sprite,
    And cannot be recurèd!'
The boy, that kissed his mother's pain,
Gan smile, and kissed her whole again;
    And made her hope assurèd.

She sucked the wound, and 'suaged the sting;
And little LOVE, ycured, did sing!
    Then let no Lover sorrow!
To-day, though grief attaint his heart;
Let him with courage bide the smart!
    Amends will come to-morrow!

My bonny Lass, thine eye,
    So sly,
Hath made me sorrow so!
    Thy crimson cheeks, my Dear!
    So clear,
Have so much wrought my woe!

Thy pleasing smiles and grace,
    Thy face,
Have ravished so my sprites,
    That life is grown to nought,
    Through thought
Of love; which me affrights.

For Fancy's flames of fire
    Aspire
Unto such furious power;
    As but the tears I shed
    Make dead,
The brands would me devour!

I should consume to nought;
    Through thought
Of thy fair shining eye,
    Thy cheeks, thy pleasing smiles,
    The wiles
That forced my heart to die!

Thy grace, thy face, the part
    Where Art
Stands gazing, still to see
    The wondrous gifts and power,
    Each hour,
That hath bewitchèd me!

ACCURST be LOVE; and they that trust his trains!
  He tastes the fruit: whilst others toil.
  He brings the lamp: we lend the oil.
  He sows distress: we yield him soil.
  He wageth war: we bide the foil.

Thomas Lodge, M.D.

Accurst be Love; and those that trust his trains!
  He lays the trap: we seek the snare.
  He threat'neth death: we speak him fair.
  He coins deceits: we foster care.
  He fav'reth pride: we count it rare.

Accurst be Love; and those that trust his trains!
  He seemeth blind: yet wounds with art.
  He vows content: he pays with smart.
  He swears relief: yet kills the heart.
  He calls for truth: yet scorns desert.

Accurst be Love; and those that trust his trains!
Whose heaven is hell; whose perfect joys are pains.

Like desert woods, with darksome shades obscured,
Where dreadful beasts, where hateful horror, reigneth;
Such is my wounded heart, whom sorrow paineth.

The trees are fatal shafts, to death inured,
That cruel Love within my breast maintaineth,
To whet my grief, when as my sorrow waneth.

The ghastly beasts, my thoughts in cares assured,
Which wage me war, whilst heart no succour gaineth,
With false suspect, and fear that still remaineth.

Thomas Lodge, M.D.

The horrors, burning sighs by cares procured,
Which forth I send, whilst weeping eye complaineth,
To cool the heat the helpless heart containeth.

But shafts, but cares, sighs, horrors, unrecured,
Were nought esteemed; if, for these pains awarded,
My faithful love, by you might be rewarded!

My PHILLIS hath the morning sun
    At first to look upon her;
And PHILLIS hath morn-waking birds,
    Her risings for to honour.

My PHILLIS hath prime-feathered flowers,
    That smile when she treads on them;
And PHILLIS hath a gallant flock,
    That leap, since she doth own them.

But PHILLIS hath so hard a heart
    (Alas, that she should have it!)
As yields no mercy to desert,
    Nor grace to those that crave it.

Sweet sun! when thou lookest on,
    Pray her regard my moan!
Sweet birds! when you sing to her,
    To yield some pity, woo her!

Thomas Lodge, M.D.

Sweet flowers! when as she treads on,
    Tell her, her beauty deads one!
And if, in life, her love she nill agree me;
Pray her, before I die, she will come see me!

Love guides the roses of thy lips,
    And flies about them, like a bee!
If I approach, he forward skips!
    And if I kiss, he stingeth me!

Love in thine eyes doth build his bower,
    And sleeps within their pretty shine:
And if I look, the Boy will lower;
    And from their orbs shoot shafts divine!

Love works thy heart within his fire;
    And in my tears doth firm the same:
And if I tempt, it will retire;
    And of my plaints doth make a game!

Love! let me cull her choicest flowers;
    And pity me, and calm her eye!
Make soft her heart! Dissolve her lowers!
    Then will I praise thy deity!

But if thou do not, Love! I'll truly serve her,
In spite of thee; and, by firm faith, deserve her!

Robert Tofte.

THE Grecians used to offer up their hair
 Unto their rivers, whom they did esteem
As mighty Gods; and them great honour bare,
 As if no virtue small in them had been.
  Do thou the like, sweet LAURA, unto me!
  Who, for my love, deserves a greater fee.

Thy golden tresses on me do bestow!
 Who hold whole rivers flowing in mine eyes:
Yet would not I, thou off shouldst cut them though!
  Dost muse! and ask, How this, thou mayst devise?
  I'll tell thee! Give thyself to me, for mine!
  So shalt thou give, uncut, thy tresses fine.

ON quicksedge, wrought with lovely eglantine,
 My LAURA laid her handkercher to dry;
Which had before snow-white ywashed been.
 But, after, when she called to memory,
That long 'twould be before, and very late,
 Ere sun could do, as would her glist'ring eyes:
She cast from them such sparkling glances straight,
 And with such force, in such a strangy guise,
As suddenly, and in one selfsame time,
She dried her cloth; but burnt this heart of mine!

GOLD upon gold, my only Joy did plate;
   Whilst she did dress her head by crystal Glass.
But whilst she looked on it, it sudden brake!
   So as, amazed thereat, much grieved she was.
      To whom I said, 'To grieve thus, 'tis in vain!
      Since what is broke, whole cannot be again!

'Look steadfastly, with both thine eyes, on me;
   Who have my heart, through love, a Glass new made!'
She on my face looked, and herself did see;
   Wherewith contented th'roughly, thus she said,
      'Most happy I! Since, for to dress my head,
      For broken Glass, of whole one I am sped!'

RICH damask roses in fair cheeks do bide
   Of my sweet Girl! like April in his prime:
But her hard heart, cold chilly snow doth hide;
   Of bitter Januar, the perfect sign.
Her hair of gold shows yellow, like the corn
   In July; when the sun doth scorch the ground:
And her fair breast, ripe fruit; which doth adorn
   September rich. So as in her are found
Both Harvest, Summer, Winter, Spring, to be;
Which you in breast, hair, heart, and face, may see!

Samuel Daniel.

SIREN.

COME, worthy Greek! ULYSSES! come,
    Possess these shores with me!
The winds and seas are troublesome;
    And here we may be free!
Here we may sit, and view their toil,
    That travail in the deep:
And joy the day in mirth the while;
    And spend the night in sleep!

ULYSSES.

Fair Nymph, if Fame, or Honour, were
    To be attained with Ease;
Then would I come and rest with thee,
    And leave such toils as these!
But here it dwells; and here must I
    With danger seek it forth!
To spend the time luxuriously
    Becomes not Men of Worth!

SIREN.

ULYSSES! O, be not deceived
    With that unreal name!
This Honour is a thing conceived;
    And rests on others' fame;
Begotten only to molest
    Our peace, and to beguile
(The best thing of our life!) our rest;
    And gives us up to toil.

Samuel Daniel.

ULYSSES.

Delicious Nymph! suppose there were
    Nor Honour, nor Report;
Yet Manliness would scorn to wear
    The time in idle sport!
For Toil doth give a better touch,
    To make us feel our joy;
And Ease finds tediousness as much
    As Labour yields annoy.

SIREN.

Then, Pleasure likewise seems the shore,
    Whereto tends all your toil;
Which you forego, to make it more,
    And perish oft the while!
Who may disport them diversely,
    Finds never tedious day!
And Ease may have variety,
    As well as Action may!

ULYSSES.

But natures of the noblest frame,
    These toils and dangers please!
And they take comfort in the same,
    As much as you in Ease:
And with the thought of actions past
    Are recreated still;
When Pleasure leaves a touch, at last,
    To shew that it was ill.

Samuel Daniel.

SIREN.

That doth Opinion only cause!
  That 's out of Custom bred;
Which makes us many other laws
  Than ever Nature did!
No widows wail for our delights!
  Our sports are without blood!
The world, we see, by warlike wights,
  Receives more hurt than good!

ULYSSES.

But yet the state of things requires
  These motions of unrest;
And these Great Spirits of high desire
  Seem born to turn them best!
To purge the mischiefs that increase,
  And all good order mar;
For oft we see a wicked Peace,
  To be well changed for War.

SIREN.

Well! Well! ULYSSES! then I see
  I shall not have thee here!
And therefore I will come to thee;
  And take my fortune there!
I must be won! that cannot win;
  Yet lost, were I not won!
For Beauty hath created been
  T' undo; or be undone!

Samuel Daniel.

Now each creature joys the other,
    Passing happy days and hours;
One bird reports unto another,
    In the fall of silver showers:
Whilst the earth, our common mother,
    Hath her bosom decked with flowers.

Whilst the greatest torch of heaven,
    With bright rays, warms FLORA's lap;
Making nights and days both even,
    Cheering plants with fresher sap:
My field, of flowers quite bereaven,
    Wants refresh of better hap!

ECHO, daughter of the Air,
    Babbling guest of rocks and hills,
Knows the name of my fierce Fair;
    And sounds the accents of my ills.
Each thing pities my despair;
    Whilst that She, her lover kills.

Whilst that She, O cruel Maid!
    Doth me and my love despise;
My life's flourish is decayed,
    That depended on her eyes:
But her will must be obeyed!
    And well he ends, for love who dies!

Samuel Daniel.

THE PROLOGUE TO
HYMEN'S TRIUMPH.

Hymen. IN this disguise and pastoral attire,
Without my saffron robe, without my torch,
Or other ensigns of my duty,
I, HYMEN, am come hither secretly,
To make Arcadia see a work of glory,
That shall deserve an everlasting story.

Here, shall I bring you, two the most entire
And constant Lovers that were ever seen,
From out the greatest suff'rings of annoy
That Fortune could inflict, to their full joy!
Wherein, no wild, no rude, no antic, sport;
But tender Passions, motions soft and grave,
The still spectators may expect to have!

For these are only CYNTHIA's recreatives
Made unto PHŒBUS, and are feminine:
And therefore must be gentle, like to her;
Whose sweet affections mildly move and stir.

And here, with this white wand, will I effect
As much as with my flaming Torch of Love!
And with the power thereof, affections move
In these fair Nymphs and Shepherds round about.

Envy. Stay, HYMEN! stay! You shall not have the day
Of this great glory! as you make account.
We will herein, as we were ever wont,
Oppose you, in the Matches you address;
And undermine them with disturbances!

Samuel Daniel.

Hymen.   Now, do thy worst, base ENVY, thou canst do!
Thou shalt not disappoint my purposes!

Avarice.   Then will I, HYMEN! In despite of thee
I will make parents cross desires of love
With those respects of wealth, as shall dissolve
The strongest knots of kindest faithfulness!

Hymen.   Hence, greedy AVARICE! I know thou art
A hag, that dost bewitch the minds of men;
Yet shalt thou have no power at all herein!

Jealousy.   Then will I, HYMEN! Do thou what thou canst;
I will steal closely into linkèd hearts,
And shake their veins with cold distrustfulness!
And ever keep them waking in their fears,
With spirits, which their imagination rears.

Hymen.   Disquiet JEALOUSY, vile Fury! Thou
That art the ugly monster of the mind!
Avaunt! begone! Thou shalt have nought to do
In this fair work of ours! nor ever more
Canst enter there, where HONOUR keeps the door.
    And therefore, hideous Furies! get you hence!
This place is sacred to Integrity
And clean desires! Your sight most loathsome is
Unto so well disposed a company!
Therefore, begone! I charge you, by my power!
We must have nothing in Arcadia sour!

Envy.   HYMEN! Thou canst not chase us so away!
For look, how long as thou mak'st Marriages;
So long will we produce incumbrances!

And we will, in the same disguise as thou,
Mix us among these Shepherds; that we may
Effect our work the better, being unknown:
For Ills shew other faces than their own!

Love is a sickness, full of woes,
    All remedies refusing;
A plant that, with most cutting, grows;
    Most barren, with best using.
        Why so?
More we enjoy it, more it dies!
If not enjoyed; it, sighing, cries,
      'Hey-ho!'
Love is a torment of the mind!
    A tempest everlasting!
And Jove hath made it of a kind,
    Not well, nor full, nor fasting!
        Why so?
More we enjoy it, more it dies! &c.

Eyes, hide my love! and do not show
    To any but to her, my notes!
Who only doth that cypher know,
    Wherewith we pass our secret thoughts.
      Belie your looks in others' sight;
      And wrong yourselves, to do her right!

Anonymous.

Happy he
Who, to sweet home retired,
Shuns glory so admired;
And to himself lives free!
Whilst he who strives, with pride, to climb the skies,
Falls down, with foul disgrace, before he rise!

Let who will
The Active Life commend;
And all his travails bend
Earth with his fame to fill!
Such fame, so forced, at last dies with his death;
Which life maintained by others' idle breath!

My delights
To dearest home confined,
Shall there make good my mind;
Not awed with Fortune's spites!
High trees, heaven blasts! Winds shake and honours fell;
When lowly plants, long time in safety dwell.

All I can,
My worldly strife shall be,
They, one day, say of me,
'He died a good old man!'
On his sad soul, a heavy burden lies,
Who, known to all, unknown to himself dies!

OUR BLESSED LADY'S LULLABY.

Upon my lap, my Sovereign sits,
    And sucks upon my breast;
Meanwhile his love sustains my life,
    And gives my body rest.
        Sing, lullaby, my little boy!
        Sing, lullaby, my life's joy!

When thou hast taken thy repast,
    Repose, my babe, on me!
So may thy Mother and thy Nurse,
    Thy Cradle also be!
        Sing, lullaby, my little boy! &c.

I grieve, that duty doth not work
    All that my wishing would;
Because I would not be to thee
    But in the best I should!
        Sing, lullaby, my little boy.! &c.

Yet as I am, and as I may,
    I must, and will, be thine!
Though all too little for thyself
    Vouchsafing to be mine.
        Sing, lullaby, my little boy! &c.

My wits, my words, my deeds, my thoughts,
    And else what is in me,
I rather will not wish to use,
    If not in serving thee!
        Sing, lullaby, my little boy! &c.

My babe, my bliss, my child, my choice,
    My fruit, my flower, and bud;
My JESUS, and my only joy!
    The sum of all my good!
        Sing, lullaby, my little boy! &c.

My sweetness, and the sweetest most
    That Heaven could Earth deliver!
Soul of my love, Spirit of my life,
    Abide with me for ever!
        Sing, lullaby, my little boy! &c.

Live still with me, and be my Love!
    And death will me refrain;
Unless thou let me die with thee,
    To live with thee again!
        Sing, lullaby, my little boy! &c.

Leave now to wail! thou luckless wight
    That wrought'st thy race's woe!
Redress is found! and foilèd is
    Thy fruit-alluring foe!
        Sing, lullaby, my little boy! &c.

Richard Verstegan.

The fruit of death, from Paradise
    Made thee, exilèd, mourn!
My fruit of life, to Paradise
    Makes joyful thy return!
        Sing, lullaby, my little boy! &c.

Grow up, good fruit! Be nourished by
    These fountains two of me!
That only flow with Maiden's milk,
    The only meat for thee!
        Sing, lullaby, my little boy! &c.

The earth is now a heaven become!
    And this base bower of mine,
A princely Palace unto me,
    My son doth make it shine!
        Sing, lullaby, my little boy! &c.

His sight gives clearness to my sight,
    When waking I him see!
And sleeping, his mild countenance
    Gives favour unto me!
        Sing, lullaby, my little boy! &c.

When I him in mine arms embrace;
    I feel my heart embraced!
E'en by the inward grace of his,
    Which he in me hath placed.
        Sing, lullaby, my little boy! &c.

And when I kiss his loving lips;
  Then his sweet-smelling breath
Doth yield a savour to my soul,
  That feeds Love, Hope, and Faith!
    Sing, lullaby, my little boy! &c.

The Shepherds left their keeping sheep,
  For joy to see my lamb!
How may I more rejoice to see
  Myself to be the dam!
    Sing, lullaby, my little boy! &c.

Three Kings their treasures hither brought,
  Of incense, myrrh, and gold;
The Heaven's treasure, and the King,
  That here they might behold.
    Sing, lullaby, my little boy! &c.

One sort, an Angel did direct;
  A star did guide the other:
And all, the fairest son to see
  That ever had a mother!
    Sing, lullaby, my little boy! &c.

This sight I see! this child I have!
  This infant I embrace!
O, endless comfort of the earth;
  And Heaven's eternal grace!
    Sing, lullaby, my little boy! &c.

Richard Verstegan.

Thee, Sanctity herself doth serve!
    Thee, Goodness doth attend!
Thee, Blessedness doth wait upon;
    And Virtues all commend!
        Sing, lullaby, my little boy! &c.

Great Kings and Prophets wishèd have
    To see that I possess!
Yet wish I never thee to see,
    If not in thankfulness!
        Sing, lullaby, my little boy! &c.

Let Heaven and Earth, and saints and men,
    Assistance give to me!
That all their most occurring aid
    Augment my thanks to thee!
        Sing, lullaby, my little boy! &c.

And let th' ensuing blessèd race,
    Thou wilt succeeding raise,
Join all their praises unto mine,
    To multiply thy praise!
        Sing, lullaby, my little boy! &c.

And take my service well in worth,
    And JOSEPH's here with me!
Who, of my husband bears the name,
    Thy servant for to be!
        Sing, lullaby, my little boy! &c.

[*? Thomas Deloney.*]

THE SPANISH LADY'S LOVE.

THE FIRST PART.

WILL you hear a Spanish Lady, how she wooed an Englishman?
Garments gay, as rich as may be, bedecked with jewels, had
    She on;
        Of a comely countenance and grace was She;
        Both by birth and parentage of high degree.

As his prisoner there he kept her; in his hands her life did lie;
CUPID's bands did tie them faster, by the liking of an eye.
        In his courteous company was all her joy;
        To favour him with any thing, she was not coy!

But, at last, there came commandment for to set all Ladies free,
With their jewels still adornèd. None to do them injury!
        'Oh! then,' said this Lady gay, 'full woe is me!'
        Oh! let me still sustain this kind captivity!

'Gallant Captain, take some pity on a woman in distress!
Leave me not within this city, for to die in heaviness!
        Thou hast set, this present day, my body free;
        But my heart in prison still remains with thee!'

'*How shouldst thou, fair Lady! love me! whom thou know'st thy
    country's foe,
Thy fair words make me suspect thee! Serpents lie where
    flowers grow!*'
        'All the harm I think on thee, most courteous Knight!
        God grant, upon my head the same may fully light!

[? *Thomas Deloney.*]

'Blessed be the time and season, that thou came on Spanish
  ground!
If you may our foes be termèd; gentle foes we have you found!
  With our city, you have won our hearts each one!
  Then to your country, bear away that is your own!'

THE SECOND PART.

'*Rest you still, most gallant Lady! Rest you still, and weep no
  more!
Of fair flowers you have plenty! Spain doth yield you wondrous
  store!
  Spaniards fraught with jealousy, we oft do find;
  But Englishmen, throughout the world, are counted kind!*'

'Leave me not unto a Spaniard! Thou alone enjoy'st my heart!
I am lovely, young, and tender! Love is likewise my desert!
  Still to have thee, day and night my mind is pressed!
  The Wife of every Englishman is counted blessed!'

'*It would be a shame, fair Lady! for to bear a woman hence;
English soldiers never carry any such, without offence.*'
  'I will quickly change myself! if it be so;
  And, like a Page, will follow thee, where'er thou go!'

'*I have neither gold, nor silver, to maintain thee, in this case;
And to travel is great charges, as you know, in every place.*'
  'My chains and jewels, every one, shall be thy own!
  And eke a hundred pounds in gold, that lies unknown.'

'*On the seas are many dangers. Many storms do there arise:
Which will be, to Ladies, dreadful; and force tears from wat'ry
  eyes.*'
  'Well in worth, I shall endure extremity;
  For I could find in heart to lose my life for thee!'

[? Thomas Deloney.]

'*Courteous Lady! leave this folly! Here comes all that breeds
    the strife!
I, in England, have already a sweet woman to my Wife.
    I will not falsify my vow, for gold, nor gain;
    Not yet for all the fairest Dames that live in Spain!*'

'O, how happy is that woman, that enjoys so true a friend!
Many happy days God send her! and of my suit I'll make
    an end;
    On my knees, I pardon crave for my offence!
    Which Love and true Affection did first commence.

'Commend me to that gallant Lady! Bear to her, this Chain
    of Gold
With these Bracelets, for a token! grieving that I was so bold.
    All my jewels, in like sort, take thou with thee!
    For they are fitting for thy Wife; but not for me.

'I will spend my days in prayer! love and all her laws defy!
In a Nunnery I will shroud me! far from any company!
    But ere my prayer have an end; be sure of this'
    To pray for thee, and for thy Love, I will not miss!

'Thus, farewell, most gallant Captain! Farewell, to my
    heart's content!
Count not Spanish Ladies wanton! though to thee my mind
    was bent.
    Joy and true prosperity remain with thee!'
    '*The like fall unto thy share, most fair Lady!*'

Henry Constable.

THE SHEPHERD'S SONG OF VENUS AND ADONIS.

VENUS fair did ride!
Silver doves, they drew her
  By the pleasant lawns,
    Ere the sun did rise.
VESTA's beauty rich
Opened wide to view her.
PHILOMEL records
    Pleasing harmonies.
  Every bird of Spring
  Cheerfully did sing.
Paphos' Goddess they salute.
  Now Love's Queen, so fair,
  Had of mirth no care;
For her son had made her mute.
  In her breast so tender,
  He a shaft did enter;
When her eyes beheld a boy.
  ADONIS was he naméd,
  By his mother shaméd;
Yet he now is VENUS' joy!

Him alone she met,
Ready bound for hunting;
  Him she kindly greets,
  And his journey stays.
Him she seeks to kiss,

Henry Constable.

No devices wanting.
Him her eyes still woo,
    Him her tongue still prays.
  He, with blushing red,
  Hangeth down the head;
Not a kiss can he afford!
  His face is turned away,
  Silence said her 'Nay!';
Still she wooed him, for a word!
  'Speak,' she said, 'thou fairest!
  Beauty thou impairest!
See me, I am pale and wan!
  Lovers all adore me!
  I for love implore thee!'
Crystal tears, with that down ran.

  Him herewith she forced
To come sit down by her.
  She his neck embraced,
    Gazing in his face.
  He, like one transformed,
Stirred no look to eye her.
  Every herb did woo him,
    Growing in that place.
  Each bird with a ditty
  Prayèd him for pity,
In behalf of Beauty's Queen.
  Waters' gentle murmur
  Cravèd him to love her.
Yet no liking could be seen.

Henry Constable.

'Boy,' she said, 'look on me!
Still I gaze upon thee!
Speak, I pray thee, my delight!'
Coldly he replied,
And, in brief, denied
To bestow on her a sight.

'I am now too young
To be won by Beauty!
Tender are my years,
I am yet a bud!'
'Fair thou art!' she said;
'Then it is thy duty,
Wert thou but a blossom,
To effect my good!
Every beauteous flower
Boasteth in my power!
Birds and beasts my laws effect!
MYRRHA, thy fair mother,
Most of any other,
Did my lovely hests respect!
Be with me delighted;
Thou shalt be requited!
Every Nymph on thee shall tend!
All the Gods shall love thee!
Man shall not reprove thee!
LOVE himself shall be thy friend!'

'Wend thee from me, VENUS!
I am not disposed!
Thou wring'st me too hard!

Henry Constable.

Prithee, let me go!
Fie! what a pain it is,
Thus to be enclosed!
If love begin with labour;
It will end in woe!'
'Kiss me! I will leave!'
'Here, a kiss receive!'
'A short kiss I do it find!
Wilt thou leave me so?
Yet thou shalt not go!
Breathe once more thy balmy wind!
It smelleth of the myrrh-tree,
That to the world did bring thee!
Never was perfume so sweet!'
When she had thus spoken,
She gave him a token;
And their naked bosoms meet.

'Now,' he said, 'let's go!
Hark, the hounds are crying!
Grisly boar is up!
Huntsmen follow fast!'
At the name of boar,
VENUS seemed dying!
Deadly coloured pale,
Roses overcast.
'Speak,' said she, 'no more
Of following the boar;
Thou, unfit for such a chase!
Course the fearful hare!

Henry Constable.

Ven'son, do not spare!
If thou wilt yield VENUS grace,
  Shun the boar, I pray thee!
  Else I still will stay thee!'
Herein, he vowed to please her mind;
  Then her arms enlarged!
  Loth she him discharged.
Forth he went, as swift as wind!

  THETIS, PHŒBUS' steeds
In the west retained,
  Hunting sport was past;
  Love her Love did seek!
Sight of him too soon,
Gentle Queen, she gained!
On the ground he lay,
  Blood had left his cheek,
  For an orpèd swine
  Smit him in the groin!
Deadly wound, his death did bring.
  Which, when VENUS found,
  She fell into a swound:
And, awaked, her hands did wring!
  Nymphs and Satyrs skipping,
  Came together tripping.
ECHO every cry exprest.
  VENUS, by her power,
  Turned him to a flower;
Which she weareth in her crest.

Henry Constable.

TO HIS FLOCKS.

FEED on, my flocks, securely!
Your Shepherd watcheth surely!
Run about, my little lambs!
Skip and wanton with your dams!
Your loving Herd with care will tend ye!

Sport on, fair flocks, at pleasure!
Nip VESTA's flow'ring treasure!
I myself will duly hark,
When my watchful dog doth bark!
From wolf and fox, I will defend ye!

MINE eye, with all the Deadly Sins is fraught.
1. First Proud, sith it presumed to look so high!
    A watchman being made, stood gazing by,
2. And Idle, took no heed, till I was caught.
3. And Envious bears envy that by thought
    Should, in his absence, be to her so nigh.
4. To Kill my heart, mine eye let in her eye;
    And so consent gave to a murder wrought!
5 And Covetous, it never would remove
    From her fair hair; gold so doth please his sight!
6. Unchaste, a bawd between my heart and love.
7. A Glutton eye, with tears drunk every night!
    These sins procurèd have a Goddess' ire;
    Wherefore my heart is damned in Love's sweet fire!

DAMELUS' SONG TO HIS DIAPHENIA.

DIAPHENIA, like the daffadowndilly,
White as the sun, fair as the lily:
   Heigh-ho! how I do love thee!
     I do love thee as my lambs
     Are belovèd of their dams!
   How blest were I! if thou wouldst prove me.

DIAPHENIA, like the spreading roses,
That in thy sweets, all sweets encloses!
   Fair Sweet! how I do love thee!
     I do love thee as each flower
     Loves the sun's life-giving power!
   For, dead, thy breath to life might move me!

DIAPHENIA, like to all things blessèd,
When all thy praises are expressèd.
   Dear Joy! how I do love thee!
     As the birds do love the Spring,
     Or the bees their careful King!
   Then, in requite, sweet Virgin, love me!

Henry Constable.

A PASTORAL SONG
BETWEEN PHILLIS AND AMARYLLIS,
TWO NYMPHS, EACH ANSWERING OTHER, LINE FOR LINE.

[PHILLIS.] FIE! on the sleights that men devise!
[AMARYLLIS.] *Heigh-ho! silly sleights!*
When simple Maids they would entice,
   Maids are Young Men's chief delights!
Nay, women, they witch with their eyes!
   Eyes like beams of burning sun!
And men, once caught, they soon despise!
   So are Shepherds oft undone!

If any Young Man win a Maid,
   Happy man is he!
By trusting him, she is betrayed!
   Fie! upon such treachery!
If Maids win Young Men with their guiles,
   Heigh-ho! guileful grief!
They deal like weeping crocodiles,
   That murder men without relief.

Henry Constable.

I know a simple country Hind;
  Heigh-ho! silly Swain!
To whom fair DAPHNE provèd kind.
  Was he not kind to her again?
He vowed, by PAN, with many an oath:
  Heigh-ho! Shepherds' God is he!
Yet, since, hath changed; and broke his troth.
  Troth-plight broke, will plaguèd be!

She had deceivèd many a Swain,
  Fie! on false deceit!
And plighted troth to them in vain.
  There can be no grief more great!
Her measure was with measure paid.
  Heigh-ho! heigh-ho! equal meed!
She was beguiled, that had betrayed.
  So shall all deceivers speed!

If every Maid were like to me;
  Heigh-ho! hard of heart!
Both Love and Lovers scorned should be!
  Scorners shall be sure of smart!
If every Maid were of my mind;
  Heigh-ho! heigh-ho! lovely Sweet!
They to their Lovers should prove kind!
  Kindness is for Maidens meet!

Methinks, Love is an idle toy.
   Heigh-ho! busy pain!
Both wit and sense it doth annoy.
   Both sense and wit thereby we gain!
Tush, Phyllis, *cease! Be not so coy!*
   Heigh-ho! heigh-ho! coy disdain!
I know you love a Shepherd's boy!
   Fie! that Maidens so should feign!

Well, Amaryllis, now I yield!
   Shepherds! pipe aloud!
Love conquers both in town and field!
   Like a tyrant fierce and proud.
The Evening Star is up, ye see!
   Vesper shines! We must away!
Would every Lover might agree!
   So we end our Roundelay.

SOME there are as fair to see too;
  But by Art, and not by Nature.
Some as tall and goodly be too;
  But want beauty to their stature.

Some have gracious, kind, behaviour;
  But are foul, or simple, creatures.
Some have wit, but want sweet favour;
  Or are proud of their good features.

Only you, in Court, or City,
Are both fair! tall! kind! and witty!

TO CUPID.

LOVE! if a God thou art;
  Then evermore thou must
  Be merciful and just!
If thou be just; O, wherefore doth thy dart
Wound mine alone; and not my Lady's heart?

If, merciful; then why
  Am I to pain reserved?
  Who have thee truly served:
While She, that by thy power sets not a fly,
Laughs thee to scorn; and lives at liberty!

Then, if a God thou wouldst accounted be;
Heal me like her! or else wound her like me!

Francis Davison.

STREPHON'S PALINODE

[In order to show the corresponding rhyme-system of these two Poems, apparently the only ones of this kind in the Literature, their answering rhymes are here numbered (1), (2), (3), &c.—E. A.]

STREPHON, upon some unkindness conceived, having made show to leave URANIA, and make love to another Nymph, was, at the next solemn assembly of Shepherds, not only frowned upon by URANIA; but commanded, with great bitterness, out of her presence. Whereupon, sorry for his offence, and desirous to regain her grace, whom he had never forsaken but in shew; upon his knees he, in this Song, humbly craves pardon: and URANIA, finding his true penitence, and unwilling to lose so worthy a Servant, receives him again into greater grace and favour than before.

SWEET! I do not pardon crave, (1)
  Till I have, (2)
By deserts, this fault amended! (3)
  This, I only this, desire, (4)
    That your ire (5)
May, with penance, be suspended! (6)

Not my will, but Fate, did fetch (7)
  Me, poor wretch! (8)
Into this unhappy error: (9)
  Which to plague, no tyrant's mind (10)
    Pain can find, (11)
Like my heart's self-guilty terror! (12)

Francis Davison.

Then, O, then, let that suffice! (13)
    Your dear eyes (14)
Need not, need not more afflict me! (15)
    Nor your sweet tongue, dipped in gall, (16)
        Need at all (17)
From your presence interdict me! (18)

Unto him that hell sustains, (19)
    No new pains (20)
Need be sought, to his tormenting! (21)
    Oh! my pains, hell's pains surpass; (22)
        Yet, alas, (23)
You are still new pains inventing! (24)

By my love, long, firm, and true, (25)
    Borne to you; (26)
By these tears, my grief expressing; (27)
    By this pipe, which, nights and days, (28)
        Sounds thy praise: (29)
Pity me! my fault confessing! (30)

Or if I may not desire (31)
    That thine ire (32)
May, with penance, be suspended; (33)
    Yet let me full pardon crave, (34)
        When I have, (35)
With soon death, my fault amended! (36)

URANIA'S ANSWER,

IN INVERTED RHYMES,

STAFF [=STANZA] FOR STAFF.

SINCE true penance hath suspended (6)
    Feignèd ire; (5)
More I'll grant than you desire! (4)
    Faults confessed are half amended; (3)
        And I have, (2)
In this half, all that I crave! (1)

Therefore, banish now the terror (12)
    Which you find (11)
In your guiltless grievèd mind! (10)
    For, though you have made an error, (9)
        From me, wretch! (8)
First beginning it did fetch! (7)

Ne'er my sight I'll interdict thee (18)
    More at all! (17)
Ne'er speak words more, dipped in gall! (16)
    Ne'er, ne'er, will I more afflict thee (15)
        With these eyes! (14)
What is past shall now suffice! (13)

Now new joys I'll be inventing! (24)
    Which, alas, (23)
May thy passèd woes surpass. (22)
    Too long thou hast felt tormenting! (21)
        Too great pains (20)
So great love and faith sustains! (19)

Let these eyes (by thy confessing, (30)
        Worthy praise!) (29)
Never see more nights, nor days! (28)
    Let my woes be past expressing! (27)
        When, to you, (26)
I cease to be kind and true. (25)

Thus are both our states amended! (36)
        For you have (35)
Fuller pardon than you crave! (34)
    And my fear is quite suspended; (33)
        Since mine ire (32)
Wrought th' effect I most desire. (31)

Francis Davison.

THAT ONLY HER BEAUTY AND VOICE PLEASE HIM.

PASSION may my judgement blear!
Therefore, sure, I will not swear
  That others are not pleasing:
    But (I speak it to my pain;
    And my life shall it maintain!)
  None else yields my heart easing!

Ladies, I do think there be,
Other some as fair as She;
  Though none have fairer features!
    But my turtle-like affection,
    Since of' her I made election,
  Scorns other fairest creatures!

Surely, I will not deny
But some others reach as high,
  With their sweet warbling voices:
    But since her notes charmed mine ear,
    Even the sweetest tunes I hear,
  To me, seem rude, harsh noises!

Francis Davison.

UPON HER PROTESTING, THAT NOW, HAVING TRIED HIS SINCERE AFFECTION, SHE LOVED HIM.

LADY! you are with beauties so enriched
    Of body and of mind;
    As I can hardly find,
Which of them all hath most my heart bewitched.

Whether your skin so white, so smooth, so tender,
    Or face so lovely fair,
    Or long heart-binding hair,
Or dainty hand, or leg and foot so slender;

Or whether your sharp wit and lively spirit,
    Where pride can find no place;
    Or your most pleasing grace;
Or speech which doth true eloquence inherit.

Most lovely, all, and each, of them doth move me
    More than words can express:
    But yet I must confess
I love you most; because you please to love me!

AT her fair hands, how have I grace intreated!
   With prayers oft repeated!
   Yet still my love is thwarted.
Heart, let her go! for She'll not be converted!
   Say, Shall She go?
      O, no, no, no, no, no!
She is most fair; though She be marble-hearted!

How often have my sighs declared mine anguish!
   Wherein I daily languish;
   Yet doth She still procure it.
Heart, let her go! for I can not endure it!
   Say, Shall She go?
      O, no, no, no, no, no!
She gave the wound; and She alone must cure it!

The trickling tears, that down my cheeks have flowed,
   My love have often showed;
   Yet still unkind I prove her!
Heart, let her go! for nought I do can move her!
   Say, Shall She go?
      O, no, no, no, no, no!
Though me She hates; I can not choose but love her!

But shall I still a true affection owe her;
   Which prayers, sighs, tears, do shew her:
   And shall She still disdain me?
Heart, let her go! if they no grace can gain me.
   Say, Shall She go?
      O, no, no, no, no, no!
She made me hers; and hers She will retain me!

Walter Davison.

But if the love that hath, and still doth, burn me,
　　No love, at length, return me;
　　Out of my thoughts I'll set her!
Heart, let her go! O, heart, I pray thee, let her!
　　Say, Shall She go?
　　　O, no, no, no, no, no!
Fixed in the heart; how can the heart forget her?
But if I weep and sigh, and often wail me,
　　Till tears, sighs, prayers, fail me;
　　Shall yet my love persèver?
Heart, let her go! if She will right thee never.
　　Say, Shall She go?
　　　O, no, no, no, no, no!
Tears, sighs, prayers, fail; but true love lasteth ever!

REASON and Love, lately, at strife contended,
　　Whose right it was to have my mind's protection?
Reason, on his side, Nature's will pretended;
　　Love's title was, my Mistress' rare perfection.
Of Power, to end this strife, each makes election;
　　Reason's pretence discoursive Thoughts defended:
But Love soon brought those Thoughts into subjection
　　By Beauty's troops; which on my Saint depended.
Yet since to rule the mind was Reason's duty,
　　On this condition, it by Love was rendered:
'That endless praise by Reason should be tendered,
　　As a due tribute to her conquering beauty!'
Reason was pleased withal; and to Love's royalty,
He pledged my heart, as hostage for his loyalty.

Anonymous.

FAIN would I change that note,
    To which fond Love hath charmed me;
Long, long, to sing by rote,
    Fancying that, that harmed me:
Yet when this thought doth come,
'Love is the perfect sum
    Of all delight!'
  I have no other choice
  Either for pen, or voice,
    To sing, or write!

O, Love! they wrong thee much,
    That say, 'Thy sweet is bitter!'
When thy ripe fruit is such,
    As nothing can be sweeter!
Fair House of Joy and Bliss,
Where truest pleasure is;
    I do adore thee!
I know thee, what thou art!
I serve thee with my heart;
    And fall before thee!

MY Love bound me, with a kiss,
    That I should no longer stay.
When I felt so sweet a bliss,
    I had less power to part away.
        Alas! that women do not know,
        Kisses make men loth to go!

Yes! She knows it but too well!
　　For I heard, when VENUS' dove,
In her ear, did softly tell,
　　'That Kisses were the Seals of Love!'
　　　　O, muse not then, though it be so,
　　　　Kisses make men loth to go!

Wherefore did She thus inflame
　　My desires, heat my blood,
Instantly to quench the same;
　　And starve whom She had given food?
　　　　I, I, [*Aye! Aye!*] the common-sense can show
　　　　Kisses make men loth to go!

Had She bid me go at first;
　　It would ne'er have grieved my heart!
Hope delayed had been the worst:
　　But, ah! to kiss; and then, to part!
　　　　How deep it struck, speak Gods! You know
　　　　Kisses make men loth to go!

FAREWELL, dear Love! since thou wilt needs be gone.
Mine eyes do shew my life is almost done.
　　　　Nay, I will never die!
　　　　So long as I can spy.
　　　　There be many mo!
　　　　Though that She do go!
　　There be many mo, I fear not!
　　Why, then, let her go! I care not! . . .

Anonymous.

Ten thousand times, farewell! Yet, stay a while!
Sweet! kiss me once! Sweet kisses, time beguile!
      I have no power to move.
      How now! Am I in love?
      Wilt thou needs be gone?
      Go, then! All is one!
Wilt thou needs be gone? O, hie thee!
Nay! stay; and do no more deny me!

Once more, farewell! I see, 'loth to depart'
Bids oft 'Adieu!' to her, that holds my heart!
      But seeing I must lose
      Thy love, which I did choose;
      Go thy ways, for me!
      Since it may not be.
Go thy ways, for me! but, Whither?
Go, O, but where I may come thither!

What shall I do? My Love is now departed!
She is as fair, as She is cruel-hearted!
      She would not be entreated,
      With prayers oft repeated!
      If She come no more;
      Shall I die therefore?
If She come no more; what care I!
Faith! let her go! or come! or tarry!

Christopher Marlow.

I WALKED along a stream, for pureness rare,
Brighter than sunshine; for it did acquaint
The dullest sight, with all the glorious prey
That in the pebble-pavèd channel lay.
No molten crystal; but a richer mine,
  Even Nature's rarest alchemy, ran there!
Diamonds resolved, and substance more divine.
  Through whose bright gliding current might appear
A thousand naked Nymphs; whose ivory shine
  Enamelling the banks, made them more dear
Than ever was that glorious Palace gate
Where the day-shining Sun, in triumph sat.

Upon this brim, the eglantine and rose,
  The tamarisk, olive, and the almond tree,
As kind companions, in one union grows;
  Folding their twindring arms, as oft we see
Turtle-taught Lovers, either, other 'close;
  Lending to dullness, feeling sympathy.
    And as a costly valance o'er a bed,
    So did their garland tops the brook o'erspread!
Their leaves, that differed both in shape and show,
  Though all were green; yet difference such in green,
Like to the chequered bent of IRIS' bow,
  Prided the running main, as it had been. . . .

Christopher Marlow.

THE PASSIONATE SHEPHERD,
TO HIS LOVE.

COME live with me, and be my Love!
And we will all the pleasures prove
That valleys, groves, and hills, and fields,
Woods, or steepy mountain, yields.

And we will sit upon the rocks,
Seeing the Shepherds feed their flocks;
By shallow rivers, to whose falls
Melodious birds sing Madrigals.

And I will make thee beds of roses,
And a thousand fragrant posies;
A cap of flowers, and a kirtle
Embroidered all with leaves of myrtle;

A gown made of the finest wool,
Which from our pretty lambs we pull;
Fair linèd slippers, for the cold,
With buckles of the purest gold;

A belt of straw and ivy buds,
With coral clasps and amber studs:
And if these pleasures may thee move,
Come live with me, and be my Love!

The Shepherds Swains shall dance and sing
For thy delight, each May morning.
If these delights thy mind may move;
Then live with me, and be my Love!

Ignoto.

[*Ignoto* is not to be taken as the pseudonym of a single Poet, but rather as that of a number of Poets who wished to remain unknown: for poems by R. BARNFIELD, F. GREVILLE Lord BROOKE, T. LODGE, Sir W. RALEGH, and A. W., have been recovered from this ascription.—E. A.]

THE NYMPH'S REPLY TO THE SHEPHERD.

IF all the World and Love were young,
And truth in every Shepherd's tongue;
These pretty pleasures might me move
To live with thee, and be thy Love.

Time drives the flocks from field to fold,
When rivers rage, and rocks grow cold;
And PHILOMEL becometh dumb;
The rest complain of cares to come.

The flowers do fade; and wanton fields,
To wayward winter reckoning yields.
A honey tongue, a heart of gall,
Is Fancy's Spring; but Sorrow's Fall.

Thy gowns, thy shoes, thy beds of roses,
Thy cap, thy kirtle, and thy posies,
Soon break! soon wither! soon forgotten!
In folly ripe; in reason rotten!

Thy belt of straw and ivy buds,
Thy coral clasps and amber studs,
All these in me no means can move
To come to thee, and be thy Love!

But could Youth last, and Love still breed;
Had Joys no date, nor Age no need:
Then these delights my mind might move
To live with thee, and be thy Love!

A NYMPH'S DISDAIN OF LOVE.

'Hey, down-a-down!' did DIAN sing,
 Amongst her virgins sitting,
'Than Love there is no vainer thing!
 For Maidens most unfitting!'
And so think I, with a down, down, derry!

When Women knew no woe,
 But lived themselves to please;
Men's feigning guiles they did not know,
 The ground of their disease.
Unborn was false Suspect!
 No thought of Jealousy!
From wanton toys and fond affect,
 The Virgin's life was free!
  'Hey, down-a-down!' did DIAN sing, &c.

At length, Men usèd charms;
  To which what Maids gave ear,
Embracing gladly endless harms,
  Anon enthrallèd were.
Thus Women welcomed Woe,
  Disguised in name of Love,
A jealous hell! a painted show!
  So shall they find, that prove!
    'Hey, down-a-down!' did DIAN sing, &c.

PHILLIDA'S LOVE CALL TO HER CORIDON; AND HIS REPLYING.

PHIL. CORIDON! arise, my CORIDON!
    TITAN shineth clear!
COR. Who is it, that calleth CORIDON?
    Who is it, that I hear?
PHIL. PHILLIDA, thy True Love, calleth thee!
    Arise, then! Arise, then!
        Arise, and keep thy flock with me!
COR. PHILLIDA, my True Love; is it she?
    I come then! I come then!
        I come, and keep my flock with thee!

PHIL. Here are cherries ripe for CORIDON;
    Eat them, for my sake!
COR. Here's my oaten pipe, my lovely one!
    Sport for thee to make!

Ignoto.

PHIL.   Here are threads, my True Love! fine as silk,
          To knit thee, to knit thee
              A pair of stockings white as milk.
COR.   Here are reeds, my True Love! fine and neat,
          To make thee, to make thee
              A bonnet, to withstand the heat.

PHIL.   I will gather flowers, my CORIDON!
          To set in thy cap!
COR.   I will gather pears, my lovely one!
          To put in thy lap!
PHIL.   I will buy my True Love garters gay,
          For Sundays! for Sundays!
              To wear about his legs so tall.
COR.   I will buy my True Love yellow say
          For Sundays! for Sundays!
              To wear about her middle small.

PHIL.   When my CORIDON sits on a hill,
          Making melody;
COR.   When my lovely one goes to her wheel,
          Singing cheerily;
PHIL.   Sure, methinks, my True Love doth excel
          For sweetness! for sweetness!
              Our PAN, that old Arcadian Knight!
COR.   And, methinks, my True Love bears the bell
          For clearness! for clearness!
              Beyond the Nymphs that be so bright.

Ignoto.

PHIL. Had my CORIDON! my CORIDON
         Been, alack! her Swain:
COR.   Had my lovely one! my lovely one
         Been in Ida plain,
PHIL. CYNTHIA, ENDYMION had refused!
         Preferring, preferring
             My CORIDON to play withal.
COR.   The Queen of Love had been excused;
         Bequeathing, bequeathing
             My PHILLIDA the golden ball.

PHIL. Yonder comes my mother, CORIDON!
         Whither shall I fly?
COR.   Under yonder beech, my lovely one!
         While she passeth by.
PHIL. Say to her, Thy True Love was not here!
         Remember! remember
             To-morrow is another day!
COR.   Doubt me not, my True Love! do not fear!
         Farewell then! farewell then!
             Heaven keep our loves alway!

SWEET Violets! Love's Paradise! that spread
  Your gracious odours (which you couchèd bear
      Within your paly faces)
  Upon the gentle wing of some calm-breathing wind
      That plays upon the plain;

Ignoto.

If, by the favour of propitious stars, you gain
Such grace, as in my Lady's bosom place to find:
    Be proud to touch those places!
And when her warmth, your moisture forth doth wear,
Whereby her dainty parts are sweetly fed,
    Your Honours of the flowery meads, I pray!
    You pretty Daughters of the Earth and Sun!
With mild and seemly breathing, straight display
    My bitter sighs! that have my heart undone.

Vermilion Roses! that, with new day's rise,
    Display your crimson folds fresh-looking fair,
        Whose radiant bright disgraces
    The rich adornèd rays of roseate rising Morn:
        Ah! if her virgin's hand
    Do pluck your pure! ere PHŒBUS view the land,
And vail your gracious pomp, in lovely Nature's scorn;
    If chance, my Mistress traces
    Fast by your flowers, to take the summer's air;
Then, woeful blushing, tempt her glorious eyes
    To spread their tears, ADONIS' death reporting,
    And tell Love's torments, sorrowing for her friend;
Whose drops of blood, within her leaves consorting,
    Report fair VENUS' moans withouten end!

Then may remorse, in pitying of my smart,
Dry up my tears; and dwell within her heart!

Ignoto.

AN INVECTIVE AGAINST WOMEN.

ARE Women *fair?* I [*Aye*] wondrous fair to see to!
Are Women *sweet?* Yea, passing sweet they be too!
Most fair and sweet to them that inly love them;
Chaste and discreet to all, save those that prove them.

Are Women *wise?* Not wise; but they be witty!
Are Women *witty?* Yea; the more the pity!
They are so witty, and in wit so wily,
That, be ye ne'er so wise, they will beguile ye!

Are Women *fools?* Not fools; but fondlings many!
Can Women *fond* be faithful unto any?
When snow-white swans do turn to colour sable,
Then Women fond will be both firm and stable!

Are Women *Saints?* No Saints; nor yet no Devils!
Are Women *good?* Not good; but needful evils!
So angel-like, that Devils I do not doubt them!
So needful ills, that few can live without them!

Are Women *proud?* I [*Aye*] passing proud, and [*if you*]
    praise them!
Are Women *kind?* I [*Aye*] wondrous kind, and [*if you*]
    please them!
Or so imperious, no man can endure them;
Or so kind-hearted, any may procure them!

THE SHEPHERD'S SLUMBER.

IN peascod time, when hound to horn
    Gives ear, till buck be killed;
And little lads, with pipes of corn,
    Sat keeping beasts afield;
I went to gather strawberries tho,
    By woods and groves full fair;
And parched my face with PHŒBUS so,
    In walking in the air,
That down I laid me, by a stream,
    With boughs all overclad;
And there I met the strangest dream
    That ever Shepherd had.

Methought, I saw each Christmas Game,
    Each Revel all and some,
And every thing that I can name,
    Or may in fancy come.
The substance of the sights I saw,
    In silence pass they shall;
Because I lack the skill to draw
    The order of them all.
But VENUS shall not pass my pen;
    Whose Maidens, in disdain,
Did feed upon the hearts of men,
    That CUPID's bow had slain.

Ignoto.

And that blind boy was all in blood
    Bebathèd to the ears;
And like a Conqueror he stood,
    And scornèd Lovers' tears.
'I have,' quoth he, 'more hearts at call
    Than CÆSAR could command;
And, like the deer, I make them fall!
    That runneth o'er the lawn.
One drops down here! another, there!
    In bushes as they groan;
I bend a scornful, careless, ear,
    To hear them make their moan.'

'Ah, Sir!' quoth HONEST MEANING then,
    'Thy boylike brags I hear!
When thou hast wounded many a man,
    As huntsman doth the deer;
Becomes it thee to triumph so!
    Thy mother wills it not;
For she had rather break thy bow,
    Than thou shouldst play the sot!'
'What saucy merchant speaketh now?'
    Said VENUS, in her rage,
'Art thou so blind, thou know'st not how
    I govern every age!

'My son doth shoot no shaft in waste!
    To me the boy is bound:

Ignoto.

He never found a heart so chaste,
  But he had power to wound!'
'Not so, fair Goddess!' quoth FREE WILL,
  'In me, there is a choice!
And cause I am of mine own ill;
  If I in thee rejoice!
And when I yield myself a slave
  To thee, or to thy son;
Such recompense I ought not have!
  If things be rightly done.'

'Why, fool!' stepped forth DELIGHT, and said,
  'When thou art conquered thus,
Then, lo, Dame LUST, that wanton Maid,
  Thy Mistress is, iwus!
And LUST is CUPID's darling Dear!
  Behold her, where she goes!
She creeps, the milk-warm flesh so near,
  She hides her under close;
Where many privy thoughts do dwell,
  A heaven here on earth!
For they have never mind of hell;
  They think so much on mirth!'

'Be still, GOOD MEANING!' quoth GOOD SPORT,
  'Let CUPID triumph make!
For, sure, his kingdom shall be short;
  If we no pleasure take!

Ignoto.

Fair Beauty and her play-feres gay,
  The Virgins Vestal too,
Shall sit, and with their fingers play,
  As idle people do.
If HONEST MEANING fall to frown,
  And I, GOOD SPORT, decay;
Then VENUS' glory will come down,
  And they will pine away!'

'Indeed,' quoth WIT, 'this your device,
  With strangeness must be wrought!
And where you see these women nice,
  And looking to be sought;
With scowling brows, their follies check;
  And so give them the fig!
Let Fancy be no more at beck!
  When Beauty looks so big.'
When VENUS heard how they conspired
  To murder women so;
Methought, indeed, the house was fired,
  With storms and lightning tho.

The thunderbolts through windows burst;
  And, in their steps, a wight
Which seemed some soul, or sprite, accurst,
  So ugly was the sight:
'I charge you, Ladies all,' said he,
  'Look to yourselves in haste!

Ignoto.

For if that men so wilful be,
  And have their thoughts so chaste,
And they can tread on Cupid's breast,
  And march on Venus' face:
Then they shall sleep in quiet rest;
  When you shall wail your case!'

With that, had Venus, all in spite,
  Stirred up the Dames to ire;
And Lust fell cold, and Beauty white
  Sat babbling with Desire;
Whose mutt'ring words I might not mark.
  Much whispering there arose;
The day did lower, the sun waxed dark,
  Away each Lady goes!
But whither went this angry flock,
  Our Lord himself doth know!
Wherewith full loudly crew the cock;
  And I awakèd so.

'A dream,' quoth I, 'a dog it is!
  I take thereon no keep!
I gage my head, such toys as this
  Doth spring from lack of sleep!'

Sir Walter Ralegh.

As you came from the holy land
  Of Walsingham,
Met you not with my True Love,
  By the way, as you came?

How shall I know your True Love,
  That have met many one,
As I went to the holy land;
  That have come, that have gone?

She is neither white, nor brown;
  But as the heavens fair!
There is none hath a form so divine,
  In the earth, or the air!

Such a one did I meet, good Sir!
  Such an angelic face;
Who like a Queen, like a Nymph, did appear
  By her gait, by her grace.

She hath left me here all alone,
  All alone, as unknown;
Who sometimes did me lead with herself,
  And me loved as her own.

Sir Walter Ralegh.

What's the cause that She leaves you alone,
    And a new way doth take?
Who loved you once as her own,
    And her joy did you make.

*I have loved her all my youth;
    But now old, as you see,
LOVE likes not the falling fruit
    From the withered tree!*

*Know, that LOVE is a careless child,
    And forgets promise past;
He is blind; he is deaf when he list,
    And in faith never fast!*

*His desire is a dureless content,
    And a trustless joy.
He is won, with a world of despair;
    And is lost, with a toy.*

*Of womenkind such indeed is the love;
    Or the word Love abused,
Under which many childish desires
    And conceits are excused.*

*But True Love is a durable fire,
    In the mind ever burning;
Never sick! never old! never dead!
    From itself never turning!*

Sir Walter Ralegh.

WHAT is our Life? A Play of Passion!
Our mirth? The Music of Division!
Our mothers' wombs, the Tiring Houses be;
Where we are dressed for this short Comedy!
Heaven, the judicious sharp Spectator is,
That sits, and marks still, Who do act amiss?
Our graves, that hide us from the searching sun,
Are like Drawn Curtains, when the Play is done.
Thus march we, Playing, to our latest rest;
Only we die in earnest! That's no jest!

FAREWELL TO THE COURT.

LIKE truthless dreams, so are my joys expired;
    And past return are all my dandled days!
My love, misled; and fancy, quite retired:
    Of all which past, the sorrow only stays!

My lost delights, now clean from sight of land,
    Have left me all alone in unknown ways.
My mind, to woe; my life in Fortune's hand:
    Of all which past, the sorrow only stays!

As in a country strange, without companion,
    I only wail the wrong of Death's delays!
Whose sweet Spring spent, whose Summer wellnigh
      is done:
    Of all which past, the sorrow only stays!

Whom care forewarns, ere age or Winter's cold,
To haste me hence, to find my fortune's fold!

Sir Walter Ralegh.

A POESY TO PROVE AFFECTION IS NOT LOVE.

CONCEIT, begotten by the eyes,
Is quickly born, and quickly dies:
For while it seeks our hearts to have,
Meanwhile there Reason makes his grave.
For many things the eyes approve,
Which yet the heart doth seldom love.

For as the seeds, in Spring-time sown,
Die in the ground, ere they be grown;
Such is Conceit! whose rooting fails,
As child that in the cradle quails;
Or else, within the mother's womb,
Hath his beginning, and his tomb.

Affection follows Fortune's wheels;
And soon is shaken from her heels!
For following Beauty, or Estate,
Her liking still is turned to hate.
For all affections have their change;
And Fancy only loves to range.

Desire himself runs out of breath;
And getting, doth but gain his death!
Desire, nor reason hath, nor rest;
And, blind, doth seldom choose the best!
Desire attained is not Desire;
But as the cinders of the fire.

Sir Walter Ralegh.

As ships, in ports desired are drowned;
As fruit, once ripe, then falls to ground;
As flies, that seek for flames, are brought
To cinders by the flames they sought:
So fond Desire, when it attains,
The life expires! the woe remains!

And yet some Poets fain would prove
Affection to be perfect Love!
And that Desire is of that kind,
No less a Passion of the mind!
As if wild beasts and men did seek
To like, to love, to choose, alike!

A REPORTING SONNET.

HER face, her tongue, her wit, so fair, so sweet, so sharp,
First bent, then drew, now hit, mine eye, mine ear, mine heart.
Mine eye, mine ear, my heart, to like, to learn, to love,
Her face, her tongue, her wit, doth lead, doth teach, doth move.
Her face, her tongue, her wit, with beams, with sound, with art,
Doth blind, doth charm, doth rule, mine eye, mine ear, my heart.

Mine eye, mine ear, my heart, with life, with hope, with skill,
Her face, her tongue, her wit, doth feed, doth feast, doth fill.
O, face, O, tongue, O, wit, with frowns, with checks, with smart,
Wring not, vex not, wound not, mine eye! mine ear! my heart!
This eye, this ear, this heart, shall joy, shall bind, shall swear,
Your face, your tongue, your wit, to serve! to love! to fear!

MELIBŒUS. SHEPHERD, *what is Love? I pray thee, tell!*
FAUSTUS.　It is that fountain, and that well,
　　　Where Pleasure and Repentance dwell.
　　　It is, perhaps, that sauncing bell
　　　That tolls all in, to heaven; or hell.
　　　　And this is Love, as I hear tell!

MEL. *Yet, what is Love? I prithee, say!*
FAU. It is a work on holiday.
　　　It is December matched with May,
　　　When lusty bloods, in fresh array,
　　　Hear ten months after of the play.
　　　　And this is Love, as I hear say!

MEL. *Yet, what is Love? Good Shepherd, sain!*
FAU. It is a sunshine mixed with rain.
　　　It is a toothache, or like pain.
　　　It is a game, where none doth gain.
　　　The Lass saith, 'No!'; and would full fain.
　　　　And this is Love, as I hear sain!

MEL. *Yet, Shepherd, what is Love? I pray!*
FAU. It is a "Yea!" It is a 'Nay!'
　　　A pretty kind of sporting fray.
　　　It is a thing will soon away!
　　　Then, Nymphs! take vantage, while ye may!
　　　　And this is Love, as I hear say!

Sir Walter Ralegh.

MEL. Yet, what is Love? Good Shepherd, show!
FAU. A thing that creeps. It cannot go.
       A prize that passeth to and fro;
       A thing for one; a thing for mo.
       And he that proves, must find it so.
         And, Shepherd, this is Love, I trow!

THE ADVICE.

MANY desire; but few, or none, deserve
  To foil the fort of thy most constant will.
Wherefore, take heed! Let fancy never swerve
  But unto him that will defend thee still!
    For this, be sure! The fort of fame once won;
    Farewell, the rest! Thy happy days are done!

Many desire; but few, or none, deserve
  To pluck the branch, and let the flower fall.
Wherefore, take heed! Let fancy never swerve
  But unto him, that will take leaves and all!
    For this, be sure! The flower once plucked away;
    Farewell, the rest! The branch will soon decay!

Many desire; but few, or none, deserve
  To cut the corn, not subject to the sickle.
Wherefore, take heed! Let fancy never swerve;
  But constant stand! for mowers' minds are fickle!
    For this, be sure! The crop being once obtained;
    Farewell, the rest! The soil will be disdained!

Sir Walter Ralegh.

Fain would I; but I dare not!
I dare; but yet I may not!
I may; although I care not
For pleasure, when I play not!

You laugh; because you like not!
I jest; and yet I joy not!
You pierce; although you strike not!
I strike; and yet annoy not!

I spy; when as I speak not!
Full oft I speak, and speed not!
But of my wounds, you reck not!
Because you see, they bleed not.

Yet bleed they, when you see not!
But you, the pains endure not!
Of noble minds, they be not,
That ever kill and cure not!

I see; when as I view not!
I wish; although I crave not!
I serve; and yet I sue not!
I hope for that I have not!

I catch; although I hold not!
I burn; although I flame not!
I seem; when as I would not;
And when I seem, I am not!

Sir Walter Ralegh.

Yours I am; though I seem not!
And will be; though I show not!
My outward deeds, then deem not;
When mine intent you know not!

But if my service prove not
Most sure, although I sue not;
Withdraw your mind, and love not!
Nor of my ruin rue not!

LIKE to a hermit poor, in place obscure,
   I mean to spend my days of endless doubt!
To wail such woes, as time cannot recure!
   Where none but LOVE shall ever find me out.

My food shall be, of care and sorrow made.
   My drink nought else but tears fall'n from mine eyes.
And for my light, in such obscurèd shade,
   The flames shall serve, which from my heart arise.

A Gown of gray my body shall attire.
   My Staff, of broken hope, whereon I'll stay.
Of late repentance, linked with long desire,
   The Couch is framed; whereon my limbs I'll lay.

    And at my Gate, Despair shall linger still,
    To let in Death; when Love and Fortune will.

THE LIE.

Go, Soul, the Body's guest,
　Upon a thankless arrant!
Fear not to touch the best!
　The truth shall be thy warrant!
　　Go, since I needs must die,
　　And give the World the lie!

Say to the Court, it glows
　And shines like rotten wood!
Say to the Church, it shows
　What's good; and doth no good!
　　If Church and Court reply;
　　Then give them both the lie!

Tell Potentates, they live
　Acting by others' action;
Not loved, unless they give;
　Not strong, but by affection.
　　If Potentates reply;
　　Give Potentates the lie!

Tell men of high condition,
　That manage the Estate,
Their purpose is ambition;
　Their practice, only hate!
　　And if they once reply;
　　Then give them all the lie!

Sir Walter Ralegh.

Tell them that brave it most;
  They beg for more, by spending!
Who, in their greatest cost,
  Like nothing but commending.
    And if they make reply;
    Then give them all the lie!

Tell Zeal, it wants devotion!
  Tell Love, it is but lust!
Tell Time, it meets but motion!
  Tell Flesh, it is but dust!
    And wish them not reply;
    For thou must give the lie!

Tell Age, it daily wasteth!
  Tell Honour, how it alters!
Tell Beauty, how she blasteth!
  Tell Favour, how it falters!
    And as they shall reply;
    Give every one the lie!

Tell Wit, how much it wrangles
  In tickle points of niceness!
Tell Wisdom, she entangles
  Herself in overwiseness!
    And when they do reply;
    Straight give them both the lie!

Sir Walter Ralegh.

Tell Physic, of her boldness;
　Tell Skill, it is prevention;
Tell Charity, of coldness;
　Tell Law, it is contention:
　　And as they do reply;
　　So give them still the lie!

Tell Fortune, of her blindness;
　Tell Nature, of decay;
Tell Friendship, of unkindness;
　Tell Justice, of delay:
　　And if they will reply;
　　Then give them all the lie!

Tell Arts they have no soundness,
　But vary by esteeming;
Tell Schools, they want profoundness,
　And stand so much on seeming.
　　If Arts and Schools reply;
　　Give Arts and Schools the lie!

Tell Faith, it's fled the City!
　Tell how the Country erreth!
Tell, Manhood shakes off pity!
　Tell, Virtue least preferrèd!
　　And if they do reply;
　　Spare not to give the lie!

So when thou hast, as I
    Commanded thee, done blabbing:
Because to give the lie
    Deserves no less than stabbing;
      Stab at thee, he that will!
      No stab, my soul can kill!

HIS PILGRIMAGE.

GIVE me my scallop-shell of quiet,
    My staff of faith to walk upon,
My scrip of joy, immortal diet!
    My bottle of salvation,
My gown of glory, hope's true gage!
And thus I'll take my Pilgrimage!

Blood must be my body's only balmer;
    No other balm will there be given!
Whilst my soul, like a quiet Palmer,
    Travelleth towards the land of Heaven,
Over the silver mountains,
Where spring the nectar fountains.

      There will I kiss
      The bowl of bliss;
And drink mine everlasting fill,
Upon every milken hill.
My soul will be a-dry before;
But, after, it will thirst no more!

Then by that happy blissful day,
    More peaceful Pilgrims I shall see;
That have cast off their rags of clay,
    And walk apparelled fresh like me.
        I'll take them, first,
        To quench their thirst,
And taste of nectar suckets,
        At those clear wells,
        Where sweetness dwells;
Drawn up by Saints in crystal buckets.

    And when our bottles and all we
Are filled with immortality;
Then, the blessèd paths we'll travel,
Strowed with rubies thick as gravel;
Ceilings of diamonds, sapphire floors,
High walls of coral, and pearly bowers.

    From thence, to Heaven's bribeless Hall:
Where no corrupted voices brawl;
No conscience molten into gold;
No forged accuser bought, or sold;
No Cause deferred, no vain-spent journey;
For there, CHRIST is the King's Attorney:
Who pleads for all, without degrees;
And he hath angels, but no fees.
    And when the Grand twelve million Jury
Of our sins, with direful fury,

Sir Walter Ralegh.

Against our souls, black verdicts give:
CHRIST pleads his death; and then we live!

Be thou my speaker, taintless Pleader!
Unblotted Lawyer! true Proceeder!
Thou giv'st salvation, even for alms!
Not with a bribèd Lawyer's palms.

And this is mine eternal plea
To Him that made heaven, and earth, and sea.
    That, since my flesh must die so soon,
    And want a head to dine next noon;
    Just, at the stroke, when my veins start
      and spread,
    Set on my soul, an everlasting head!

Then am I ready, like a Palmer fit,
To tread those blest paths; which before I writ.

Anonymous.

  SHALL I (like a hermit) dwell
On a rock, or in a cell,
Calling home the smallest part
That is missing of my heart,
To bestow it, where I may
Meet a rival every day?
  If She undervalue me;
  What care I, how fair She be!

  Were her tresses angel-gold;
If a stranger may be bold,
Unrebukèd, unafraid,
To convert them to a braid;
And, with little more ado,
Work them into bracelets too!
  If the mine be grown so free;
  What care I, how rich it be!

  Were her hands as rich a prize
As her hairs, or precious eyes;
If She lay them out to take
Kisses, for good manners' sake!
And let every Lover skip
From her hand, unto her lip!
  If She seem not chaste to me;
  What care I, how chaste She be!

  No! She must be perfect snow,
In effect as well as show!
Warming but as snowballs do;
Not, like fire, by burning too!

But when She, by change, hath got
To her heart, a second lot;
　Then, if others share with me,
　Farewell, her! whate'er She be!

　I SAW my Lady weep!
And Sorrow proud! to be advancèd so
In those fair eyes, where all perfections keep.
　Her face was full of Woe!
But such a Woe (believe me!) as wins more hearts
Than Mirth can do, with her inticing parts!

　Sorrow was there made fair!
And Passion, wise! Tears, a delightful thing!
Silence, beyond all Speech, a wisdom rare!
　She made her sighs to sing;
And all things, with so sweet a sadness move;
As made my heart, at once, both grieve and love!

　O, fairer than aught else
The world can show! leave off in time to grieve!
Enough! enough! your joyful look excels!
　Tears kill the heart, believe!
O, strive not to be excellent in Woe;
Which only breeds your beauty's overthrow!

DAMŒTAS' JIG,
IN PRAISE OF HIS LOVE.

JOLLY Shepherd, Shepherd on a hill,
    On a hill so merrily,
    On a hill so cheerily,
Fear not, Shepherd, there to pipe thy fill!
Fill every dale! fill every plain!
Both sing, and say, 'Love feels no pain!'

Jolly Shepherd, Shepherd on a green,
    On a green so merrily,
    On a green so cheerily,
Be thy voice shrill! be thy mirth seen!
Heard to each Swain! seen to each Trull!
Both sing, and say, 'Love's joy is full!'

Jolly Shepherd, Shepherd in the sun,
    In the sun so merrily,
    In the sun so cheerily,
Sing forth thy songs! and let thy rhymes run
Down to the dales, from the hills above!
Both sing, and say, 'No life, to Love!

John Wootton.

Jolly Shepherd, Shepherd in the shade,
    In the shade so merrily,
    In the shade so cheerily,
Joy in thy life, life of Shepherd's trade!
Joy in thy love! love full of glee!
Both sing, and say, 'Sweet Love for me!'

Jolly Shepherd, Shepherd here or there,
    Here or there so merrily,
    Here or there so cheerily,
Or in thy chat, either at thy cheer,
In every jig, in every lay,
Both sing, and say, 'Love lasts for aye!'

Jolly Shepherd! Shepherd, DAPHNIS' Love!
    DAPHNIS' Love so merrily,
    DAPHNIS' Love so cheerily,
Let thy fancy never more remove!
Fancy be fixed; fixed not to fleet!
Still sing, and say, 'Love's yoke is sweet!'

DAMŒTAS' MADRIGAL,
IN PRAISE OF HIS DAPHNIS.

TUNE on my pipe, the praises of my Love!
  Love fair and bright!
Fill earth with sound, and airy heavens above,
  Heavens, JOVE's delight,
   With DAPHNIS' praise!

To pleasant Tempe groves and plains about,
  Plains, Shepherds' pride!
Resounding echoes of her praise ring out!
  Ring far and wide
   My DAPHNIS' praise!

When I begin to sing, begin to sound!
  Sound loud and shrill!
Do make each note unto the skies rebound!
  Skies calm and still,
   With DAPHNIS' praise!

Her Tresses are like wires of beaten gold!
  Gold bright and sheen!
Like NISUS' golden hair, that SCYLLA polled!
  SCYLL. o'erseen,
   Through MINOS' love.

Her Eyes like shining lamps, in midst of night!
  Night dark and dead;
Or as the stars, that give the seamen light!
  Light for to lead
   Their wand'ring ships.

John Wootton.

Amidst her Cheeks, the rose and lily strive,
  Lily snow-white;
When their contend doth make their colour thrive,
  Colour too bright
   For Shepherds' eyes!

Her Lips like scarlet of the finest dye!
  Scarlet blood-red.
Teeth white as snow, which on the hills doth lie,
  Hills overspread
   By winter's force.

Her Skin as soft as is the finest silk!
  Silk soft and fine:
Of colour like unto the whitest milk!
  Milk of the kine
   Of DAPHNIS' herd.

As swift of Foot as is the pretty roe!
  Roe swift of pace,
When yelping hounds pursue her to and fro;
  Hounds fierce in chase,
   To 'reave her life.

Cease, tongue! to tell of any more compares!
  Compares too rude!
APHNIS' deserts and beauty are too rare!
  Then here, conclude
   Fair DAPHNIS' praise!

A FICTION, HOW CUPID MADE A NYMPH WOUND HERSELF WITH HIS ARROWS.

It chanced, of late, a Shepherd's Swain,
    That went to seek a strayèd sheep,
Within a thicket, on the plain,
    Espied a dainty Nymph asleep.

Her golden hair o'erspread her face,
    Her careless arms abroad were cast,
Her quiver had her pillow's place,
    Her breast lay bare to every blast.

The Shepherd stood, and gazed his fill!
    Nought durst he do! nought durst he say!
When chance, or else perhaps his will,
    Did guide the God of Love that way.

The crafty boy, that sees her sleep,
    Whom, if She waked, he durst not see,
Behind her closely seeks to creep,
    Before her nap should ended be.

There come; he steals her shafts away;
    And puts his own into their place:
Ne dares he any longer stay;
    But, ere She wakes, hies hence apace!

Scarce was he gone, when She awakes,
    And spies the Shepherd standing by;
Her bended bow in haste She takes,
    And at the simple Swain lets fly.

Forth flew the shaft, and pierced his heart,
    That to the ground he fell with pain;
Yet up again forthwith he start,
    And to the Nymph he ran amain.

Amazed to see so strange a sight,
    She shot! and shot! but all in vain:
The more his wounds, the more his might!
    Love yielded strength, in midst of pain.

Her angry eyes are great with tears,
    She blames her hands! She blames her skill!
The bluntness of her shafts She fears;
    And try them on herself She will!

'Take heed, sweet Nymph! Try not the shaft!
    Each little touch will prick the heart!
Alas, thou know'st not CUPID's craft!
    Revenge is joy; the end is smart!'

Yet try She will, and prick some bare!
    Her hands were gloved; and, next to hand,
Was that fair breast, that breast so rare!
    That made the Shepherd senseless stand.

That breast She pricked; and, through that breast,
   Love finds an entry to her heart.
At feeling of this new-come guest,
   Lord! how this gentle Nymph doth start!

She runs not now! She shoots no more!
   Away She throws both shafts and bow!
She seeks for that She shunned before!
   She thinks the Shepherd's haste too slow!

Though mountains meet not; Lovers may!
   So others do; and so do they!
The God of Love sits on a tree,
   And laughs, that pleasant sight to see.

TO TIME.

ETERNAL Time, that wasteth without waste!
   That art, and art not! diest, and livest still!
Most slow of all; and yet of greatest haste!
   Both ill, and good; and neither good, nor ill!
      How can I justly praise thee, or dispraise!
      Dark are thy nights; but bright and clear thy days!

Both free and scarce, thou giv'st and tak'st again!
   Thy womb, that all doth breed, is tomb to all!
Whatso by thee hath life, by thee is slain!
   From thee, do all things rise; by thee, they fall!
      Constant, inconstant, moving, standing still;
      WAS, IS, SHALL BE, do thee both breed and kill.

Anomos, i.e. A. W.

I lose thee, when I seek to find thee out!
The farther off, the more I follow thee!
The faster hold, the greater cause of doubt!
WAS, IS, I know; but SHALL, I cannot see!
All things by thee are measured; thou, by none!
All are in thee! Thou, in thyself alone!

WHERE HIS LADY KEEPS HIS HEART.

SWEET LOVE, mine only treasure!
   For service long unfeigned,
   Wherein I nought have gained,
Vouchsafe this little pleasure!
   To tell me, In what part
   My Lady keeps my heart?

If in her Hair so slender,
   Like golden nets untwined,
   Which fire and Art have fined;
Her thrall my heart I render!
   For ever to abide
   With locks so dainty tied!

If in her Eyes, She bind it;
   Wherein that fire was framed,
   By which it is inflamed;
I dare not look to find it!
   I only wish it sight,
   To see that pleasant light!

But if her Breast have deignèd
    With kindness to receive it;
    I am content to leave it,
Though death thereby were gainèd;
    Then, Lady! take your own!
    That lives for you alone.

CUPID'S MARRIAGE WITH DISSIMULATION.

A NEW-FOUND Match is made of late,
  Blind CUPID needs will change his wife!
New-fangled LOVE doth PSYCHE hate!
  With whom so long he led his life.
      DISSEMBLING, she
      The Bride must be,
    To please his wanton eye!
      PSYCHE laments
      That LOVE repents
His choice! without cause, Why?

Cytheron sounds with music strange,
  Unknown unto the Virgins nine.
From flat to sharp, the tune doth range;
  Too base, because it is too fine.
      See how the Bride,
      Puffed up with pride,

Can mince it passing well!
She trips on toe!
Full fair to show:
Within doth poison dwell!

Now wanton LOVE at last is sped!
DISSEMBLING is his only joy!
Bare TRUTH, from VENUS' Court is fled!
Dissembling pleasures hide annoy.
It were in vain
To talk of pain;
The wedding yet doth last!
But pain is near;
And will appear
With a dissembling cast!

Despair and Hope are joined in one;
And Pain with Pleasure linkèd sure:
Not one of these can come alone!
No certain hope! no pleasure pure!
Thus sour and sweet,
In love do meet;
DISSEMBLING likes it so!
Of sweet, small store!
Of sour, the more!
Love is a pleasant woe!

Amor et mellis et fellis.

DISPRAISE OF LOVE, AND LOVERS' FOLLIES.

If Love be life, I long to die!
    Live they that list, for me!
And he that gains the most thereby,
    A fool, at least, shall be!
But he that feels the sorest fits,
'Scapes with no less than loss of wits!
      Unhappy life they gain,
      Which Love do entertain!

In day, by feignèd looks they live;
    By lying dreams in night!
Each frown, a deadly wound doth give;
    Each smile, a false delight!
If 't hap their Lady pleasant seem;
It is for others' love! they deem:
      If void She seem of joy,
      Disdain doth make her coy!

Such is the peace that Lovers find!
    Such is the life they lead!
Blown here and there, with every wind,
    Like flowers in the mead!
Now, war! Now, peace! Then, war again!
Desire! Despair! Delight! Disdain!
      Though dead, in midst of life!
      In peace; and yet at strife!

Anomos, i.e. A. W.

THE TOMB OF DEAD DESIRE.

When Venus saw Desire must die,
  Whom high Disdain
  Had justly slain,
For killing Truth with scornful eye;
The Earth she leaves, and gets her to the sky.
  Her golden hairs she tears.
  Black weeds of woe she wears.
For help, unto her father doth she cry!
  Who bids her stay a space,
  And hope for better grace.

To save his life, she hath no skill.
  Whom should she pray!
  What do! or say!
But weep, for wanting of her will!
Meantime, Desire hath ta'en his last farewell:
  And in a meadow fair,
  To which the Nymphs repair,
His breathless corpse is laid, with worms to dwell.
  So Glory doth decay,
  When Death takes life away!

When morning star had chased the night,
  The Queen of Love
  Looked from above,
To see the grave of her delight;

And as, with heedful eye, she viewed the place,
    She spied a flower unknown,
    That on his grave was grown,
Instead of learnèd Verse, his tomb to grace.
    If you the name require;
    Heart's-ease, from dead DESIRE.

A DEFIANCE TO DISDAINFUL LOVE.

Now, have I learned, with much ado, at last,
  By true disdain to kill desire!
This was the mark at which I shot so fast!
  Unto this height I did aspire!
    Proud LOVE; now do thy worst, and spare not!
    For thee, and all thy shafts, I care not!

What hast thou left, wherewith to move my mind!
  What life, to quicken dead desire!
I count thy words and oaths as light as wind!
  I feel no heat in all thy fire!
    Go, change thy bow; and get a stronger!
    Go, break thy shafts; and buy thee longer!

In vain, thou bait'st thy hook with Beauty's blaze!
  In vain, thy wanton eyes allure!
These are but toys for them that love to gaze!
  I know what harm thy looks procure!
    Some strange conceit must be devised;
    Or thou, and all thy skill, despised!

Anomos, i.e. A. W.

A REPENTANT POEM.

Though late, my heart! yet turn at last;
  And shape thy course another way!
'Tis better lose thy labour past;
  Than follow on to sure decay!
    What though thou long have strayed awry;
    In hope of grace, for mercy cry!

Though weight of Sin doth press thee down,
  And keep thee grov'lling on the ground;
Though black Despair, with angry frown,
  Thy wit and judgement quite confound;
    Though Time and Wit have been misspent;
    Yet grace is left, if thou repent!

Weep, then, my heart! weep still, and still!
  Nay, melt to floods of flowing tears!
Send out such shrieks as Heaven may fill;
  And pierce thine angry Judge's ears!
    And let thy soul, that harbours Sin,
    Bleed streams of blood, to drown it in

Anomos, i.e. A. W.

Then shall thine angry Judge's face
  To cheerful looks itself apply!
Then shall thy soul be filled with grace;
  And Fear of Death constrained to fly
    Even so, my GOD! O, when? How long?
    I would! but Sin is too too strong!

I strive to rise; Sin keeps me down!
  I fly from Sin; Sin follows me!
My will doth reach at Glory's crown:
  Weak is my strength, it will not be!
    See, how my fainting soul doth pant!
    O, let thy strength supply my want!

Anonymous.

THE BONNY EARL OF MURRAY.

Ye Highlands, and ye Lawlands!
    O, where have you been?
They have slain the Earl of Murray;
    And they laid him on the green!

Now wae be to thee, Huntley!
    And wherefore did you sae?
I bade you, bring him wi' you;
    But forbad you him to slay!

He was a braw gallant;
    And he rid at the ring!
And the bonny Earl of Murray,
    O, he might have been a King!

He was a braw gallant;
    And he play'd at the ba'!
And the bonny Earl of Murray
    Was the flower amang them a'!

He was a braw gallant;
    And he played at the gluve!
And the bonny Earl of Murray,
    O, he was the Queen's Luve!

Oh! lang will his Lady
    Look o'er the Castle Down,
Ere she see the Earl of Murray
    Come sounding through the town!

A MAN, of late, was put to death,
    For that he had his part
Of stolen goods. Should you then 'scape,
    That stolen have my heart!

The Law, you see, would you condemn
    If I should plead my case:
But, sure, to work you such despite,
    I cannot have the face!

Yet Reason would, I should have 'mends!
    For that, in any wise,
To have mine own restored again;
    It will not me suffice!

You had my heart, when it was whole;
    And sound, I know, you found it!
Would you, then, give it back again,
    When you have all-to-wound it!

The Old Law biddeth, tooth for tooth
    And eye for eye restore!
Give, then, your heart to me, for mine;
    And I will ask no more!

THE WOODMAN'S WALK[S].

Through a fair forest, as I went
    Upon a summer's day,
I met a Woodman quaint and gent;
    Yet in a strange array.

I marvelled much at his disguise
    Whom I did know so well;
But thus, in terms both grave and wise,
    His mind he gan to tell:

'Friend, muse not at this fond array;
    But list awhile to me!
For it hath holp me to survey
    What I shall shew to thee.

'Long lived I in this forest fair
    Till, weary of my weal,
Abroad in walks, I would repair;
    As now I will reveal.

'My first day's walk was to the Court,
    Where Beauty fed mine eyes;
Yet found I that the Courtly sport
    Did mask in sly disguise.

'For Falsehood sat in fairest looks;
    And friend to friend was coy.
Court Favour filled but empty books;
    And there I found no joy.

'Desert went naked in the cold;
    When crouching Craft was fed.
Sweet words were cheaply bought and sold;
    But none that stood in stead.

'Wit was imployed for each man's own;
    Plain Meaning came too short.
All these devices seen and known,
    Made me forsake the Court.

'Unto the City next I went,
    In hope of better hap;
Where liberally I launched and spent,
    As set on Fortune's lap.

'The little stock I had in store,
    Methought, would ne'er be done!
Friends flocked about me more and more;
    As quickly lost as won!

'For when I spent; they then were kind!
    But when my purse did fail;
The foremost man came last behind!
    Thus love with wealth doth quail.

'Once more for footing yet I strove,
    Although the World did frown;
But they before that held me up,
    Together trod me down!

'And lest, once more, I should arise;
    They sought my quite decay!
Then got I into this disguise;
    And thence I stole away!

'And in my mind, methought, I said,
    "Lord bless me from the City!
Where simpleness is thus betrayed;
    And no remorse, or pity."

'Yet would I not give over so;
    But, once more, try my fate!
And to the Country then I go,
    To live in quiet state.

'There, did appear no subtle shows;
    But "Yea!" and "Nay!" went smoothly!
But, Lord! how country folks can gloze!
    When they speak most soothly.

'More craft was in a buttoned cap,
    And in an old wife's rail,
Than, in my life, it was my hap
    To see on down, or 'dale.

'There was no open forgery!
   But underhanded gleaning;
Which they call Country Policy,
   But hath a worser meaning.

'Some good Bold-face bears out the wrong;
   Because he gains thereby:
The poor man's back is cracked ere long;
   Yet there he lets him lie!

'And no degree, among them all,
   But had such close intending;
That I upon my knees did fall,
   And prayed for their amending.

'Back to the woods I got again,
   In mind perplexèd sore:
Where I found ease of all this pain;
   And mean to stray no more!

'There, City, Court, nor Country too,
   Can any way annoy me!
But, as a Woodman ought to do,
   I freely may imploy me!

'There live I quietly alone,
   And none to trip my talk:
Wherefore, when I am dead and gone,
   Think on the Woodman's Walk!'

Shepherd Tony.

THE SHEPHERD'S SUN.

Fair Nymphs! sit ye here by me
  On this flow'ry green;
While we, this merry day, do see
  Some things but seldom seen..
Shepherds all! now come, sit around
  On yond chequered plain;
While, from the woods, we hear resound
  Some com[fort] for Love's pain.
    Every bird sits on his bough
      As brag as he that is the best;
    Then, sweet Love! reveal how
      Our minds may be at rest!
        Echo thus replied to me,
          'Sit under yonder beechen-tree;
        And there, Love will shew thee,
    How all may be redrest!'

Hark! Hark! Hark, the Nightingale!
  In her mourning lay,
She tells her story's woeful tale,
  To warn ye, if she may.
'Fair Maids! take ye heed of Love!
  It is a per'lous thing!
As Philomel herself did prove,
  Abusèd by a King.
    If Kings play false, believe no men
      That make a seemly outward show!

But, caught once, beware then;
  For then begins your woe!
They will look babies in your eyes,
  And speak so fair as fair may be;
But trust them in no wise!
  Example take by me!'

'Fie! Fie!' said the Threstlecock,
  'You are much to blame,
For one man's fault, all men to blot!
  Impairing their good name.
Admit you were usèd amiss,
  By that ungentle King;
It follows not, that you, for this,
  Should all men's honours wring!
    There be good; and there be bad!
      And some are false; and some are true!
    As good choice is still had
      Amongst us men, as you!
      Women have faults as well as we!
      Some say, for our one, they have three!
    Then smite not! nor bite not!
    When you as faulty be.'

'Peace! peace!' quoth MADGE Howlet then,
  Sitting out of sight,
'For women are as good as men;
  And both are good alike!'

'Not so!' said the little Wren,
  'Difference there may be!
The cock alway[s] commands the hen;
  Then men shall go for me!'
    Then Robin Redbreast, stepping in,
      Would needs take up this tedious strife;
    Protesting, 'True loving
      In either, lengthened life!
        If I love you; and you love me;
        Can there be better harmony!
      Thus ending contending,
        Love must the umpire be!'

Fair Nymphs! Love must be your guide!
  Chaste, unspotted, Love
To such as do your thralls betide,
  Resolved, without remove.
Likewise, jolly Shepherd Swains!
  If you do respect
The happy issue of your pains;
  True Love must you direct!
    You hear the birds contend for love!
      The bubbling springs do sing sweet love!
    The mountains and fountains
      Do echo nought but love!   [all!
        Take hands, then, Nymphs and Shepherds
        And to this river's music's fall,
      Sing, 'True Love and Chaste Love
        Begins our Festival!'

Thomas Armstrong.

ARMSTRONG'S GOOD NIGHT!

This night is my departing night;
  For here nae langer must I stay!
There 's neither friend, nor foe, o' mine,
  But wishes me away!

What I have done, thro' lack of wit,
  I never, never, can recall!
I hope ye're a' my friends as yet;
  Good Night! and joy be with you all!

Thomas Decker.

Art thou poor; yet hast thou golden slumbers?
    O, sweet content!
Art thou rich; yet is thy mind perplexed?
    O, punishment!
Dost thou laugh, to see how fools are vexed
To add to golden numbers, golden numbers?
    O, sweet content! O, sweet content!

Work apace! apace! apace! apace!
Honest labour bears a lovely face!
Then Hey noney, noney! Hey noney, noney!

Canst drink the waters of the crispèd spring?
    O, sweet content!   [tears?
Swim'st thou in wealth; yet sink'st in thine own
    O, punishment!
Then he that patiently want's burden bears,
No burden bears; but is a King! a King!
    O, sweet content! O, sweet content!

Work apace! apace! apace! apace! &c.

THE FIRST THREE-MEN'S SONG.

O, THE month of May! the merry month of May!
  So frolic! so gay! and so green! so green! so green!
O, and then did I, unto my True Love say,
  'Sweet PEG, thou shalt be my Summer's Queen!

'Now the nightingale! the pretty nightingale!
  The sweetest singer in all the forest's quire, [tale!
Entreats thee, sweet PEGGIE! to hear thy True Love's
  Lo, yonder she sitteth; her breast against a briar!

'But O, I spy the cuckoo! the cuckoo! the cuckoo!
  See, where she sitteth! Come away, my Joy!
Come away, I prithee! I do not like the cuckoo
  Should sing, where PEGGIE and I kiss and toy!'
O, the month of May! the merry month of May! &c.

THE SECOND THREE-MEN'S SONG.

COLD 's the wind, and wet 's the rain;
  Saint HUGH be our good speed!
Ill is the weather that bringeth no gain;
  Nor helps good hearts in need!

Troll the bowl! the jolly nut-brown bowl!
  And here, kind mate, to thee!
    [*As often as there be men to drink.*]
Let 's sing a dirge for Saint HUGH's soul;
  And drown it merrily!

Down a down! Hey down a down!
  Hey derry derry down a down!
Ho, well done, to let me come!
  Ring compass, gentle joy!
    [*At last, when all have drunk, this verse.*]
Cold 's the wind, and wet 's the rain; &c.

TO HIS DEAREST SON,
HENRY THE PRINCE.

GOD gives not Kings the style of Gods in vain;
   For, on his throne, his sceptre do they sway!
   And as their subjects ought them to obey;
So Kings should fear and serve their GOD again!
If, then, ye would enjoy a happy reign,
   Observe the statutes of your heavenly King!
   And from his law, make all your laws to spring;
Since his Lieutenant here, ye should remain!
Reward the just! Be steadfast, true, and plain!
   Repress the proud! maintaining aye the right!
   Walk always so, as ever in his sight;
Who guards the godly, plaguing the profane!
   And so ye shall in princely virtues shine;
   Resembling right your mighty King divine.

Anonymous.

WILLY, prithee, go to bed!
For thou wilt have a drowsy head!
To-morrow, we must a hunting;
And betimes be stirring!
    With a hey trolly, lolly, lo!
    Trolly, lolly, lo!

It is like to be fair weather;
Couple up all thy hounds together!
Couple Jolly and Little Jolly!
Couple Troll with Old Tolly!
    With a hey trolly, lolly, lo! &c.

Couple Finch with Black Troll!
Couple Chaunter with Jumboll!
Let Beauty go at liberty;
For she doth know her duty!
    With a hey trolly, lolly, lo! &c.

Let Merry go loose! It makes no matter!
For Cleanly, sometimes she will clatter:
And yet, I am sure, she will not stray;
But keep with us still, all the day!
    With a hey trolly, lolly, lo! &c.

With O, masters! and wot you where?
This other day I start a hare
On what-call Hill, upon the knoll;
And there she started before Troll!
    With a hey trolly, lolly, lo! &c.

And down she went the common dale;
With all the hounds at her tail!
With 'Yeaffe a yaffe! Yeaffe a yaffe!'
'Hey Troll! Hey Chaunter! Hey Jumboll!'
 With a hey trolly, lolly, lo! &c.

See, how Chooper chops it in!
And so doth Gallant now begin!
Look, how Troll begins to tattle!
Tarry a while, ye shall hear him prattle!
 With a hey trolly, lolly, lo! &c.

For Beauty begins to wag her tail!
Of Cleanly's help, we shall not fail!
And Chaunter opens very well!
But Merry, she doth bear the bell!
 With a hey trolly, lolly, lo! &c.

Go, prick the path; and down the lane,
She useth still her old train!
She is gone to what-call Wood;
Where we are like to do no good!
 With a hey trolly, lolly, lo! &c.

THE MARRIAGE OF THE FROG AND THE MOUSE.

IT was the Frog in the Well;
 Humble dum! Humble dum!
And the merry Mouse in the Mill.
 Tweedle, tweedle, twino!

Anonymous.

The Frog would a wooing ride;
    Humble dum! Humble dum!
Sword and buckler by his side.
    Tweedle, tweedle, twino!

When he was upon his high horse set;
    Humble dum! Humble dum!
His boots, they shone as black as jet!
    Tweedle, tweedle, twino!

When he came to the merry Mill-pin,
    Humble dum! Humble dum!
'Lady Mouse, be you within?'
    Tweedle, tweedle, twino!

Then came out the dusty Mouse,
    Humble dum! Humble dum!
'I am Lady of the house!'
    Tweedle, tweedle, twino!

'Hast thou any mind of me?'
    Humble dum! Humble dum!
'I have e'en great mind of thee!'
    Tweedle, tweedle, twino!

'Who shall this marriage make?'
    Humble dum! Humble dum!
'Our Lord, which is the Rat!'
    Tweedle, tweedle, twino!

Anonymous.

'What shall we have to our supper?'
   Humble dum! Humble dum!
'Three beans in a pound of butter!'
   Tweedle, tweedle, twino!

When supper they were at,
   Humble dum! Humble dum!
The Frog, the Mouse, and even the Rat.
   Tweedle, tweedle, twino!

Then came in GIB our Cat,
   Humble dum! Humble dum!
And catched the Mouse, e'en by the back.
   Tweedle, tweedle, twino!

Then did they separate;
   Humble dum! Humble dum!
And the Frog leaped on the floor so flat.
   Tweedle, tweedle, twino!

Then came in DICK our Drake;
   Humble dum! Humble dum!
And drew the Frog, even to the lake.
   Tweedle, tweedle, twino!

The Rat ran up the wall.
   Humble dum! Humble dum!
A goodly company! The Devil go with all!
   Tweedle, tweedle, twino!

Francis Beaumont.

TRUE BEAUTY.

May I find a woman fair;
And her mind as clear as air!
If her beauty go alone,
'Tis to me, as if 'twere none!

May I find a woman rich;
And not of too high a pitch!
If that pride should cause disdain,
Tell me, Lover! Where's thy gain?

May I find a woman wise;
And her falsehood not disguise!
Hath She wit, as She hath will,
Double-armed She is to ill!

May I find a woman kind;
And not wavering like the wind!
How should I call that Love mine,
When 'tis his! and his! and thine!

May I find a woman true!
There is Beauty's fairest hue!
There is Beauty, Love, and Wit;
Happy he can compass it!

LIKE a ring, without a finger,
Or a bell, without a ringer;
Like a horse was never ridden,
Or a feast, and no guest bidden;
Like a well, without a bucket,
Or a rose, if no man pluck it:
    Just such as these, may She be said,
      That lives, ne'er loves; but dies a Maid!

The ring, if worn, the finger decks!
The bell, pulled by the ringer, speaks!
The horse doth ease, if he be ridden!
The feast doth please, if guests be bidden!
The bucket draws the water forth!
The rose, when plucked, is still most worth!
    Such is the Virgin, in my eyes,
      That lives, loves, marries, ere She dies.

Like to a stock not grafted on,
Or like a lute not played upon;
Like a jack, without a weight,
Or a bark, without a freight;
Like a lock, without a key,
Or a candle in the day:
    Just such as these, may She be said,
      That lives, ne'er loves; but dies a Maid!

Francis Beaumont.

The grafted stock doth bear best fruit!
There 's music in the fingered lute!
The weight doth make the jack go ready!
The freight doth make the bark go steady!
The key, the lock doth open right!
The candle 's useful in the night!
  Such is the Virgin, in my eyes,
   That lives, loves, marries, ere She dies.

Like a call, without 'Anon, Sir!'
Or a question, and no answer;
Like a ship was never rigged,
Or a mine was never digged;
Like a wound, without a tent,
Or civet-box, without a scent:
  Just such as these, may She be said,
   That lives, ne'er loves; but dies a Maid!

Th' 'Anon, Sir!' doth obey the call!
The question answered, pleaseth all!
Who rigs a ship, sails with the wind!
Who digs a mine, doth treasure find!
The wound, by wholesome tent, hath ease!
The box perfumed, the senses please!
  Such is the Virgin, in my eyes,
   That lives, loves, marries, ere She dies.

Francis Beaumont.

Like marrow-bone was never broken,
Or commendations, and no token;
Like a fort, and none to win it;
Or like the Moon, and no Man in it;
Like a school, without a Teacher;
Or like a pulpit, and no Preacher:
    Just such as these, may She be said,
    That lives, ne'er loves; but dies a Maid!

The broken marrow-bone is sweet!
The token doth adorn the greet!
There 's triumph in the fort being won!
The Man rides glorious in the Moon!
The school is, by the Teacher stilled!
The pulpit, by the Preacher filled!
    Such is the Virgin, in my eyes,
    That lives, loves, marries, ere She dies.

Like a cage, without a bird,
Or a thing too long deferred;
Like the gold was never tried,
Or the ground unoccupied;
Like a house, that 's not possessed,
Or the book was never pressed:
    Just such as these, may She be said,
    That lives, ne'er loves; but dies a Maid!

The bird in cage doth sweetly sing!
Due season prefers every thing!
The gold that's tried, from dross is pured!
There's profit in the ground manured!
The house is by possession graced!
The book, when pressed, is then embraced!
    Such is the Virgin, in my eyes,
    That lives, loves, marries, ere She dies.

ON THE TOMBS IN
WESTMINSTER ABBEY.

MORTALITY, behold and fear!
What a change of flesh is here!
Think, how many royal bones
Sleep within this heap of stones!
    Here they lie, had realms and lands;
Who now want strength to stir their hands:
Where, from their pulpits, sealed with dust,
They preach, 'In greatness is no trust!'
    Here's an acre sown indeed
With the richest, royall'st, seed,
That the earth did e'er suck in;
Since the First Man died for sin.
    Here the bones of birth have cried,
'Though Gods they were; as Men they died!'
    Here are sands, ignoble things,
Dropped from the ruined sides of Kings!
    Here's a World of pomp and State
Buried in dust; once dead by Fate.

Francis Beaumont.

MASTER FRANCIS BEAUMONT'S
LETTER TO BEN JONSON,

Written before he and Master FLETCHER *came to London, with two of the precedent Comedies, then not finished; which deferred their merry meetings at the 'Mermaid.'*

THE sun (which doth the greatest comfort bring
To absent friends; because the selfsame thing
They know they see, however absent) is
Here our best haymaker! Forgive me this!
It is our country's style. In this warm shine,
I lie; and dream of your full *Mermaid* Wine!
O, we have Water mixed with Claret Lees!
Drink apt to bring in drier heresies
Than Beer! good only for the Sonnet's strain,
With fustian metaphors to stuff the brain!
So mixed, that, given to the thirstiest one,
'Twill not prove alms, unless he have the stone!
I think, with one draught, man's invention fades!
Two cups had quite spoiled HOMER's *Iliads*!
'Tis liquor that will find out SUTCLIFF's wit,
Lie where he will; and make him write worse yet!
Filled with such moisture, in most grievous qualms,
Did ROBERT WISDOM write his singing *Psalms*!
And so must I do this! and yet I think
It is a potion sent us down to drink,
By special Providence. Keeps us from fights
Makes us not laugh, when we make legs to Knights!

'Tis this that keeps our minds fit for our states;
A medicine to obey our Magistrates!
 For we do live more free than you! No hate,
No envy at one another's happy state,
Moves us! We are all equal every whit!
 Of land that GOD gives men, here is their wit!
If we consider fully, for our best,
And gravest man will, with his main house-jest
Scarce please you! We want subtlety to do
The City tricks; lie! hate! and flatter too!
Here, are none that can bear a painted show!
Strike, when you wince; and then lament the blow!
Who (like mills set the right way for to grind)
Can make their gains alike, with every wind!
Only some fellow, with the subtlest pate
Amongst us, may perchance equivocate
At selling of a horse; and that's the most!

 Methinks, the little wit I had, is lost
Since I saw you! For wit is like a rest
Held up at tennis! which men do the best
With the best gamesters. What things have we seen
Done at the *Mermaid*[1]! heard words that have been

---

[1] 1. THOMAS FULLER, in his *Worthies of England* (p. 126, Warwickshire), London, 1662, fol., thus refers generally to the two great Dramatists:
 'Many were the Wit Combats betwixt SHAKESPEARE and BEN JONSON! which two I behold like a Spanish great Galleon, and an English Man of War. Master JONSON, like the former, was built far higher in Learning; solid, but slow in his performances. SHAKESPEARE, with the English Man of War, lesser in bulk but lighter in sailing, could turn with all tides,

So nimble, and so full of subtle flame,
As if that every one (from whence they came)
Had meant to put his whole wit in a jest;
And had resolved to live a fool, the rest
Of his dull life! Then, when there hath been thrown
Wit able enough to justify the Town
For three days past! Wit, that might warrant be
For the whole City to talk foolishly
Till that were cancelled! And, when we were gone,
We left an air behind us; which alone
Was able to make the two next companies
Right witty! though but downright fools, more wise!

tack about, and take advantage of all winds, by the quickness of his Wit and Invention.'

2. THOMAS CORYATE, at p. 37 of his *Traveller for the English Wits, Greeting*, London, 1616, 4to, addresses a letter from Ajmere, dated Wednesday, November 8, 1615 [*O. S.*]:

'To the High Seneschal of the Right Worshipful Fraternity of Sirenaical Gentlemen, that meet the first Friday of every month, at the sign of the *Mermaid*, in Bread Street, in London;'

and thus concludes it:

'The Gentleman that bringeth this letter unto you, was Preacher to the English Merchants conversant at the Court of the aforesaid mighty Monarch, in the town of Ajmere, in this Eastern India: and in divers loving offices hath been so kind unto me, that I intreat your generosities to entertain him friendly for my sake; to exhilarate him with the purest quintessence of the Spanish, French, and Rhenish grape, which the *Mermaid* yieldeth; and either one in the name of you all, or else the total universality of the one after another, to thank him heartily, according to the quality of his merits. Farewell, noble Sirenaicks!'

3. It is interesting also to remember that, from 1608 onwards, in this same Bread Street, London, JOHN MILTON was living as a little child.

4. What a confluence of gifted minds did those first Fridays of the months witness in that street! SHAKESPEARE, MILTON, JONSON, BEAUMONT, FLETCHER, &c., &c.

Francis Beaumont.

 When I remember this, and see that now
The Country Gentlemen begin to allow
My wit for dry bobs; then I needs must cry,
'I see my days of Ballating grow nigh!'
 I can already riddle; and can sing
Catches, sell bargains: and I fear shall bring
Myself to speak the hardest words I find,
Over as oft as any, with one wind,
That takes no medicines! But one thought of thee
Makes me remember all these things to be
The wit of our young men! fellows that show
No part of good; yet utter all they know!
Who, like trees of the Guard, have growing souls.
 Only strong Destiny, which all controls,
I hope hath left a better fate in store
For me, thy friend! than to live ever poor,
Banished unto this home! Fate, once again,
Bring me to thee! who canst make smooth and plain
The Way of Knowledge for me; and then I
(Who have no good, but in thy company!)
Protest it will, my greatest comfort be,
To acknowledge all I have, to flow from thee!
 BEN, when these Scenes are perfect, we'll taste wine!
I'll drink thy Muse's health! thou shalt quaff mine!

[It has been thought that BEN JONSON's poem on page 214 was his reply to this poetical Letter of BEAUMONT to him.—E. A.]

THE MASQUE.

Night rises in mists.

Our reign is come! For in the raging sea,
The Sun is drowned; and, with him, fell the Day!
Bright Cynthia, hear my voice! I am the Night!
For whom thou bear'st about thy borrowed light.
Appear! No longer thy pale visage shroud!
But strike thy silver horns quite through a cloud;
And send a beam upon my swarthy face!
By which I may discover all the place
And persons; and how many longing eyes
Are come to wait on our Solemnities.

[*Enter* Cynthia.]

How dull and black am I! I could not find
This beauty without thee; I am so blind!
Methinks, they shew like to those eastern streaks
That warn us hence, before the Morning breaks.
Back, my pale servant! for these eyes know how
To shoot far more, and quicker, rays than thou!

Cynthia.

Great Queen! they be a troop, for whom alone,
One of my clearest moons I have put on!
A troop that looks as if thyself and I
Had plucked our reins in, and our whips laid by
To gaze upon these mortals; that appear
Brighter than we!

Night.

> Then let us keep them here;
> And never more our chariots drive away!
> But hold our places, and outshine the Day!

Cynthia.

> Great Queen of Shadows! you are pleased to speak
> Of more than may be done! We may not break
> The Gods' decrees; but, when our time is come,
> Must drive away! and give the Day our room.
> Yet, whilst our reign lasts, let us stretch our power
> To give our servants one contented hour!
> With such unwonted solemn grace and State,
> As may, for ever after, force them hate
> Our brother's glorious beams; and wish the night,
> Crowned with a thousand stars, and our cold light.
> For almost all the world their service bend
> To Phœbus: and in vain my light I lend!
> Gazed on, unto my sitting from my rise,
> Almost of none, but of unquiet eyes.

Night.

> Then, shine at full, fair Queen! and by thy power
> Produce a birth, to crown this happy hour
> Of Nymphs and Shepherds! Let their Songs discover,
> Easy and sweet, who is the happy Lover!
> Or if thou woo't, then call thine own Endymion
> From the sweet flow'ry bed he lies upon,

On Latmus' top! thy pale beams drawn away;
And of this long night, let him make this day!

CYNTHIA.

Thou dream'st, dark Queen! That fair boy was not
    mine ;
Nor went I down to kiss him! Ease and wine
Have bred these bold tales! Poets, when they rage,
Turn Gods to men ; and make an hour, an Age!

    CUPID, pardon what is past ;
    And forgive our sins at last!
Then we will be coy no more ;
But thy deity adore!
Troths, at fifteen we will plight!
And will tread a dance, each night,
In the fields, or by the fire,
With the youths that have desire!

Given earrings, we will wear!
Bracelets of our Lovers' hair ;
Which they on our arms shall twist,
With their names carved, on our wrist.
All the money that we owe [*own*],
We in tokens will bestow!
And learn to write that (when 'tis sent)
Only our Loves know what is meant!
    O, then pardon what is past ;
    And forgive our sins at last!

COME you whose Loves are dead!
    And, whiles I sing,
    Weep, and wring
Every hand; and every head
Bind with cypress and sad yew!
Ribands black, and candles blue;
For him that was, of men most true!

Come, with heavy mourning!
    And, on his grave,
    Let him have
Sacrifice of sighs and groaning!
Let him have fair flowers enow!
White and purple, green and yellow!
For him that was, of men most true!

LAY a garland on my hearse, of the dismal yew!
Maidens, willow branches bear! say, I dièd true!
My Love was false; but I was firm, from the hour
    of my birth.
Upon my buried body lie lightly, gentle earth!

I COULD never have the power
To love one above an hour;
But my heart would prompt mine eye,
On some other man to fly!
VENUS, fix mine eyes fast!
Or, if not, give me all that I shall see at last!

FRANCKE.	TELL me, dearest! What is Love?
CLORA.	'Tis a lightning from above!
	'Tis an arrow! 'Tis a fire!
	'Tis a boy they call Desire!
BOTH.	'Tis a grave
	Gapes to have
	Those poor fools, that long to prove!
FRANCKE.	Tell me more! Are women true?
CLORA.	Yes, some are! and some as you!
	Some are willing! some are strange,
	Since you men first taught to change!
BOTH.	And till troth
	Be in both;
	All shall love, to love anew!
FRANCKE.	Tell me more yet! Can they grieve?
CLORA.	Yes, and sicken sore; but live!
	And be wise, and delay;
	When you men are as wise as they!
BOTH.	Then I see,
	Faith will be
	Never till they both believe!

    COME, Shepherds! come!
      Come away, without delay,
        Whilst the gentle time doth stay!
      Green woods are dumb:

And will never tell to any
Those dear kisses; and those many
Sweet embraces that are given!
Dainty pleasures, that would even
Raise in coldest Age a fire;
And give virgin blood desire!
   Then, if ever,
   Now or never,
  Come and have it!
   Think not I
   Dare deny;
  If you crave it!

Away, delights! Go, seek some other dwelling!
  For I must die!
Farewell, false Love! Thy tongue is ever telling
  Lie after lie!
For ever let me rest now from thy smarts!
  Alas, for pity, go,
  And fire their hearts
That have been hard to thee! Mine was not so!

Never again deluding Love shall know me!
  For I will die!
And all those griefs, that think to overgrow me,
  Shall be as I!
For ever will I sleep! while poor Maids cry,
  'Alas, for pity, stay!
  And let us die
With thee! Men cannot mock us in the clay!'

Roses, their sharp spines being gone,
Not royal in their smells alone,
    But in their hue!
Maiden Pinks, of odour faint!
Daisies smell-less; yet most quaint!
    And sweet Time true!

Primrose, firstborn child of VER,
Merry Spring-time's Harbinger,
    With her bells dim!
Oxlips, in their cradles growing!
Marigolds, on death-beds blowing!
    Larks'-heels trim!

All dear Nature's children sweet- [*Strew flowers!*]
Ly [strew] 'fore Bride and Bridegroom's feet;
    Blessing their sense.
Not an angel of the air,
Bird melodious, or bird fair,
    Is absent hence!

The Crow, the sland'rous Cuckoo, nor
The boding Raven, nor Chough hoar,
    Nor chattering Pie,
May on our Bride-House perch, or sing!
Or with them, any discord bring;
    But from it fly!

John Fletcher.

[*A HYMN TO PAN.*]

ALL ye woods, and trees, and bowers!
All ye Virtues, and ye Powers,
That inhabit in the lakes!
In the pleasant springs! or brakes!
    Move your feet
      To our sound;
    Whilst we greet
      All this ground,
With his honour and his name;
That defends our flocks from blame.

He is great; and he is just!
He is ever good! and must
Thus be honoured! Daffadillies,
Roses, Pinks, and lovèd Lilies,
    Let us fling!
    Whilst we sing,
    'Ever holy!
    Ever holy!
Ever honoured! Ever young!'
Thus great PAN is ever sung!

John Fletcher.

[*ANOTHER HYMN TO PAN.*]

Sing his praises, that doth keep
    Our flocks from harm!
Pan, the father of our sheep!
    And, arm in arm,
Tread we softly, in a round;
Whilst the hollow neighbouring ground
Fills the music, with her sound.

'Pan! O, great God, Pan! to thee
    Thus do we sing!
Thou that keep'st us chaste and free,
    As the young Spring!
Ever be thy honour spoke,
From that place, the Morn is broke;
To that place, Day doth unyoke!'

TO FRANCIS BEAUMONT.

How I do love thee, BEAUMONT, and thy Muse;
That unto me, dost such religion use!
How I do fear myself! that am not worth
The least indulgent thought thy pen drops forth!
At once, thou mak'st me happy; and unmak'st!
And giving largely to me, more thou tak'st!
What fate is mine, that so itself bereaves!
What art is thine, that so thy friend deceives!
When, even there, where most thou praisest me,
For writing better, I must envy thee!

[It has been thought that the above was JONSON's answer to BEAUMONT's poetical letter printed at pages 201–204.—E. A.]

LOVE is blind, and a wanton!
In the whole world, there is scant one
    Such another;
    No, not his mother!

He hath plucked her doves and sparrows,
To feather his sharp arrows:
    And alone prevaileth;
    Whilst sick VENUS waileth!

But if CYPRIS once recover
The Wag; it shall behove her
    To look better to him;
    Or she will undo him!

Ben Jonson.

[ECHO MOURNING THE DEATH OF NARCISSUS.]

SLOW, slow, fresh fount! Keep time with my salt tears!
   Yet slower, yet! O, faintly! gentle springs!
List to the heavy part the music bears!
   'Woe weeps out her division, when she sings!'
     Droop, herbs and flowers!
     Fall, grief in showers!
   'Our beauties are not ours!'
     O, I could still,
Like melting snow upon some craggy hill,
     Drop! drop! drop! drop!
Since Nature's Pride is now a withered daffodil.

THE KISS.

O, THAT joy so soon should waste!
   Or so sweet a bliss
     As a kiss
   Might not for ever last!
So sugared! so melting! so soft! so delicious!
   The dew that lies on roses,
   When the Morn herself discloses,
     Is not so precious!
O, rather than I would it smother;
Were I to taste such another,
   It should be my wishing,
   That I might die, kissing!

EPITAPH ON S. P. [SALATHIEL PAVY], A CHILD OF QUEEN ELIZABETH'S CHAPEL.

WEEP with me, all you that read
    This little story;
And know, for whom a tear you shed,
    Death's self is sorry!
'Twas a child, that so did thrive
    In grace and feature,
As Heaven and Nature seemed to strive
    Which owned the creature!

Years he numbered scarce thirteen,
    When Fates turned cruel;
Yet three filled Zodiacs had he been
    The Stage's jewel!
And did act, what now we moan,
    Old Men so duly;
As, sooth, the PARCÆ thought him one,
    He played so truly!

So, by error, to his fate
    They all consented!
But viewing him since (alas, too late!),
    They have repented;
And have sought, to give new birth,
    In baths to steep him:
But, being so much too good for Earth;
    Heaven vows to keep him!

Queen and Huntress, chaste and fair!
  Now the sun is laid to sleep,
Seated in thy silver chair,
  State in wonted manner keep!
    Hesperus intreats thy light,
    Goddess excellently bright!

Earth, let not thy envious shade
  Dare itself to interpose!
Cynthia's shining orb was made,
  Heaven to clear, when day did close.
    Bless us then with wishèd sight,
    Goddess excellently bright!

Lay thy bow of pearl apart;
  And thy crystal shining quiver!
Give unto the flying hart
  Space to breathe, how short soever!
    Thou, that mak'st a day of night;
    Goddess excellently bright!

———

  Still to be neat! Still to be drest,
As you were going to a feast!
Still to be powdered! still, perfumed!
Lady, it is to be presumed
(Though Art's hid causes are not found!)
All is not sweet! all is not sound!

Give me a look, give me a face,
That makes simplicity a grace!
Robes loosely flowing! hair as free!
Such sweet neglect more taketh me,
Than all th' adulteries of Art!
They strike mine eyes; but not my heart!

IF I freely may discover
What would please me in my Lover;
   I would have her fair and witty,
   Savouring more of Court than City;
   A little proud, but full of pity;
   Light and humorous in her toying;
   Oft building hopes, and soon destroying;
   Long, but sweet, in the enjoying;
Neither too easy, nor too hard:
All extremes I would have barred!

She should be allowed her Passions;
So they were but used as fashions!
   Sometimes froward, and then frowning;
   Sometimes sickish, and then swooning!
   Every fit, with change still crowning!
   Purely jealous, I would have her!
   Then only constant, when I crave her!
   'Tis a virtue should not save her.
Thus: nor her delicates would cloy me
Neither her peevishness annoy me!

Ben Jonson.

TO CELIA.

DRINK to me, only with thine eyes;
  And I will pledge with mine!
Or leave a kiss but in the cup;
  And I'll not look for wine!
The thirst that from the soul doth rise,
  Doth ask a drink divine:
But might I, of JOVE's nectar sup;
  I would not change for thine!

I sent thee, late, a rosy wreath;
  Not so much honouring thee,
As giving it a hope, that there
  It could not withered be.
But thou, thereon didst only breathe;
  And sent'st it back to me:
Since when it grows; and smells, I swear,
  Not of itself, but thee!

TO CELIA.

COME, my CELIA, let us prove,
While we can, the sports of Love!
Time will not be ours for ever!
He, at length, our good will sever!
Spend not then his gifts in vain!
Suns that set, may rise again;
But if, once, we lose this light,
'Tis, with us, perpetual night!

Why should we defer our joys?
Fame and Rumour are but toys!
Cannot we delude the eyes
Of a few poor household spies?
Or his easier ears beguile,
Thus removèd by our wile?
'Tis no sin, Love's fruit to steal;
But the sweet thefts to reveal!
To be taken! To be seen!
These have, crimes accounted been!

FOOLS! They are the only nation
Worth men's envy, or admiration!
Free from care, or sorrow-taking;
Themselves and others merry making;
All they speak, or do, is sterling.
  Your Fool, he is your Great Man's darling;
And your Lady's sport and pleasure!
Tongue and Bauble are his treasure.
His very face begetteth laughter;
And he speaks truth, free from slaughter!
  He's the grace of every feast;
And, sometimes, the chiefest guest!
Hath his trencher, and his stool;
When Wit shall wait upon the Fool!
    O, who would not be
      'Hee! Hee! Hee!'

[THE GLOVE OF THE DEAD LADY.]

THOU more than most sweet Glove
Unto my more sweet Love!
Suffer me to store with kisses
This empty lodging; that now misses
The pure rosy hand that ware thee,
Whiter than the kid that bare thee!
Thou art soft; but that was softer!
 Cupid's self hath kissed it ofter,
Than e'er he did his mother's doves!
Supposing her, the Queen of Loves,
That was thy Mistress! best of Gloves!

THAT WOMEN ARE BUT MEN'S SHADOWS.

FOLLOW a shadow, it still flies you!
 Seem to fly it, it will pursue!
So court a Mistress, she denies you!
 Let her alone, she will court you!
  Say, are not Women truly then
  Styled but the shadows of us Men?

At morn and even, shades are longest;
 At noon, they are, or short, or none:
So Men, at weakest; they are strongest!
 But grant us perfect; they're not known!
  Say, are not Women truly then
  Styled but the shadows of us Men?

ON LUCY [RUSSELL], COUNTESS OF BEDFORD.

This morning, timely rapt with holy fire,
  I thought to form unto my zealous Muse,
What kind of creature I could most desire
  To honour! serve! and love! as Poets use.

I meant to make her fair, and free, and wise;
  Of greatest blood; and yet more good than great!
I meant the Day Star should not brighter rise;
  Nor lend like influence from his lucent seat!

I meant she should be courteous, facile, sweet;
  Hating that solemn vice of Greatness, Pride;
I meant each softest virtue, there should meet;
  Fit in that softer bosom to reside!

Only a learned, and a manly, soul
  I purposed her! that should, with even powers,
The rock, the spindle, and the shears, control
  Of Destiny; and spin her own free hours!

Such, when I meant to feign, and wished to see;
My Muse bade, 'BEDFORD write!'; and that was she!

Anonymous.

Since first I saw your face, I resolved to honour and renown ye!
If now I be disdained; I wish my heart had never known ye!
What! I that loved, and you that liked; shall we begin to wrangle?
No! No! No! my heart is fast; and cannot disentangle!

If I admire, or praise, you too much; that fault you may
    forgive me!
Or if my hands had strayed but a touch; then justly might you
    leave me!
I asked you leave! You bade me, love! Is 't now a time to
    chide me?
No! No! No! I'll love you still; what fortune e'er betide me!

The sun, whose beams most glorious are, rejecteth no beholder!
And your sweet beauty, past compare! made my poor eyes the bolder!
Where Beauty moves, and Wit delights, and signs of Kindness
    bind, me;
There, O, there! where'er I go, I'll leave my heart behind me!

There is a Lady sweet and kind,
Was never face so pleased my mind!
I did but see her passing by;
And yet I love her till I die!

Her gesture, motion, and her smiles;
Her wit, her voice, my heart beguiles!
Beguiles my heart, I know not, Why?
And yet I love her till I die!

Her free behaviour, winning looks,
Will make a Lawyer burn his books!
I touched her not, alas, not I;
And yet I love her till I die! . . .

Should I remain confinèd there,
So long as PHŒBUS in his Sphere;
I to request, She to deny:
Yet would I love her till I die!

CUPID is wingèd, and doth range!
Her country so, my Love doth change!
But change She earth, or change She sky;
Yet will I love her till I die!

COME away! come, sweet Love!
  The golden morning breaks!
All the earth, all the air,
  Of Love and Pleasure speaks!
Teach thine arms then to embrace,
  And sweet rosy lips to kiss;
  And mix our souls in mutual bliss!
Eyes were made for Beauty's grace,
  Viewing, rueing, Love's long pain;
  Procured by Beauty's rude disdain.

Come away! come, sweet Love!
  The golden morning wastes!
While the sun, from his Sphere,
  His fiery arrows casts;
Making all the shadows fly.
  Playing, staying, in the grove
  To entertain the stealth of love.
Thither, sweet Love! let us hie!
  Flying, dying, in desire,
  Winged with sweet hopes and heavenly fire!

Anonymous.

Come away! come, sweet Love!
  Do not in vain adorn
Beauty's grace! that should rise
  Like to the naked morn.
Lilies on the river's side,
  And fair Cyprian flowers new-blown,
  Desire no beauties but their own!
Ornament is Nurse of Pride!
  Pleasure measures Love's delight;
  Haste then, sweet Love! our wishèd flight!

  In dew of roses steeping
Her lovely cheeks, LYCORIS thus sat weeping:
'Ah! DORUS false! that hast my heart bereft me;
  And now, unkind, hast left me!
    Hear, alas, O, hear me!
      Ay me! ay me!
  Cannot my beauty move thee!
    Pity! then pity me;
    Because I love thee!
Ay me! Thou scorn'st, the more I pray thee!
And this thou dost; and all to slay me!
Ah! do then kill me; and vaunt thee!
Yet my ghost still shall haunt thee!'

Sir David Murray.

THE COMPLAINT OF THE SHEPHERD HARPALUS.

Poor Harpalus, oppressed with love,
    Sat by a crystal brook;
Thinking his sorrows to remove,
    Ofttimes therein did look;

And hearing how, on pebble stones,
    The murmuring river ran,
As if it had bewailed his groans,
    Unto it thus began:

'Fair stream!' quoth he, 'that pities me,
    And hears my matchless moan;
If thou be going to the sea,
    As I do so suppone,

'Attend my plaints, past all relief!
    Which dolefully I breathe,
Acquaint the Sea Nymphs with my grief!
    Which still procures my death.

'Who, sitting on the craggy rocks,
    May in their Songs express,
While as they comb their golden locks,
    Poor Harpalus' distress.

Sir David Murray.

'And so, perhaps, some passenger,
    That passeth by the way,
May stay and listen, for to hear
    Them sing this doleful Lay':

Poor HARPALUS, a Shepherd Swain,
    More rich in youth than store,
Loved fair PHILENA, hapless man!
    PHILENA, Oh! therefore!

Who still, remorseless-hearted Maid,
    Took pleasure in his pain;
And his good-will, poor soul! repaid
    With undeserved disdain.

Ne'er Shepherd loved a Shepherdess
    More faithfully than he!
Ne'er Shepherd yet belovèd less
    Of Shepherdess could be!

How oft, with dying looks, did he
    To her his woes impart!
How oft his sighs did testify
    The dolour of his heart!

How oft from valleys to the hills,
    Did he his griefs rehearse!
How oft re-echoed they his ills
    Aback again, alas!

Sir David Murray.

How oft, on barks of stately pines,
 Of beech, of hollen green,
Did he ingrave, in mournful lines,
 The dole he did sustain.

Yet all his plaints could have no place
 To change PHILENA's *mind!*
The more his sorrows did increase,
 The more she proved unkind!

'The thought whereof, through very care,
 Poor HARPALUS *did move,*
That, overcome with high despair,
 He quat both life and love!

BEAUTY, being long a resident above,
 With importune celestial suits was deaved,
 Of sacred Sprites, who still her favour craved,
That she, from thence resolvèd to remove:
And so, at last, from top of all the Rounds,
 LOVE, on his wings, convoyed her here below;
 Where she, not willing any should her know,
Sought out the North, to be her resting bounds.
There she remains, her name being changed; yet still
 For beauty now, fair CÆLIA she is called!
 Whose sight sometimes, as it the Gods all thralled;
So now her looks, poor human souls doth kill!
 And O, no wonder, if they thus do end;
 Since they but fail, where Gods could not defend!

Thomas Campion, M.D.

My sweetest LESBIA, let us live and love!
And though the sager sort our deeds reprove;
Let us not weigh them! Heaven's great lamps do dive
Into their west; and straight again revive:
But soon as once is set our little light;
Then must we sleep one ever-during night!

If all would lead their lives in love like me,
Then bloody swords and armour should not be!
No drum, nor trumpet, peaceful sleeps should move;
Unless alarm came from the Camp of Love!
But fools do live, and waste their little light;
And seek with pain their ever-during night!

When timely death, my life and fortunes ends;
Let not my hearse be vexed with mourning friends!
But let all Lovers, rich in triumph, come;
And with sweet pastimes grace my happy tomb!
And, LESBIA! close up thou, my little light;
And crown with love my ever-during night!

Now winter nights enlarge
    The number of their hours;
And clouds their storms discharge
    Upon the airy towers.

Let now the chimneys blaze,
    And cups o'erflow with wine!
Let well-tuned words amaze,
    With harmony divine!
Now yellow waxen lights
    Shall wait on honey Love!
While youthful Revels, Masques, and Courtly sights,
    Sleep's leaden spells remove.

This time doth well dispense
    With Lovers' long discourse!
Much speech hath some defence;
    Though Beauty, no remorse.
All do not all things well.
    Some measures comely tread!
Some knotted riddles tell!
    Some poems smoothly read!
The Summer hath his joys;
    And Winter his delights:
Though LOVE and all his pleasures are but toys;
    They shorten tedious nights!

O, SWEET delight! O, more than human bliss!
With her to live that ever loving is.
To hear her speak, whose words so well are placed,
That She by them, as they by her, are graced.
Those looks to view, that feast the viewer's eye:
How blessed is he, that may so live and die!

Such love as this, the Golden Times did know!
When all did reap; yet none took care to sow.
Such love as this, an endless Summer makes!
And all distaste, from frail affection takes.
So loved, so blessed in my beloved, am I;
Which, till their eyes ache, let iron men envy!

AND would you see my Mistress' face?
It is a flow'ry Garden place;
Where knots of beauties have such grace,
That all is work, and nowhere space.

It is a sweet, delicious, Morn;
Where day is breeding, never born!
It is a Meadow, yet unshorn;
Which thousand flowers do adorn.

It is the Heaven's bright reflex;
Weak eyes to dazzle and to vex!
It is th' Idæa of her sex;
Envy of whom doth World perplex.

It is a face of Death that smiles;
Pleasing, though it kills the whiles:
Where Death and Love, in pretty wiles,
Each other mutually beguiles.

Thomas Campion, M.D.

It is fair Beauty's freshest youth,
It is the feigned Elysium's truth,
The Spring, that wintered hearts renew'th:
And this is that, my soul pursu'th!

IF thou long'st so much to learn, sweet boy! what 'tis to love?
Do but fix thy thought on me; and thou shalt quickly prove!
    Little suit, at first, shall win
      Way to thy abashed desire!
    But then, will I hedge thee in,
      Salamander-like, with fire!

With thee, dance I will! and sing! and thy fond dalliance bear!
We, the grovy hills will climb; and play the wantons there!
    Other whiles we'll gather flowers,
      Lying dallying on the grass!
    And thus our delightful hours,
      Full of waking dreams, shall pass!

When thy joys were thus at height; my love should turn from thee!
Old acquaintance then should grow as strange as strange might be!
    Twenty rivals thou shouldst find,
      Breaking all their hearts for me!
    When to all, I'll prove more kind
      And more forward, than to thee!

Thus, thy silly youth enraged, would soon my love defy!
But, alas, poor soul, too late! Clipt wings can never fly!
    Those sweet hours which we had past,
      Called to mind, thy heart would burn!
    And couldst thou fly ne'er so fast,
      They would make thee straight return!

TURN all thy thoughts to eyes!
　Turn all thy hairs to ears!
Change all thy friends to spies;
　And all thy joys to fears!
　　True Love will yet be free!
In spite of jealousy.

Turn darkness into day!
　Conjectures into truth!
Believe, what th' envious say!
　Let Age interpret Youth!
　　True Love will yet be free!
In spite of jealousy.

Wrest every word and look!
　Rack every hidden thought!
Or fish with golden hook!
　True Love can not be caught!
　　For that will still be free!
In spite of jealousy.

GIVE Beauty all her right!
　She's not to one form tied.
Each shape yields fair delight,
　Where her perfections 'bide.
　　HELEN, I grant, might pleasing be;
　　And ROS'MOND was as sweet as she!

Some, the quick eye commends!
  Some, smelling lips and red!
Pale looks have many friends;
  Through sacred sweetness bred.
    Meadows have flowers that pleasure move;
    Though Roses are the Flowers of Love.

Free Beauty is not bound
  To one unmovèd clime!
She visits ev'ry ground;
  And favours ev'ry time!
    Let the old Loves with mine compare;
    My Sovereign is as sweet and fair!

———

Awake! Awake! thou heavy sprite!
  That sleep'st the deadly sleep of sin!
Rise now, and walk the Ways of Light!
  'Tis not too late yet to begin.
    Seek heaven, early! Seek it, late!
    True Faith still finds an open gate!

Get up! Get up! thou leaden man!
  Thy tracks to endless joy, or pain,
Yield but the model of a span!
  Yet burns out thy life's lamp in vain!
    One minute bounds thy bane, or bliss;
    Then watch, and labour, while time is!

KIND are her answers;
But her performance keeps no day:
    Breaks time, as dancers
From their own music when they stray.
All her free favours and smooth words
    Wing my hopes in vain!
O, did ever voice so sweet but only feign!
    Can True Love yield such delay,
    Converting joy to pain?

    Lost is our freedom,
When we submit to Women so!
    Why do we need them?
When, in their best, they work our woe!
    There is no wisdom
Can alter ends, by Fate prefixed!
O, why is the good of Man with evil mixed?
    Never were days yet callèd two;
    But one night went betwixt!

WHETHER men do laugh, or weep;
Whether they do wake, or sleep;
Whether they die young, or old;
Whether they feel heat, or cold;
There is, underneath the sun,
Nothing in true earnest done!

All our pride is but a jest!
None are worst; and none are best!
Grief and Joy, and Hope and Fear,
Play their Pageants everywhere!
Vain Opinion all doth sway;
And the World is but a Play!

Powers above, in clouds do sit,
Mocking our poor apish wit;
That so lamely, with such State,
Their high glory imitate.
No ill can be felt but pain;
And that, happy men disdain!

THINK'ST thou to seduce me then, with words that have no meaning!
Parrots so can learn to prate our speech, by pieces gleaning!
Nurses teach their children so, about the time of weaning!

Learn to speak first; then to woo! To wooing much pertaineth!
He that courts us, wanting Art, soon falters when he feigneth;
Looks asquint on his discourse; and smiles when he complaineth.

Skilful Anglers hide their hooks! fit baits for every season!
But with crooked pins fish'st thou! as babes do, that want reason.
Gudgeons only can be caught with such poor tricks of treason!

Ruth forgive me, if I erred, from human heart's compassion!
When I laughed sometimes too much to see thy foolish fashion:
But, alas, who less could do, that found so good occasion!

WHEN thou must home, to shades of underground;
  And there arrived, a new admirèd guest,
The beauteous Spirits do ingirt thee round,
  White IOPE, blithe HELEN, and the rest,
    To hear the stories of thy finished love,
    From that smooth tongue; whose music, Hell can move!

Then wilt thou speak of Banqueting delights,
  Of Masques and Revels, which sweet Youth did make;
Of Tourneys and great Challenges of Knights;
  And all these Triumphs, for thy beauty's sake!
    When thou hast told these honours done to thee;
    Then, tell! O tell, how thou didst murder me!

  SHALL I come, sweet Love! to thee,
    When the evening beams are set?
  Shall I not excluded be?
    Will you find no feignèd let?
      Let me not, for pity! more
      Tell the long hours at your door!

Who can tell, what thief, or foe,
  In the covert of the night,
For his prey, will work my woe;
  Or through wicked foul despite!
    So may I die unredressed,
    Ere my long love be possessed!

But to let such dangers pass,
   Which a Lover's thoughts disdain!
'Tis enough, in such a place,
   To attend Love's joys in vain!
     Do not mock me, in thy bed;
     While these cold nights freeze me dead!

WHAT is it all, that men possess, among themselves conversing?
Wealth, or Fame, or some such boast; scarce worthy the rehearsing!
Women only are Men's good; with them in love conversing!
If weary; they prepare us rest! If sick; their hand attends us!
When with grief our hearts are 'pressed; their comfort best befriends us!
Sweet, or sour, they willing go, to share what Fortune sends us!
What pretty babes! with pain they bear; our name and form presenting.
What we get, how wise they keep! by sparing, wants preventing.
Sorting all their household cares to our observed contenting.
All this, of whose large use I sing, in two words is expressed.
GOOD WIFE is the good I praise! if by good men possessed.
Bad with bad, in ill suit well; but good with good live blessed!

THERE is a garden in her face,
   Where roses and white lilies grow.
A heavenly Paradise is that place,
   Wherein all pleasant fruits doth flow.
     There, cherries grow, which none may buy,
     Till 'Cherry ripe!' themselves do cry.

Those cherries fairly do enclose
  Of orient pearl a double row;
Which when her lovely laughter shows,
  They look like rosebuds filled with snow.
    Yet them, nor Peer, nor Prince, can buy,
    Till 'Cherry ripe!' themselves do cry.

Her eyes, like Angels, watch them still;
  Her brows, like bended bows do stand,
Threatening with piercing frowns to kill
  All that attempt, with eye, or hand,
    Those sacred cherries to come nigh!
    Till 'Cherry ripe!' themselves do cry.

  JACK and JOAN, they think no ill;
  But loving live, and merry still!
  Do their week-day's work; and pray
  Devoutly on the Holy Day.
  Skip and trip it on the green,
  And help to choose the Summer Queen.
  Lash out, at a Country Feast,
  Their silver penny with the best.

  Well can they judge of nappy ale;
  And tell, at large, a winter tale.
  Climb up to the apple-loft;
  And turn the crabs till they be soft.
  TIB is all the father's joy;
  And little TOM, the mother's boy.
  All their pleasure is Content;
  And care, to pay their yearly rent.

JOAN can call by name, her cows;
And deck her windows with green boughs.
She can wreaths and tutties make;
And trim with plums a bridal cake.
JACK knows what brings gain, or loss;
And his long flail can stoutly toss:
Makes the hedge, which others break;
And ever thinks, what he doth speak.

Now, you Courtly Dames and Knights,
That study only strange delights!
Though you scorn the homespun gray,
And revel in your rich array;
Though your tongues dissemble deep,
And can your heads from danger keep:
Yet, for all your pomp and train,
Securer lives the silly Swain!

———

FOLLOW thy fair Sun, unhappy Shadow!
  Though thou be black as night,
  And She made all of light;
Yet follow thy fair Sun, unhappy Shadow!

Follow her, whose light thy light depriveth!
  Though here thou liv'st disgraced,
  And She in heaven is placed;
Yet follow her, whose light the world reviveth!

Follow those pure beams; whose beauty burneth!
    That so have scorchèd thee;
    As thou still black must be,
Till her kind beams, thy black to brightness turneth!

Follow her, while yet her glory shineth!
    There comes a luckless night,
    That will dim all her light;
And this, the black unhappy Shade divineth!

Follow still! since so thy Fates ordainèd.
    The Sun must have his Shade,
    Till both at once do fade;
The Sun still proved, the Shadow still disdainèd!

    WHEN to her lute CORINNA sings,
Her voice revives the leaden strings;
And doth in highest notes appear,
As any challenged echo clear:
But when she doth of mourning speak;
E'en with her sighs, the strings do break!

    And as her lute doth live, or die,
Led by her Passion; so must I!
For when of Pleasure she doth sing,
My thoughts enjoy a sudden Spring!
But if she doth of Sorrow speak;
E'en from my heart, the strings do break!

HER fair inflaming Eyes,
  Chief authors of my cares,
I prayed, in humblest wise,
  With grace to view my tears!
    They beheld me, broad awake;
    But, alas, no ruth would take!

Her Lips, with kisses rich
  And words of fair delight,
I fairly did beseech
  To pity my sad plight!
    But a voice from them brake forth,
    As a whirlwind from the North!

Then to her Hands I fled,
  That can give heart and all;
To them I long did plead;
  And loud for pity call!
    But, alas, they put me off,
    With a touch worse than a scoff!

So back I straight returned;
  And at her Breast I knocked!
Where long in vain I mourned;
  Her heart so fast was locked!
    Not a word could passage find;
    For a rock enclosed her mind!

Then down my prayers made way
      To those most comely parts
   That make her fly, or stay,
      As they affect deserts!
         But her angry Feet, thus moved,
         Fled with all the parts I loved!

Yet fled they not so fast
   As her enragèd Mind,
Still did I after haste!
   Still was I left behind!
      Till I found, 'twas to no end
      With a Spirit to contend!

BLAME not my cheeks, though pale with love they be!
   The kindly heat unto my heart is flown,
To cherish it, that is dismayed by thee;
   Who art so cruel and unsteadfast grown!
      For Nature, called for by distressèd hearts,
      Neglects, and quite forsakes, the outward parts!

But they, whose cheeks with careless blood are stained,
   Nurse not one spark of love within their hearts!
And when they woo, they speak with Passion feigned;
   For their fat love lies in their outward parts!
      But in their breasts, where LOVE his Court should hold,
      Poor CUPID sits, and blows his nails for cold!

SILLY boy, 'tis full moon yet ! Thy night, as day shines clearly !
Had thy youth but wit to fear ; thou couldst not love so dearly!
Shortly, wilt thou mourn ! when all thy pleasures are bereaved:
Little knows he how to love, that never was deceived!

This is thy first maiden flame, that triumphs yet unstained.
All is artless now you speak ! Not one word yet, is feigned !
All is heaven that you behold ; and all your thoughts are blessèd !
But no Spring can want his Fall! Each TROILUS hath his CRESSEID !

Thy well-ordered locks, ere long shall rudely hang neglected ;
And thy lively pleasant cheer read grief, on earth dejected !
Much then wilt thou blame thy Saint ! that made thy heart so holy :
And, with sighs, confess, ' In love, that too much faith is folly!'

Yet be just, and constant still ! Love may beget a wonder !
Not unlike a Summer's frost, or Winter's fatal thunder.
He that holds his Sweetheart true, unto his day of dying,
Lives, of all that ever breathed, most worthy the envying !

———

Now, let her change, and spare not!
Since She proves strange, I care not!
Feigned love charmed so my delight,
That still I doted on her sight:
But She is gone! new joys embracing;
And my desires disgracing.

When did I err in blindness;
Or vex her with unkindness!
If my cares served her alone;
Why is She thus untimely gone?
True Love abides to th' hour of dying!
False Love is ever flying!

False! then, farewell for ever!
Once false, proves faithful never!
He that boasts now of thy love,
Shall soon my present fortunes prove!
Were he as fair as bright ADONIS;
Faith is not had, where none is!

AWAKE, thou spring of speaking grace!
    Mute rest becomes not thee!
The fairest women while they sleep,
    And pictures, equal be.
O, come and dwell in Love's discourses;
    Old renewing, new creating!
The words which thy rich tongue discourses
    Are not of common rating!

Thy voice is as an echo clear;
    Which music doth beget!
Thy speech is as an oracle;
    Which none can counterfeit!
For thou alone, without offending,
    Hast obtained power of enchanting!
And I could hear thee, without ending!
    Other comfort never wanting.

Some little reason, brutish lives
　　With human glory share:
But language is our proper grace;
　　From which they severed are.
As brutes in reason Man surpasses;
　　Men in speech excel each other!
If speech be then the best of graces;
　　Do it not in slumber smother!

———

COME, you pretty false-eyed wanton!
　　Leave your crafty smiling!
Think you, to escape me now,
　　With slipp'ry words beguiling!
No, you mocked me th' other day;
　　When you got loose, you fled away!
But since I have caught you now;
　　I'll clip your wings, for flying!
Smoth'ring kisses fast I'll heap!
　　And keep you so from crying.

Sooner may you count the stars,
　　And number hail down pouring;
Tell the osiers of the Thames,
　　Or Goodwin Sands devouring:
Than the thick-showered kisses here,
　　Which now thy tired lips must bear!
Such a harvest never was,
　　So rich and full of pleasure!
But 'tis spent as soon as reaped;
　　So trustless is Love's treasure!

Thomas Campion, M.D.

THE man upright of life, whose guiltless heart is free
From all dishonest deeds, or thought of vanity;
That man, whose silent days in harmless joys are spent,
Whom hopes cannot delude, nor sorrow discontent:
That man needs neither towers, nor armour, for defence;
Nor secret vaults, to fly from thunder's violence.

He, only, can behold, with unaffrighted eyes,
The horrors of the deep, and terrors of the skies.
Thus scorning all the cares that Fate, or Fortune, brings,
He makes the heavens his Book; his Wisdom, heavenly things;
Good thoughts, his only Friends; his Wealth, a well-spent age;
The earth, his sober Inn, and quiet Pilgrimage.

    WHAT if a day, or a month, or a year,
Crown thy delights, with a thousand sweet contentings!
    Cannot a chance of a night, or an hour,
Cross thy desires, with as many sad tormentings?
    Fortune, Honour, Beauty, Youth, are but blossoms dying!
    Wanton Pleasure, doting Love, are but shadows flying!
      All our joys are but toys; idle thoughts deceiving!
      None have power, of an hour, in their life's bereaving!

    Earth's but a point to the world; and a man
Is but a point to the world's comparèd centre!
    Shall then, a point of a point be so vain
As to triumph in a silly point's adventure!
    All is hazard that we have! There is nothing biding!
    Days of pleasure are like streams, through fair meadows
        gliding!
      Weal and woe, Time doth go! Time is never turning!
      Secret fates guide our states; both in mirth and mourning!

So many Loves have I neglected;
  Whose good parts might move me:
That now I live, of all rejected.
  There is none will love me!
Why is maiden heat so coy?
  It freezeth, when it burneth!
Loseth what it might enjoy;
  And having lost it, mourneth!

Should I then woo, that have been wooed;
  Seeking them that fly me!
When I, my faith with tears have vowed,
  And when all deny me,
Who will pity my disgrace;
  Which love might have prevented?
There is no submission base;
  Where error is repented.

O, happy men! whose hopes are licensed
  To discourse their Passion;
While women are confined to silence,
  Losing wished occasion.
Yet our tongues than theirs, men say,
  Are apter to be moving:
Women are more dumb than they;
  But in their thoughts more moving!

When I compare my former strangeness
  With my present doting;
I pity men, that speak in plainness
  Their true heart's devoting;
While we (with repentance!) jest
  At their submissive Passion.
Maids, I see, are never blest,
  That strange be, but for fashion!

Never love! unless you can
  Bear with all the faults of Man.
Men sometimes will jealous be,
  Though but little cause they see;
    And hang the head, as discontent,
    And speak what, straight, they will repent!

Men that but one Saint adore,
  Make a show of love to more!
Beauty must be scorned in none;
  Though but truly served in one.
    For what is Courtship but disguise!
    True hearts may have dissembling eyes.

Men, when their affairs require,
Must a while themselves retire:
Sometimes hunt, and sometimes hawk;
And not ever sit and talk!
    If these, and such like, you can bear;
    Then like! and love! and never fear!

Thomas Campion, M.D.

FOLLOW your Saint! Follow, with accents sweet!
Haste you, sad notes! Fall at her flying feet!
There, wrapped in cloud of sorrow, pity move!
And tell the ravisher of my soul, I perish for her love!
But if She scorns my never-ceasing pain;
Then, burst with sighing in her sight; and ne'er return again!

All that I sang, still to her praise did tend!
Still She was first! Still She my Songs did end!
Yet She, my love and music both doth fly!
The music that her echo is, and beauty's sympathy.
Then let my notes pursue her scornful flight!
It shall suffice, that they were breathed, and died, for her delight!

THOU art not fair! for all thy red and white,
  For all those rosy ornaments in thee;
Thou art not sweet! though made of mere delight:
  Nor fair, nor sweet, unless thou pity me!
    I will not soothe thy fancies! Thou shalt prove
    That beauty is no beauty without love!

Yet love not me! nor seek thou to allure
  My thoughts with beauty, were it more divine!
Thy smiles and kisses, I can not endure!
  I'll not be wrapped up in those arms of thine!
    Now shew it! if thou be a woman right;
    Embrace, and kiss, and love, me, in despite!

COME, O, come, my life's delight!
　Let me not in languor pine!
Love loves no delay! Thy sight,
　　The more enjoyed, the more divine!
　　　O, come! and take from me
　　　The pain of being deprived of thee!

Thou all sweetness dost inclose,
　Like a little World of Bliss!
Beauty guards thy looks! The rose,
　In them pure and eternal is!
　　　Come, then! and make thy flight
　　　As swift to me as heavenly light!

THRICE, toss these oaken ashes in the air!
Thrice, sit thou mute in this inchanted chair!
Then, thrice three times, tie up this true-love's knot;
And murmur soft, 'She will! or She will not!'

Go, burn these pois'nous weeds in yon blue fire!
These screech-owl's feathers! and this prickling briar!
This cypress, gathered at a dead man's grave!
That all thy fears and cares an end may have.

Then come, you Fairies, dance with me a round!
Melt her hard heart, with your melodious sound!
In vain, are all the Charms I can devise!
She hath an Art to break them with her eyes.

Anonymous.

SHOOT, false LOVE! I care not!
Spend thy shafts, and spare not!
    Fa, la, la, la!
I fear not, I, thy might!
And less I weigh thy spite!
All naked, I unarm me;
If thou canst, now shoot, and harm me!
So lightly I esteem thee;
And now as child I deem thee!
    Fa, la, la, la!

Long thy bow did fear me;
While thy pomp did blear me!
    Fa, la, la, la!
But now I do perceive
Thy art is to deceive!
And every simple Lover,
All thy falsehood can discover!
Then weep, LOVE; and be sorry!
For thou hast lost thy glory!
    Fa, la, la, la!

THERE is a jewel, which no Indian mines can buy;
 Nor chemic art can counterfeit!
It makes men rich in greatest poverty!
Makes water, wine! turns wooden cups to gold!
The homely whistle, to sweet music's strain!
Seldom it comes! To few, from Heaven sent!
That much in little, all in naught, 's CONTENT.

Michael Drayton.

FAR in the country of Arden,
There woned a Knight, hight CASSAMEN,
   As bold as ISENBRAS.
     Fell was he; and eager bent
     In battle, and in tournament,
   As was the good Sir TOPAS.

He had, as antique stories tell,
A daughter clepèd DOWSABELL;
   A Maiden fair and free;
     And for she was her father's heir,
     Full well she was yconed the leir
   Of mickle courtesy!

The silk well couth she twist and twine,
And make the fine marchpine;
   And, with the needle work!
     And she couth help the Priest to say
     His Matins on a Holy Day;
   And sing a Psalm in Kirk.

She ware a frock of frolic green,
Might well become a Maiden Queen!
   Which seemly was to see.
     A hood to that, so neat and fine;
     In colour like the columbine,
   Ywrought full featuously.

Her feature all as fresh above,
As is the grass that grows by Dove;
  And lithe as Lass of Kent!
    Her skin as soft as Lemster wool,
    As white as snow on Peakish hill,
  Or swan that swims in Trent!

This Maiden, in a morn betime,
Went forth, when May was in the prime,
  To get sweet setywall,
    The honeysuckle, the harlock,
    The lily, and the lady-smock,
  To deck her Summer Hall.

Thus as she wandered here and there,
And picked off the bloomy briar,
  She chancèd to espy
    A Shepherd sitting on a bank,
    Like Chanticleer he crowèd crank;
  And piped full merrily!

He leared his sheep, as he him list,
When he would whistle in his fist,
  To feed about him round:
    Whilst he, full many a Carol sang;
    Until the fields and meadows rang,
  And all the woods did sound!

Michael Drayton.

In favour, this same Shepherd Swain
Was like the bedlam TAMBURLAINE;
  Which held proud Kings in awe:
    But meek as any lamb mought be;
    And innocent of ill as he,
Whom his lewd brother slaw!

The Shepherd ware a sheep-gray cloak;
Which was of the finest lock
  That could be cut with shear:
    His mittens were of bauzen's skin,
    His cockers were of cordiwin,
His hood, of miniver.

His awl and lingel in a thong,
His tar-box on his broad belt hung;
  His breech of Co'entry blue.
    Full crisp and curlèd were his locks,
    His brows as white as Albion rocks;
So like a Lover true!

And piping still, he spent the day,
So merry as the popinjay!
  Which likèd DOWSABELL;
    That, would she ought, or would she nought,
    This Lad would never from her thought!
She in love-longing fell!

At length, she tuckèd up her frock,
White as the lily was her smock,
   She drew the Shepherd nigh:
      But then, the Shepherd piped a-good!
      That all his sheep forsook their food,
To hear his melody!

'Thy sheep,' quoth she, 'can not be lean!
That have a jolly Shepherd Swain;
   The which can pipe so well!'
      'Yea, but,' saith he, 'their Shepherd may!
      If, piping thus, he pine away,
In love of DOWSABELL!'

'Of love, fond boy! take thou no keep!'
Quoth she, 'Look well unto thy sheep;
   Lest they should hap to stray!'
      Quoth he, 'So had I done full well;
      Had I not seen fair DOWSABELL
Come forth to gather May!'

With that, she gan to vail her head:
Her cheeks were like the roses red;
   But not a word she said!
      With that, the Shepherd gan to frown.
      He threw his pretty pipes adown;
And on the ground him laid.

Michael Drayton.

Saith she, 'I may not stay till night,
And leave my Summer Hall undight;
   And all for love of thee!'
     'My cot,' saith he, 'nor yet my fold,
     Shall neither sheep nor shepherd hold;
   Except thou favour me!'

Saith she, 'Yet lever I were dead,
Than I should lose my maidenhead;
   And all for love of men!'
     Saith he, 'Yet are you too unkind;
     If, in your heart, you cannot find
   To love us now and then!

'And I to thee will be as kind,
As COLIN was to ROSALIND;
   Of courtesy the flower!'
     'Then will I be as true,' quoth she,
     'As ever Maiden yet might be
   Unto her paramour!'

With that, she bent her snow-white knee,
Down by the Shepherd kneelèd she;
   And him she sweetly kist!
     With that, the Shepherd whooped for joy!
     Quoth he, 'There's never Shepherd's boy
   That ever was so blest!'

Michael Drayton.

'MAIDENS! why spare ye?
Or whether not dare ye
  Correct the blind Shooter!'
  'Because wanton VENUS,
    So oft that doth pain us,
Is her son's tutor!

'Now, in the Spring,
He proveth his wing!
  The field is his Bower;
    And as the small bee,
    About flyeth he
From flower to flower!

'And wantonly roves
Abroad in the groves,
  And in the air hovers;
    Which when it him deweth,
    His feathers he meweth
In sighs of true Lovers.

'And since doomed by Fate,
(That well knew his hate!)
  That he should be blind;
    For very despite,
    Our eyes be his White!
So wayward his kind!

'If his shafts losing
(Ill his mark choosing!),
  Or his bow broken;
    The moan that VENUS maketh,
    And care that she taketh,
Cannot be spoken!

'To VULCAN commending
Her love; and straight sending
  Her doves and her sparrows,
    With kisses, unto him:
    And all but to woo him,
To make her son arrows!

'Telling what he hath done,
Saith she, "Right mine own son!"
  In her arms, she him closes!
    Sweets on him fans!
    Laid in down of her swans!
His sheets, leaves of roses!

'And feeds him with kisses;
  Which, oft, when he misses,
    He ever is froward!
      The mother's o'erjoying
      Makes, by much coying,
    The child so untoward!'

Yet in a fine net,
That a spider set,
  The Maidens had caught him!
  Had she not been near him,
  And chancèd to hear him,
  More good they had taught him!

Since there's no help; come, let us kiss, and part!
  Nay, I have done! You get no more of me!
And I am glad; yea, glad with all my heart,
  That thus so cleanly, I myself can free!
Shake hands, for ever! Cancel all our vows!
  And, when we meet at any time again,
Be it not seen, in either of our brows,
  That we one jot of former love retain.
Now, at the last gasp of Love's latest breath,
  When, his pulse failing, Passion speechless lies,
When Faith is kneeling by his bed of death,
  And Innocence is closing up his eyes;
Now (if thou wouldst!), when all have given him over,
From death to life thou might'st him yet recover!

Michael Drayton.

Upon a bank, with roses set about,
  Where pretty turtles, joining bill to bill;
And gentle springs steal softly murmuring out,
  Washing the foot of Pleasure's sacred hill:
    There, little Love, sore wounded, lies!
    His bow and arrows broken,
    Bedewed with tears from Venus' eyes.
    Oh! grievous to be spoken!

Bear him my heart! slain with her scornful eye;
  Where sticks the arrow that poor heart did kill;
With whose sharp pile, request him, ere he die,
  About the same, to write his latest Will!
    And bid him send it back to me,
    At instant of his dying;
    That cruel, cruel She may see
    My faith, and her denying!

His Chapel be a mournful cypress shade;
  And for a Chantry, Philomel's sweet lay!
Where prayers shall continually be made
  By pilgrim Lovers, passing by that way:
    With Nymphs' and Shepherds' yearly moan,
    His timeless death beweeping,
    In telling, that my heart alone
    Hath his last Will in keeping.

Michael Drayton.

TO THE VIRGINIAN VOYAGE [OF 1606].

You, brave heroic minds,
   Worthy your country's name,
     That Honour still pursue,
     Go, and subdue!
Whilst loitering hinds
   Lurk here at home with shame.

Britans, you stay too long!
   Quickly aboard bestow you!
     And with a merry gale
     Swell your stretched sail,
With vows as strong
   As the winds that blow you.

Your course securely steer!
   West-and-by-South forth keep!
     Rocks, lee shores, nor shoals,
     When ÆOLUS scowls,
You need not fear;
   So absolute the deep!

And cheerfully at sea,
   Success you still entice
     To get the pearl and gold!
     And ours to hold,
Virginia,
   Earth's only Paradise!

Michael Drayton.

Where Nature hath in store,
   Fowl, venison, and fish!
      And the fruitfull'st soil,
      Without your toil,
Three harvests more;
   All greater than your wish!

And the ambitious vine
   Crowns, with his purple mass,
      The cedar reaching high
      To kiss the sky.
The cypress, pine,
   And useful sassafras.

To whom, the Golden Age
   Still Nature's laws doth give!
      No other cares attend,
      But them to defend
From Winter's rage;
   That long there doth not live.

When as the luscious smell
   Of that delicious land,
      Above the sea that flows,
      The clear wind throws,
Your hearts to swell,
   Approaching the dear strand.

In kenning of the shore.
  (Thanks to GOD first given!)
    O, you, the happiest men,
    Be frolic then!
Let cannons roar!
  Frighting the wide heaven.

And in regions far
  Such heroes bring ye forth,
    As those from whom we came!
    And plant our name
Under the Star,
  Not known unto our North!

And where, in plenty grows
  The laurel everywhere,
    APOLLO's sacred tree!
    Your days may see
A Poet's brows
  To crown! that may sing there.

Thy *Voyages* attend,
  Industrious HAKLUYT!
    Whose reading shall inflame
    Men to seek fame;
And much commend
  To after Times, thy wit!

Anonymous.

SISTER, awake! Close not your eyes!
  The Day her light discloses!
And the bright Morning doth arise
  Out of her bed of roses.

See the clear sun, the world's bright eye,
  In at our window peeping!
Lo, how he blusheth to espy
  Us, idle wenches, sleeping!

Therefore, awake! Make haste, I say,
  And let us, without staying,
All in our gowns of green so gay,
  Into the Park a Maying!

So saith my fair and beautiful LYCORIS,
  When, now and then, She talketh
    With me, of LOVE:
'LOVE is a Spirit that walketh!
    That soars! and flies!
And none alive can hold him!
Nor touch him! nor behold him!'

  Yet when her eyes she turneth;
  I spy where he sojourneth!
    In her eyes, there he flies!
  But none can catch him,
  Till from her lips he fetch him!

John Chalkhill.

CORIDON'S SONG.

O, THE sweet contentment
  The Countryman doth find!
High trololly, lolly, loe! High trololly, lee!
  That quiet contemplation
  Possesseth all my mind!
Then, Care, away! and wend along with me!

For Courts are full of flattery,
  As hath too oft been tried!
High trololly, lolly, loe! High trololly, lee!
  The City, full of wantonness:
  And both are full of pride!
Then, Care, away! and wend along with me!

But O, the honest Countryman
  Speaks truly from his heart!
High trololly, lolly, loe! High trololly, lee!
  His pride is in his tillage,
  His horses, and his cart!
Then, Care, away! and wend along with me!

Our clothing is good sheepskins;
  Grey russet for our wives!
High trololly, lolly, loe! High trololly, lee!
  'Tis warmth, and not gay clothing,
  That doth prolong our lives!
Then, Care, away! and wend along with me!

John Chalkhill.

The Ploughman, though he labour hard,
  Yet, on the holiday,
High trololly, lolly, loe! High trololly, lee!
  No Emperor so merrily
  Does pass his time away!
Then, Care, away! and wend along with me!

To recompense our tillage,
  The heavens afford us showers!
High trololly, lolly, loe! High trololly, lee!
  And for our sweet refreshments,
  The earth affords us bowers!
Then, Care, away! and wend along with me!

The cuckoo and the nightingale
  Full merrily do sing;
High trololly, lolly, loe! High trololly, lee!
  And, with their pleasant Roundelays,
  Bid welcome to the Spring!
Then, Care, away! and wend along with me!

This is not half the happiness
  The Countryman enjoys!
High trololly, lolly, loe! High trololly, lee!
  Though others think they have as much;
  Yet he that says so, lies!
Then, come away! Turn Countryman with me!

Joshua Sylvester.

THE Poets feign, that, when the world began,
  Both Sexes in one body did remain;
Till JOVE, offended with this Double Man,
  Caused VULCAN to divide him into twain
In this division, he the heart did sever;
  But cunningly he did indent the heart,
That, if there were a reuniting ever,
  Each Part might know which was his Counterpart.
See then, dear Love! th' Indenture of my heart!
  And read the Cov'nants, writ with holy fire!
See, if your heart be not the Counterpart
  Of my true heart's indented chaste desire!
And if it be; so may it ever be!
Two hearts in one, 'twixt you, my Love, and me!

WERE I as base as is the lowly plain,
  And you, my Love, as high as heaven above!
Yet should the thoughts of me, your humble Swain,
  Ascend to heaven! in honour of my love.
Were I as high as heaven above the plain;
  And you, my Love, as humble and as low
As are the deepest bottoms of the Main:
  Wheresoe'er you were, with you my love should go!
Were you the Earth, dear Love! and I, the Skies;
  My love should shine on you, like to the sun!
And look upon you, with ten thousand eyes,
  Till heaven waxed blind! and till the world were done!
Wheresoe'er I am! below, or else above, you!
Wheresoe'er you are! my heart shall truly love you!

Joshua Sylvester.

A CONTENTED MIND.

I WEIGH not Fortune's frown or smile!
   I joy not much in earthly joys!
I seek not State! I reck not style!
   I am not fond of Fancy's toys!
     I rest so pleased with what I have;
     I wish no more! no more I crave!

I quake not at the thunder's crack!
   I tremble not at noise of war!
I swound not at the news of wrack!
   I shrink not at a blazing star!
     I fear not loss! I hope not gain!
     I envy none! I none disdain!

I see Ambition never pleased!
   I see some TANTAL's starved in store!
I see gold's dropsy seldom eased!
   I see even MIDAS gape for more!
     I neither want; nor yet abound!
     Enough's a feast! Content is crowned!

I feign not friendship, where I hate!
   I fawn not on the Great (in show)!
I prize, I praise, a mean estate;
   Neither too lofty, nor too low!
     This, this, is all my choice, my cheer;
     A mind content! A conscience clear!

EVEN as the timely sweet heat-temp'ring showers
  Feed the faint earth, and fill it all with flowers green;
Green grain, and grass, and plants, and fruits, and flowers:
  Whereby the beauty of the world is seen.
      Even so, my tears, temp'ring mine inward fire,
      Do feed my love, and foster my desire!

And as a sudden and a stormy rain
  Makes FLORA's children hang their painted heads:
And beateth down the pride of CERES' plain;
  Drowning the pastures, and the flow'ry meads.
      Even so, my tears, that overflow my fire,
      Drown my delight; but not my love's desire!

And as a little water, cast upon
  A forge, doth force the flame to mount the more;
Which being by the panting bellows blown,
  It glows, and grows much hotter than before!
      Even so, my tears, cast on mine inward fire,
      Blown by my sighs, augment my high desire!

And as a brook, that meadows undermines,   [fair;
  Doth make them seem more green, more fresh, more
And as the dew, before bright PHŒBUS shines,
  Gives the sweet rose a more delightful air:
      Even so, my tears, wat'ring mine inward fire,
      Adorn my love, and garnish my desire!

Thus, then, though weeping waste my life away,
　And drench my soul in ever-floods of care ;
Yet, by my tears, I do my faith display !
　Whereby my merits still recorded are :
　　So that my tears refresh mine inward fire ;
　　And yet my tears quench not my high desire !

THE FRUITS OF A CLEAR CONSCIENCE.

To shine in silk, and glister all in gold,
　To flow in wealth, and feed on dainty fare,
To have thy houses stately to behold,
　Thy Prince's favour, and the people's care :
　　The groaning gout, the colic, or the stone,
　　Will mar thy mirth, and turn it all to moan !

But, be it, that thy body subject be
　To no such sickness, or the like annoy ;
Yet if thy Conscience be not firm and free,
　Riches are trash ! and Honours but a toy !
　This Peace of Conscience is the perfect joy,
　　Wherewith GOD's children in the world be blest :
　　Wanting the which, as good want all the rest !

The want thereof made ADAM hide his head !
　The want of this made CAIN to wail and weep !
This want, alas, makes many go to bed ;
　When they, God wot ! have little list to sleep.
　Strive, O, then strive to entertain and keep
　　So rich a jewel, and so rare a guest !
　　Which being had ; a rush for all the rest !

George Wither.

THE AUTHOR'S RESOLUTION.

SHALL I, wasting in despair,
Die because a woman's fair?
Or make pale my cheeks with care,
'Cause another's rosy are?
    Be She fairer than the Day,
    Or the flow'ry Meads in May;
    If She think not well of me,
    What care I, how Fair She be!

Shall my silly heart be pined,
'Cause I see a woman kind?
Or a well-disposed nature
Joined with a lovely feature?
    Be she meeker, kinder, than
    Turtle-dove, or pelican;
    If She be not so to me,
    What care I, how Kind She be!

Shall a woman's virtue move
Me to perish for her love?
Or her well-deservings known,
Make me quite forget mine own?
    Be She with that goodness blest,
    Which may merit name of best;
    If She be not such to me,
    What care I, how Good She be!

'Cause her fortune seems too high;
Shall I play the fool, and die?
She that bears a noble mind,
If not outward helps She find,
    Thinks what, with them, He would do;
    That, without them, dares her woo.
    And unless that mind I see,
    What care I, how Great She be!

Great, or Good, or Kind, or Fair;
I will ne'er the more despair!
If She love me, (this believe!)
I will die ere She shall grieve!
    If She slight me, when I woo;
    I can scorn, and let her go!
    For if She be not for me,
    What care I, for whom She be!

[*A PRISON SONG.*]

I, THAT erstwhile the world's sweet air did draw,
Graced by the Fairest ever mortal saw;
Now closely pent with walls of ruthless stone,
Consume my days and nights, and all alone.

When I was wont to sing of Shepherds' loves,
My walks were fields, and downs, and hills, and groves:
But now, alas, so strict is my hard doom,
Fields, downs, hills, groves, and all,'s but one poor room!

George Wither.

Each morn, as soon as daylight did appear,
With Nature's music, birds would charm mine ear:
Which now, instead of their melodious strains,
Hear rattling shackles, gyves, and bolts, and chains.

But though that all the world's delights forsake me;
I have a Muse, and she shall music make me!
Whose airy notes, in spite of closest cages,
Shall give content to me, and after Ages!

Nor do I pass for all this outward ill!
My heart's the same; and undejected still!
And (which is more than some in freedom win)
I have true rest, and peace, and joy within!

And then, my Mind, that (spite of prison) 's free,
Whene'er she pleases, anywhere can be!
She's, in an hour, in France, Rome, Turkey, Spain,
In Earth, in Hell, in Heaven; and here again!

Yet there's another comfort in my woe;
My Cause is spread! and all the World doth know
My fault's no more but speaking truth and reason!
Not debt, nor theft, nor murder, rape, nor treason.

Nor shall my foes, with all their might and power,
Wipe out their shame; nor yet this fame of our!
Which when they find; they shall my fate envy
Till they grow lean, and sick, and mad, and die!

Then though my body here in prison rot,
And my poor *Satires* seem a while forgot:
Yet, when both fame and life have left those men,
My verse and I'll revive, and live again!

So, thus enclosed, I bear Affliction's load;
But with more true content than some abroad!
For whilst their thoughts do feel my Scourge's sting;
In bands, I'll leap! and dance! and laugh! and sing!

JOHN WEBSTER.

CALL for the robin redbreast, and the wren!
   Since o'er shady groves they hover;
   And with leaves and flowers do cover
The friendless bodies of unburied men.

   Call unto his funeral dole,
The ant, the field-mouse, and the mole
To rear him hillocks that shall keep him warm;
And (when gay tombs are robbed) sustain no harm.
But keep the wolf far thence! that's foe to men;
For with his nails, he'll dig them up again!

Let Holy Church receive him duly;
Since he paid the Church tithes truly.

William Browne.

One of the Sirens sings this Song.

STEER hither! steer your wingèd pines,
  All beaten mariners!
Here lie LOVE's undiscovered mines,
  A prey to passengers!
Perfumes far sweeter than the best
Which make the Phœnix' urn and nest!
  Fear not your ships!
Nor any to oppose you, save our lips!
  But come on shore!
Where no joy dies, till LOVE hath gotten more!

CHORUS.

But come on shore!
Where no joy dies, till LOVE hath gotten more!

For swelling waves; our panting breasts,
  Where never storms arise,
Exchange! and be a while our guests!
  For stars; gaze on our eyes!
The Compass, LOVE shall hourly sing;
And, as he goes about the ring,
  We will not miss
To tell each point he nameth, with a kiss!

CHORUS.

Then come on shore!
Where no joy dies, till LOVE hath gotten more!

William Browne.

Welcome! Welcome! do I sing!
Far more welcome than the Spring!
He that parteth from you never,
Shall enjoy a Spring for ever!

He that to the Voice is near,
  Breaking from your iv'ry pale,
Need not walk abroad to hear
  The delightful nightingale.
     Welcome! Welcome! do I sing! &c.

He that looks still on your Eyes,
  Though the Winter have begun
To benumb our arteries,
  Shall not want the Summer's sun!
     Welcome! Welcome! do I sing! &c.

He that still may see your Cheeks,
  Where all rareness still reposes,
Is a fool, if e'er he seeks
  Other lilies! other roses!
     Welcome! Welcome! do I sing! &c.

He, to whom your soft Lip yields,
  And perceives your breath in kissing,
All the odours of the fields
  Never, never, shall be missing!
     Welcome! Welcome! do I sing! &c.

William Browne.

He that question would anew,
  What fair Eden was of old?
Let him rightly study you;
  And a brief of that behold!
    Welcome! Welcome! do I sing! &c.

LOVE who will; for I'll love none!
  There's fools enough beside me!
Yet if each woman have not one;
  Come to me, where I hide me!
    And if she can the place attain;
    For once, I'll be her fool again!

It is an easy place to find;
  And women, sure, should know it!
Yet thither serves not every wind;
  Nor many men can show it!
    It is the Storehouse, where doth lie
    All women's truth and constancy.

If the journey be so long,
  No woman will adventure!
But dreading her weak vessel's wrong;
  The voyage will not enter!
    Then may she sigh, and lie alone!
    In love with all; yet loved of none!

THYRSIS' PRAISE OF HIS MISTRESS.

On a hill, that graced the plain,
Thyrsis sat, a comely Swain;
Comelier Swain ne'er graced a hill!
    Whilst his flock, that wandered nigh,
    Cropped the green grass busily;
Thus he tuned his oaten quill!

'Ver hath made the pleasant field
Many sev'ral odours yield,
Odours aromatical.
    From fair Astra's cherry lip,
    Sweeter smells for ever skip!
They, in pleasing, passen all.

'Leavy groves now mainly ring
With each sweet bird's sonneting,
Notes that make the echoes long;
    But when Astra tunes her voice,
    All the mirthful birds rejoice,
And are list'ning to her Song.

'Fairly spreads the damask rose;
Whose rare mixture doth disclose
Beauties, pencils cannot feign;
    Yet if Astra pass the bush,
    Roses have been seen to blush!
She doth all their beauties stain.

'PHŒBUS, shining bright in sky,
Gilds the floods, heats mountains high,
With his beams' all-quick'ning fire;
    ASTRA's eyes, most sparkling ones!
    Strike a heat in hearts of stones,
And inflames them with desire.

'Fields are blest with flow'ry wreath;
Air is blest, when she doth breathe!
Birds make happy ev'ry grove;
    She each bird, when she doth sing!
    PHŒBUS' heat to earth doth bring;
She makes marble fall in love!

'Those, blessings of the earth! we Swains do call:
ASTRA can bless those blessings, earth, and all!'

NOT long agone a youthful Swain,
Much wrongèd by a Maid's disdain,
Before LOVE's altar came, and did implore,
That he might like her less; or She love more!

The God him heard; and She began
To dote on him. He, foolish man!   [before,
Cloyed with much sweets, thus changed his note
'O let her love me less; or I like more!'

William Browne.

SHALL I tell you, whom I love?
  Hearken then a while to me!
And if such a woman move,
  As I now shall versify;
    Be assured, 'tis She, or none,
    That I love, and love alone!

Nature did her so much right,
  As She scorns the help of Art;
In as many virtues dight
  As e'er yet embraced a heart!
    So much good, so truly tried,
    Some for less were deified!

Wit She hath; without desire
  To make known how much She hath!
And her anger flames no higher
  Than may fitly sweeten wrath!
    Full of pity as may be;
    Though perhaps not so, to me!

Reason masters every sense;
  And her virtues grace her birth!
Lovely, as all excellence!
  Modest, in her most of mirth!
    Likelihood enough to prove
    Only Worth could kindle Love!

Such She is! and if you know
  Such a one as I have sung;

Be She brown! or fair! or so
   That She be but somewhile young:
      Be assured, 'tis She, or none,
      That I love, or love alone!

Venus, by Adonis' side,
Crying kissed, and kissing cried,
Wrung her hands, and tore her hair;
For Adonis dying there.

'Stay!' quoth she, 'O, stay and live!
Nature, surely, doth not give
To the earth her sweetest flowers,
To be seen but some few hours!'

On his face, still as he bled,
For each drop, a tear she shed!
Which she kissed, or wiped, away;
Else had drowned him where he lay.

'Fair Proserpina,' quoth she,
'Shall not have thee yet from me!
Nor thy soul, to fly begin;
While my lips can keep it in!'

Here she ceased again. And some
Say, Apollo would have come
To have cured his wounded limb;
But that she had smothered him!

Samuel Rowlands.

I CHANCED, of late, an ancient book to view
As good as *BEVIS*, and as strange and true,
Of lions, leopards, tigers, bears, and boars,
And such ill faces as in forest roars.
  Amongst the rest was one, that had a den
Piled, like a wood-wharf, with the bones of men.
He had a head most fearful to behold,
Wherein two eyes, like globes of fire, rolled;
Teeth terrible, to bite through flesh and bone;
A forkèd tongue, the like was never known!
Claws past compare, to scratch down trees withal;
A sting in 's tail, would enter through a wall!
  I do protest, I was almost afraid
To read the strange description that was made
Of this den-Devil; sure, he was no less!
As by the story any man would guess.
Yet by a valiant Knight, this same hot-shot
Was hewed as small as flesh unto the pot.

  Then, in that book, a Dragon I do find,
The like is not among the Dragons' kind!
Th' enchanted Dragon of the darksome shade,
Of seven metals all composed and made.

Samuel Rowlands.

And that the World shall witness I am read
('Gainst melancholy vexings in my head!)
In ancient stories, courage to provoke;
Not spending all my time in taking smoke:
Although my Worship's scandalled, now and then,
Amongst the ruder sort of vulgar men.
  But that I turn, and overturn again,
Old books, wherein the worm-holes do remain,
Containing Acts of ancient Knights and Squires,
That fought with Dragons spitting forth wild fires;
The history unto you shall appear,
Even, by myself, *verbatim* set down here.

As thus.

Sir EGLAMORE, that worthy Knight,
He took his sword, and went to fight;
And as he rode both hill and dale,
Armèd upon his shirt of mail,
A Dragon came out of his den,
Had slain, God knows, how many men!

When he espied Sir EGLAMORE,
O, if you had but heard him roar;
And seen how all the trees did shake!
The Knight did tremble, horse did quake,
The birds betake them all to peeping:
It would have made you fall a weeping!

But now, it is in vain to fear;
Being come unto, 'fight dog! fight bear!'
To it, they go! and fiercely fight
A life-long day, from morn till night.
The Dragon had a plaguy hide;
And could the sharpest steel abide.

No sword will enter him with cuts,
Which vexed the Knight unto the guts:
But, as in choler he did burn,
He watched the Dragon a good turn;
And, as a yawning he did fall,
He thrust his sword in, hilts and all!

Then, like a coward, he to fly
Unto his den, that was hard by;
And there he lay all night, and roared.
The Knight was sorry for his sword;
But, riding thence, said, 'I forsake it!
He that will fetch it; let him take it!'

And so, I hope, to the judicious wise,
Thus much of this rare story shall suffice
To prove, how I in worthy Works am read;
Howe'er illiterate censures are misled!

HARK! jolly Shepherds!
   Hark you, yon lusty ringing!
How cheerfully the bells dance;
   The whilst the Lads are springing!
Go then! Why sit we here delaying;
And all yon merry wanton Lasses playing?
   How gaily FLORA leads it;
      And sweetly treads it!
   The woods and groves they ring!
      Loudly resounding
   With echo sweet rebounding!

ONCE did my thoughts both ebb and flow;
   As Passion did them move!
Once did I hope! straight fear again!
   And then I was in love!

Once did I, waking, spend the night;
   And tell how many minutes move!
Once did I, wishing, waste the day;
   And then I was in love!

Once, by my carving True Love's knot,
   The weeping trees did prove
That wounds and tears were both our lot;
   And then I was in love!

Anonymous.

Once did I breathe another's breath;
    And in my Mistress move!
Once was I not mine own at all;
    And then I was in love!

Once wore I bracelets made of hair;
    And collars did approve;
Once wore my clothes made out of wax;
    And then I was in love!

Once did I sonnet to my Saint;
    My soul in Numbers move!
Once did I tell a thousand lies;
    And then I was in love!

Once in my ear did dangling hang
    A little turtle-dove!
Once, in a word, I was a fool;
    And then I was in love!

APRIL is in my Mistress' face,
And July in her eyes hath place:
Within her bosom is September;
But in her heart a cold December.

I KNOW that all beneath the moon decays;
   And what by mortals, in this world is brought,
   In Time's great periods, shall return to nought!
That fairest States have fatal nights and days.
I know how all the Muses' heavenly Lays
   (With toil of sp'rit which are so dearly bought!)
   As idle sounds, of few, or none, are sought;
And that naught lighter is, than airy praise!
I know frail Beauty, like the purple flower,
   To which one morn of birth and death affords!
   That Love, a jarring is of minds' accords;
Where Sense and Will invassal Reason's power!
     Know what I list, this all can not me move!
     But that, O, me! I both must write, and love!

SWEET Spring! thou turn'st, with all thy goodly Train,
   Thy head, with flames; thy mantle bright with flowers!
The Zephyrs curl the green locks of the plain,
   The clouds, for joy, in pearls weep down their showers.
Thou turn'st, sweet Youth! but, ah! my pleasant hours
   And happy days, with thee come not again!
   The sad memorials only of my pain
Do with thee turn; which turn my sweets in sours!
Thou art the same, which still thou wast before,
   Delicious, wanton, amiable, fair!
   But She, whose breath embalmed thy wholesome air,
Is gone! nor gold, nor gems, her can restore!
     Neglected Virtue! seasons go and come;
     While thine forgot lie closèd in a tomb!

William Drummond.

O, SACRED Blush, impurpling cheeks' pure skies
   With crimson wings, which spread thee like the Morn!
O, bashful Look, sent from those shining eyes;
   Which, though cast down on earth, couldst heaven
O, Tongue, in which most luscious nectar lies; [adorn!
   That can, at once, both bless and make forlorn!
Dear coral Lip, which Beauty beautifies,
   That trembling stood, ere that her words were born.
And you, her Words! Words, no! but Golden Chains;
   Which did captive mine ears, ensnare my soul!
Wise image of her mind! Mind that contains
   A power, all power of senses to control.
     Ye all from love dissuade so sweetly me,
     That I love more! if more my love could be.

SLEEP! Silence's child! Sweet father of soft Rest!
   Prince, whose approach, peace to all mortals brings;
   Indifferent host to Shepherds and to Kings:
Sole comforter of minds, with grief opprest.
Lo, by thy charming rod, all breathing things
   Lie slumb'ring, with forgetfulness possest:
And yet, o'er me to spread thy drowsy wings
   Thou spar'st, alas! who cannot be thy guest.
Since I am thine, O, come! but with that face
   To inward light, which thou art wont to show.
   With feignèd solace ease a true-felt woe!
Or if, deaf God! thou do deny that grace;
   Come as thou wilt! and what thou wilt, bequeath!
   I long to kiss the Image of my Death!

SHE, whose fair flowers no Autumn makes decay,
  Whose hue celestial earthly hues doth stain,
  Into a pleasant odoriferous plain
Did walk alone, to brave the pride of May.
And whilst, through chequered Lists She made her way;
  Which smiled about, her sight to entertain;
  Lo, unawares, where LOVE did hid remain
She spied; and sought to make of him her prey.
For which, of golden locks a fairest hair
  (To bind the Boy) She took: but he, afraid,
At her approach, sprang swiftly in the air;
  And, mounting far from reach, looked back, and said,
    'Why shouldst thou, Sweet! me seek in chains to [bind;
    Sith in thine eyes I daily am confined!'

ALEXIS! here, She stayed! Among these pines,
  Sweet Hermitress! She did alone repair!
  Here, did She spread the treasure of her hair,
More rich than that brought from the Colchian mines.
She set her by these musket eglantines;
  The happy place, the print seems yet to bear!
Her voice did sweeten here thy sugared lines;
  To which, winds, trees, beasts, birds, did lend their ear.
Me here, She first perceived; and here, a Morn
  Of bright carnations did o'erspread her face!
Here, did She sigh! Here, first my hopes were born;
  And I first got a pledge of promised grace!
    But, ah! what served it to be happy so!
    Sith passèd pleasures double but new woe!

PANGLORY'S WOOING SONG.

Therefore, above the rest, Ambition sat.
  His Court with glitterant pearl was all enwalled;
And round about the wall, in Chairs of State
    And most majestic splendour, were installed
    A hundred Kings: whose temples were impaled
In golden diadems, set here and there
With diamonds, and gemmèd everywhere;
And of their golden verges none disceptered were.

High over all, Panglory's blazing throne,
  (In her bright turret, all of crystal wrought)
Like Phœbus' lamp in the midst of heaven shone:
    Whose starry top (with pride infernal fraught)
    Self-arching columns, to uphold were taught.
In which her image still reflected was,
By the smooth crystal; that, most like her glass,
In beauty, and in frailty, did all others pass.

A silver wand, the Sorceress did sway:
  And for a crown of gold, her hair she wore;
Only a garland of rosebuds did play
    About her locks; and in her hand she bore
    A hollow globe of glass, that long before
She full of emptiness had bladderèd,
And all the world therein depicturèd;
Whose colours, like the rainbow, ever vanishèd.

Such wat'ry orbicles young boys do blow
  Out from their soapy shells; and much admire
The swimming world, which tenderly they row
  With easy breath, till it be waved higher:
  But if they chance but roughly once aspire,
The painted bubble instantly doth fall!
Here, when she came, she gan for music call;
And sang this Wooing Song, to welcome Him withal

    'LOVE is the blossom, where there blows
Every thing that lives, or grows!
Love doth make the heavens to move;
And the sun doth burn in love!
Love the strong and weak doth yoke,
And makes the ivy climb the oak;
Under whose shadows lions wild,
Softened by Love, grow tame and mild!
    'LOVE no med'cine can appease!
He burns the fishes in the seas.
Not all the skill, his wounds can stench!
Not all the sea, his fire can quench!
    'Love did make the bloody spear
Once a leavy coat to wear;
While, in his leaves, there shrouded lay
Sweet birds, for Love that sing and play!
    'And of all Love's joyful flame,
 I the bud and blossom am!
        'Only bend thy knee to me;
        Thy Wooing shall thy Winning be!

'See, see the flowers, that below
Now as fresh as morning blow;
And of all, the virgin Rose,
That as bright AURORA shows;
How they all unleavèd die,
Losing their virginity:
Like unto a summer shade;
But now born, and now they fade!
Every thing doth pass away!
There is danger in delay!
Come, come, gather then the Rose!
Gather it; or it you lose!
 'All the sand of Tagus' shore,
Into my bosom casts his ore!
All the valleys' swimming corn,
To my house is yearly borne!
Every grape of every vine
Is gladly bruised, to make me wine!
While ten thousand Kings, as proud
To carry up my train, have bowed;
And a world of Ladies send me,
In my chambers, to attend me!
 'All the stars in heaven that shine,
  And ten thousand more, are mine!
   'Only bend thy knee to me;
    Thy Wooing shall thy Winning be!'

Giles Fletcher the Younger, B.D.

Thus sought the dire Enchantress, in his mind
  Her guileful bait to have embossomèd:
But He, her charms dispersèd into wind;
  And, her of insolence admonishèd!
  And all her optic glasses shatterèd!
So, with her Sire, to Hell she took her flight
(The starting air flew from the damnèd sprite!);
Where deeply both, aggrieved, plungèd themselves in
    night.

But to their LORD, now musing in his thought,
  A heavenly volley of light Angels flew;
And from his Father, him a banquet brought
  Through the fine Element: for well they knew,
  After his Lenten Fast, he hungry grew.
And as he fed, the holy Quires combine
To sing a Hymn of the celestial Trine:
All thought to pass; and each was, past all thought,
    divine.

The birds' sweet notes, to sonnet out their joys,
  Attempered to the Lays Angelical!
And to the birds, the winds attune their noise!
  And to the winds, the waters hoarsely call!
  And ECHO, back again revoicèd all!
That the whole valley rang with Victory!
But now our LORD, to rest doth homeward fly.
See, how the Night comes stealing from the mountains
    high!

Ye little birds, that sit and sing
  Amidst the shady valleys,
And see how PHILLIS sweetly walks
  Within her garden alleys,
Go, pretty birds, about her bower!
Sing, pretty birds, she may not lower!
Ah! me! methinks, I see her frown!
    Ye pretty wantons, warble!

Go, tell her, through your chirping bills,
  As you by me are bidden,
To her is only known my love;
  Which from the World is hidden.
Go, pretty birds, and tell her so!
See that your notes strain not too low!
For still, methinks, I see her frown!
    Ye pretty wantons, warble!

Go, tune your voices' harmony;
  And sing, I am her Lover!
Strain loud and sweet, that every note
  With sweet content may move her!
And she that hath the sweetest voice,
Tell her, I will not change my choice!
Yet still, methinks, I see her frown!
    Ye pretty wantons, warble!

O, fly! Make haste! See, see, she falls
   Into a pretty slumber!
Sing round about her rosy bed,
   That, waking, she may wonder!
Say to her, 'Tis her Lover true,
That sendeth love to you! to you!
And when you hear her kind reply;
     Return with pleasant warblings!

[LONDON TAVERNS.]

THE Gentry to the *King's Head*,
   The Nobles to the *Crown*,
The Knights unto the *Golden Fleece*,
   And to the *Plough*, the Clown.

The Churchman to the *Mitre*,
   The Shepherd to the *Star*,
The Gardener hies him to the *Rose*,
   To the *Drum*, the man of war.

To the *Feathers*, Ladies you! The *Globe*,
   The Seaman doth not scorn!
The Usurer to the *Devil*; and
   The Townsman to the *Horn*.

The Huntsman to the *White Hart*,
   To the *Ship*, the Merchant goes:
But you that do the Muses love,
   The *Swan*, called river Po.

Thomas Heywood.

The Bankrupt to the *World's End*,
　　The Fool to the *Fortune* hie;
Unto the *Mouth*, the Oyster Wife;
　　The Fidler to the *Pie*. . . .

PACK, clouds, away; and welcome, day!
　　With night, we banish sorrow!
Sweet air, blow soft! Mount, Lark, aloft;
　　To give my Love 'Good morrow!'
Wings from the wind, to please her mind;
　　Notes from the Lark, I'll borrow!
Bird, prune thy wing! Nightingale, sing!
　　To give my Love 'Good morrow!'
　　　　To give my Love 'Good morrow!'
　　Notes from them all, I'll borrow!

Wake from thy nest, Robin Redbreast!
　　Sing, birds, in every furrow!
And from each bill, let music shrill
　　Give my fair Love 'Good morrow!'
Blackbird and Thrush, in every bush,
　　Stare, Linnet, and Cock Sparrow;
You pretty Elves, among yourselves,
　　Sing my fair Love 'Good morrow!'
　　　　To give my Love 'Good morrow!'
　　Sing, birds, in every furrow!

Sir Henry Wotton.

AN ELEGY OF A WOMAN'S HEART.

O, FAITHLESS World! and thy more faithless part,
    A Woman's Heart!
The true Shop of Variety! where sits
    Nothing but fits
And fevers of Desire, and pangs of Love;
    Which toys remove!
Why was She born to please! or I, to trust
    Words writ in dust!
Suff'ring her eyes to govern my despair;
    My pain, for air!
And fruit of time rewarded with untruth,
    The food of Youth!
Untrue She was: yet I believed her eyes,
    (Instructed spies!)
Till I was taught, that Love was but a School
    To breed a Fool!
Or sought She more, by triumphs of denial,
    To make a trial,
How far her smiles commanded my weakness!
    Yield, and confess!
Excuse no more thy folly! But, for cure,
    Blush, and endure
As well thy shame, as Passions that were vain!
    And think, 'tis gain
To know, That Love, lodged in a Woman's Heart,
    Is but a guest!

Sir Henry Wotton.

How happy is he born and taught,
　　That serveth not another's will!
Whose armour is his honest thought;
　　And simple truth, his utmost skill!

Whose Passions, not his masters are!
　　Whose soul is still prepared for death!
Untied unto the World by care
　　Of public fame, or private breath!

Who envies none that chance doth raise;
　　Nor vice hath ever understood!
(How deepest wounds are given by praise!)
　　Nor rules of State, but rules of good!

Who hath his life from rumours freed!
　　Whose conscience is his strong retreat!
Whose state can neither flatterers feed,
　　Nor ruin make oppressors great!

Who, GOD doth, late and early, pray,
　　More of his grace, than gifts, to lend!
And entertains the harmless day
　　With a religious book, or friend!

This man is freed from servile bands
　　Of hope to rise, or fear to fall!
Lord of himself, though not of lands;
　　And having nothing, yet hath all!

Sir Henry Wotton.

ON THE SUDDEN RESTRAINT OF [ROBERT CARR], EARL OF SOMERSET;
THEN FALLING FROM FAVOUR.

DAZZLED thus with height of Place,
    Whilst our hopes, our wits beguile;
No man marks the narrow space
    'Twixt a Prison and a Smile!

Then, since Fortune's favours fade,
    You that in her arms do sleep,
Learn to swim, and not to wade;
    For the hearts of Kings are deep.

But if Greatness be so blind
    As to trust in Towers of Air:
Let it be with Goodness lined,
    That, at least, the Fall be fair.

Then, though darkened, you shall say,
    When friends fail, and Princes frown:
'Virtue is the roughest way;
    But proves, at night, a bed of down!'

THE END OF THE SHAKESPEARE ANTHOLOGY.

FIRST LINES AND NOTES.

Many of these Poems became immediately popular; and appeared in other contemporary editions than those here quoted, often with great variations in the texts.
All the Works herein quoted, were published in London; unless otherwise stated.
Where a text is found associated with music, (M.) is put after its date.

	PAGE
Accurst be Love; and they that ..	89
T. LODGE, M.D. In R. S.'s *Phœnix Nest*, 1593.	
Alexis! here, She stayed! Among	290
W. DRUMMOND. *Poems*, Edin., 1616.	
All that glisters is not gold	5
W. SHAKESPEARE. *Merchant of Venice*, 1600.	
All ye woods, and trees, and	212
J. FLETCHER. *Faithful Shepherdess* [1610].	
A man, of late, was put to death ..	180
ANON. *MS. Harl.* 6910, in British Museum.	
And would you see my Mistress' ..	231
T. CAMPION, M.D. In P. ROSSETER's *Airs*, 1601. (M.)	
A new-found Match is made of late	172
A. W. In F. DAVISON's *Poetical Rhapsody*, 1602.	
April is in my Mistress' face	287
ANON. In T. MORLEY's *Madrigals*, 1594. (M.)	
Are women fair? I wondrous fair	141
IGNOTO. In F. DAVISON's *Poetical Rhapsody*, 1602.	
Art thou poor; yet hast thou......	189
T. DECKER. *Patient Grissill* [*Griselda*], 1603.	
As Diane hunted on a day	43
E. SPENSER. *Amoretti*, &c., 1595.	
As I, in hoary winter's night	65
Rev. R. SOUTHWELL, S.J. *St. Peter's Complaint* [before 1619].	
As it fell upon a day	19
R. BARNFIELD. *Poems*, 1598.	
As you came from the holy land ..	147
Sir W. RALEGH. *MS. Rawl. Poet.* 85, in Bodleian Library.	
As you went to Walsingham—see As you came from the holy land	
At her fair hands, how have I	128
W. DAVISON. In F. DAVISON's *Poetical Rhapsody*, 1602.	
Awake! Awake! thou heavy....	234
T. CAMPION, M.D. *Airs*, I [1613]. (M.)	
Awake, thou spring of speaking ..	245
T. CAMPION, M.D. *Airs*, III [1616]. (M.)	
Away, delights! Go, seek some ..	210
J. FLETCHER. *The Captain*, in BEAUMONT and FLETCHER's *Comedies*, &c., 1647.	

	PAGE
Beauty, being long a resident......	228
Sir D. MURRAY. *Sophonisba*, 1611.	
Before my face the picture hangs	60
Rev. R. SOUTHWELL, S.J. *Mœonia*, 1595.	
Behold, a silly tender Babe	64
Rev. R. SOUTHWELL, S.J. *St. Peter's Complaint* [before 1619].	
Betwixt mine Eye and Heart, ...	4
W. SHAKESPEARE. *Sonnets*, 1609.	
Blame not my cheeks, though pale	243
T. CAMPION, M.D. In P. ROSSETER's *Airs*, 1601. (M.)	
Blow, blow, thou winter wind!....	15
W. SHAKESPEARE. *As You Like It*, in *Comedies*, &c., 1623.	
Call for the robin redbreast, and the	275
J. WEBSTER. *White Devil*, 1612.	
Change thy mind! since She doth	84
R. DEVEREUX, Earl of ESSEX. *MS. Rawl. Poet.* 85, in Bodleian Library, for text: and R. DOWLAND's *Musical Banquet*, 1610 (M.), for authorship.	
Chaucer is dead; and Gower......	22
R. BARNFIELD. *Poems*, 1598.	
Cold's the wind, and wet's the rain	193
T. DECKER. *Shoemakers' Holiday*, 1600.	
Come away, come away, death! ..	15
W. SHAKESPEARE. *Twelfth Night*, in *Comedies*, &c., 1623.	
Come away! come, sweet Love! ..	224
ANON. In J. DOWLAND's *Songs*, I, 1600. (M.)	
Come, live with me, and be my	134
C. MARLOW. In J. BODENHAM's *England's Helicon*, 1600.	
Come, my Celia, let us prove	219
B. JONSON. *Volpone*, 1607.	
Come, O, come, my life's delight!	251
T. CAMPION, M.D. *Airs*, III [1616]. (M.)	
Come, Shepherds! come!	209
J. FLETCHER. *Faithful Shepherdess* [1610].	
Come, Shepherd Swains! that	81
ANON. In J. WILBYE, *Madrigals*, II, 1604. (M.)	
Come unto these yellow sands	13
W. SHAKESPEARE. *Tempest*, in *Comedies*, &c., 1623.	
Come, worthy Greek! Ulysses! ..	95
S. DANIEL. *Certain small Poems*, 1605.	

301

First Lines and Notes.

	PAGE
Come, you pretty false-eyed	246
T. CAMPION, M.D. *Airs*, II [1613]. (M.)	
Come you whose Loves are dead!	208
BEAUMONT and FLETCHER. *Knight of the Burning Pestle*, 1613.	
Conceit, begotten by the eyes	150
Sir W. RALEGH. In F. DAVISON'S *Poetical Rhapsody*, 1602.	
Coridon! arise, my Coridon!	137
IGNOTO. In J. BODENHAM'S *England's Helicon*, 1600.	
Cupid, pardon what is past	207
BEAUMONT and FLETCHER. *Cupid's Revenge*, 1615.	
Dazzled thus with height of Place	300
Sir H. WOTTON. *Reliquiæ Wottonianæ*, 1651.	
Diaphenia, like the daffadowndilly	117
H. CONSTABLE. In J. BODENHAM'S *England's Helicon*, 1600.	
Distance of place, my Love and me	40
G. FLETCHER the Elder, LL.D. *Licia* [1593].	
Drink to me, only with thine eyes	219
B. JONSON. *The Forest*, in *Works*, I, 1616.	
Eternal Time, that wasteth	170
A. W. In F. DAVISON'S *Poetical Rhapsody*, 1602.	
Even as the timely sweet	270
J. SYLVESTER. *Works*, 1641.	
Eyes, hide my love! and do not	101
S. DANIEL. *Hymen's Triumph*, 1615.	
Fain would I; but I dare not!	154
Sir W. RALEGH. *MS. Rawl. Poet.* 85, in Bodleian Library.	
Fain would I change that note	130
ANON. In Capt. T. HUME'S *Airs*, I, 1605. (M.)	
Fair Nymphs! sit ye here by me	185
SHEPHERD TONY. In J. BODENHAM'S *England's Helicon*, 1600.	
Farewell, dear Love! since thou	131
ANON. In R. JONES' *Songs*, I, 1601.(M.)	
Far in the country of Arden	253
M. DRAYTON. *Fourth Eclogue*, in *Poems* [1606].	
Fear no more the heat o' th' sun	7
W. SHAKESPEARE. *Cymbeline*, in *Comedies, &c.*, 1623.	
Feed on, my flocks, securely!	116
H. CONSTABLE. In J. BODENHAM'S *England's Helicon*, 1600.	
Fie! on the sleights that men	118
H. CONSTABLE. In J. BODENHAM'S *England's Helicon*, 1600.	
Follow a shadow, it still flies you!	221
B JONSON. *The Forest*, in *Works*, I, 1616.	
Follow thy fair Sun, unhappy	240
T. CAMPION, M.D. In P. ROSSETER'S *Airs*, 1601. (M.)	

	PAGE
Follow your Saint! Follow, with	250
T. CAMPION, M.D. In P. ROSSETER'S *Airs*, 1601. (M.)	
Fools! They are the only nation	220
B. JONSON. *Volpone*, 1607.	
Full fathom five thy father lies	1
W. SHAKESPEARE. *Tempest*, in *Comedies, &c.*, 1623.	
Give Beauty all her right!	233
T. CAMPION, M.D. *Airs*, II [1613]. (M.)	
Give me my scallop-shell of quiet	159
Sir W. RALEGH. There does not appear to be any authoritative and satisfactory text of this Poem in existence.	
God gives not Kings the style of	191
King JAMES I. *Works*, 1616.	
Gold upon gold, my only Joy did	94
R. TOFTE. *Laura*, 1597.	
Good Muse! rock me asleep with	77
N. BRETON. *Bower of Delights*, 1597.	
Go, Soul, the Body's guest	156
Sir W. RALEGH. In F. DAVISON'S *Poetical Rhapsody*. 3rd Ed., 1611.	
Happy he	102
ANON. In R. JONES' *Ultimum Vale*, 1608. (M.)	
Hark! Hark! The lark at heaven's	9
W. SHAKESPEARE. *Cymbeline*, in *Comedies, &c.*, 1623.	
Hark, jolly Shepherds!	286
ANON. In T. MORLEY'S *Madrigals*, 1594. (M.)	
Her face, her tongue, her wit, so	151
Sir W. RALEGH. In F. DAVISON'S *Poetical Rhapsody*, 1602.	
Her fair inflaming eyes	242
T. CAMPION,M.D. *Airs*,IV[1616]. (M.)	
'Hey, down-a-down!' did Dian	136
IGNOTO. In J. BODENHAM'S *England's Helicon*, 1600.	
Hide, O, hide those hills of snow	16
B. J. F. (J. FLETCHER). *Bloody Brother*, 1639. From C. C. GALLUS.	
How happy is he born and taught	299
Sir H. WOTTON. *Reliquiæ Wottonianæ*, 1651.	
How I do love thee, Beaumont	214
B. JONSON. *Epigrams*, in *Works*, I, 1616.	
How should I, your True Love	9
W. SHAKESPEARE. *Hamlet*, 1605.	
I chanced, of late, an ancient book	283
S. ROWLANDS. *Melancholy Knight*, 1615.	
I could never have the power	208
BEAUMONT and FLETCHER. *Maid's Tragedy*, 1622.	
I dwell in Grace's Court	56
Rev. R. SOUTHWELL, S.J. *St. Peter's Complaint*, 1595.	
If all the World and Love were	135
IGNOTO. In J. BODENHAM'S *England's Helicon*, 1600.	

First Lines and Notes.

	PAGE
If I freely may discover............	218
B. JONSON. *Poetaster*, 1602.	
If Love be life, I long to die!	174
A. W. In F. DAVISON's *Poetical Rhapsody*, 1602.	
If Music and sweet Poetry agree ..	21
R. BARNFIELD. *Poems*, 1598.	
If thou long'st so much to learn, ...	232
T. CAMPION, M.D. *Airs*, III [1616]. (M.)	
I know that all beneath the moon	288
W. DRUMMOND. *Poems*, Edin., 1616.	
In dew of roses steeping	225
ANON. In T. MORLEY's *Madrigals*, 1594. (M.)	
In peascod time, when hound to ..	142
IGNOTO. In J. BODENHAM's *England's Helicon*, 1600.	
In pride of youth, in midst of May	86
T. LODGE, M.D. In J. BODENHAM's *England's Helicon*, 1600.	
In the merry month of May	70
N. BRETON. In J. BODENHAM's *England's Helicon*, 1600.	
In this disguise and pastoral attire	99
S. DANIEL. *Hymen's Triumph*, 1615.	
In youth, before I waxed old, ...	43
E. SPENSER. *Amoretti*, &c., 1595.	
I pray thee, Love I say, Whither is	45
ANON. In R. S.'s *Phœnix Nest*, 1593.	
I saw, in secret, to my Dame	43
E. SPENSER. *Amoretti*, &c., 1595.	
I saw my Lady weep!	163
ANON. In J. DOWLAND's *Songs*, II, 1600. (M.)	
It chanced, of late, a Shepherd's ..	168
A. W. In F. DAVISON's *Poetical Rhapsody*, 1602.	
I, that erstwhile the world's sweet	273
G. WITHER. *The Shepherds' Hunting*, 1615.	
It was the Frog in the Well	193
ANON. In T. RAVENSCROFT's *Melismata*, 1611. (M.)	
I walked along a stream, for	133
C. MARLOW. In R. A. [ROBERT ALLOT]'s *England's Parnassus*, 1600.	
I weigh not Fortune's frown or	269
J. SYLVESTER. *Works*, 1641.	
Jack and Joan, they think no ill ..	239
T. CAMPION, M.D. *Airs*, I [1613]. (M.)	
Jog on! jog on the foot-path way	9
W. SHAKESPEARE. *Winter's Tale*, in *Comedies*, &c., 1623.	
Jolly Shepherd, Shepherd on a hill	164
J. WOOTTON. In J. BODENHAM's *England's Helicon*, 1600.	
Kind are her answers	235
T. CAMPION, M.D. *Airs*, III [1616]. (M.)	
Lady! you are with beauties so ..	127
F. DAVISON. *Poetical Rhapsody*, 1602.	
Laugh not too much! Perhaps, you	79
N. BRETON. *Bower of Delights*, 1597.	

	PAGE
Lay a garland on my hearse	208
BEAUMONT and FLETCHER. *Maid's Tragedy*, 1622.	
Let me not, to the marriage of true	4
W. SHAKESPEARE. *Sonnets*, 1609.	
Like a ring, without a finger	197
F. BEAUMONT. *Poems*, 1640.	
Like as a huntsman, after weary ..	42
E. SPENSER. *Amoretti*, &c., 1595.	
Like desert woods, with darksome	90
T. LODGE, M.D. In R. S.'s *Phœnix Nest*, 1593.	
Like Memnon's rock, touched with	39
G. FLETCHER the Elder, LL.D. *Licia* [1593].	
Like to a hermit poor, in place	155
Sir W. RALEGH. In R. S.'s *Phœnix Nest*, 1593.	
Like truthless dreams, so are my	149
Sir W. RALEGH. In R. S.'s *Phœnix Nest*, 1593.	
Live, Spenser, ever in thy 'Fairy	23
R. BARNFIELD. *Poems*, 1598.	
Long have I lived in Court: yet ..	36
Sir J. DAVIES. In F. DAVISON's *Poetical Rhapsody*, 3rd Ed., 1611.	
Love and my Mistress were at	74
N. BRETON. *Bower of Delights*, 1597.	
Love guides the roses of thy lips	92
T. LODGE, M.D. *Phillis*, 1593.	
Love! if a God thou art............	121
F. DAVISON. *Poetical Rhapsody*, 1602.	
Love is a sickness, full of woes ..	101
S. DANIEL. *Hymen's Triumph*, 1615.	
Love is blind, and a wanton!	214
B. JONSON. *Poetaster*, 1607.	
Lovely Maya, Hermes' mother	66
B. BARNES. *Parthenope*, &c. [1593].	
Love, Mistress is of many minds ..	52
Rev. R. SOUTHWELL, S.J. *St. Peter's Complaint*, 1595.	
Love's Queen (long waiting for her	81
ANON. In J. BODENHAM's *England's Helicon*, 1600.	
Love who will; for I'll love none!	278
W. BROWNE. *Lansdowne MS. 777*, in the British Museum.	
Maidens! why spare ye?	258
M. DRAYTON. *Poems* [1606].	
Many desire; but few, or none	153
Sir W. RALEGH. *MS. Rawl. Poet.* 85, in Bodleian Library.	
Mark, when She smiles with	44
E. SPENSER. *Amoretti*, &c., 1595.	
May I find a woman fair	196
F. BEAUMONT. *Poems*, 1640.	
Mine eye, with all the Deadly Sins	116
H. CONSTABLE. In F. DAVISON's *Poetical Rhapsody*, 1602.	
Mortality, behold and fear!	200
F. BEAUMONT. In *Wit's Recreations*, 2nd Ed., 1641.	
My bonny Lass, thine eye	88
T. LODGE, M.D. In R. S.'s *Phœnix Nest*, 1593.	

First Lines and Notes.

	PAGE
My flocks feed not! My ewes breed R. BARNFIELD. In J. BODENHAM's *England's Helicon*, 1600.	18
My Love bound me, with a kiss ANON. In R. JONES' *Songs*, II, 1601. (M.)	130
My love is strengthened, though.. W. SHAKESPEARE. *Sonnets*, 1609.	8
My Love lay sleeping, where...... G. FLETCHER the Elder, LL.D. *Licia* [1593].	41
My Phillis hath the morning sun.. T. LODGE, M.D. *Phillis*, 1593.	91
My sweetest Lesbia, let us live.... T. CAMPION, M.D. In P. ROSSETER's *Airs*, 1601. (M.) From CATULLUS.	229
My Thoughts are winged with.. ANON. In J. DOWLAND's *Songs*, I, 1600. (M.)	26
Never love! unless you can........ T. CAMPION, M.D. *Airs*, III [1616]. (M.)	249
News from the heavens! All wars N. BRETON. *Bower of Delights*, 1597.	76
Not long agone a youthful Swain W. BROWNE. *Lansdowne MS.* 777.	280
Not marble, nor the gilded .... W. SHAKESPEARE. *Sonnets*, 1609.	12
Now each creature joys the other S. DANIEL. *Certain small Poems*, 1605.	98
Now, have I learned, with much.. A. W. In F. DAVISON's *Poetical Rhapsody*, 1602.	176
Now, let her change, and spare.... T. CAMPION, M.D. *Airs*, III [1616]. (M.)	244
Now winter nights enlarge .... T. CAMPION, M.D. *Airs*, III [1616]. [M.]	229
O, faithless World! and thy more Sir H. WOTTON. In F. DAVISON's *Poetical Rhapsody*, 1602. The present text is from *Rel. Wott.*, 1651.	298
O, Life! what lets thee from a .... Rev. R. SOUTHWELL, S.J. *St. Peter's Complaint*, 1595.	55
O, Mistress mine, where are you .. W. SHAKESPEARE. *Twelfth Night*, in *Comedies*, &c., 1623.	13
On a hill, that graced the plain.... W. BROWNE. In J. BODENHAM's *England's Helicon*, 2nd Ed., 1614.	279
'On a hill there grows a flower .. N. BRETON. In J. BODENHAM's *England's Helicon*, 1600.	75
Once did my thoughts both ebb .. ANON. In R. JONES' *The Muses' Garden*, &c., 1610. (M.)	286
One day, I wrote her name upon .. E. SPENSER. *Amoretti*, &c., 1595.	42
One night, I did attend my sheep .. B. BARNES. *Parthenope*, &c., [1593]. From ANACREON.	68

	PAGE
One of her hands one of her ...... W. SHAKESPEARE. In Sir J. SUCKLING's *Fragmenta Aurea*, 1646.	17
On quicksedge, wrought with...... R. TOFTE. *Laura*, 1597.	93
Orpheus, with his lute, made trees W. SHAKESPEARE. *Henry VIII*, in *Comedies*, &c., 1623.	14
O, sacred Blush, impurpling...... W. DRUMMOND. *Poems*, Edin., 1616.	289
O, sweet delight! O, more than.... T. CAMPION, M.D. *Airs*, III [1616]. (M.)	230
O, that joy so soon should waste! B. JONSON. *Cynthia's Revels*, in *Works*, I, 1616.	215
O, the month of May! the merry .. T. DECKER. *Shoemakers' Holiday*, 1600.	189
O, the sweet contentment .... J. CHALKHILL. In I. WALTON's *Complete Angler*, 1653.	266
Our reign is come! For in the .... BEAUMONT and FLETCHER. *Maid's Tragedy*, 1622.	205
Pack, clouds, away; and welcome T. HEYWOOD. *Rape of Lucrece*, 1608.	297
Passion may my judgement blear F. DAVISON. *Poetical Rhapsody*, 1602.	126
Poor Harpalus, oppressed with .. Sir D. MURRAY. *Sophonisba*, 1611.	226
Pretty twinkling starry eyes! .... N. BRETON. *Passionate Shepherd*, 1604.	71
Queen and Huntress, chaste and.. B. JONSON. *Cynthia's Revels*, in *Works*, I, 1616.	217
Reason and Love, lately, at strife W. DAVISON. In F. DAVISON's *Poetical Rhapsody*, 1602.	129
Rich damask roses in fair cheeks R. TOFTE. *Laura*, 1597.	94
Roses, their sharp spines being .. J. FLETCHER. *Two Noble Kinsmen*, 1634.	211
Sad, all alone, not long I musing .. G. FLETCHER the Elder, LL.D. *Licia* [1593].	39
Say, that I should say, 'I love ye!' N. BRETON. In J. BODENHAM's *England's Helicon*, 1600.	77
Shall I come, sweet Love! to thee T. CAMPION, M.D. *Airs*, III [1613]. (M.)	237
Shall I (like a hermit) dwell........ ANON. *London Magazine*, III, 444, for August, 1734.	162
Shall I tell you, whom I love ? .... W. BROWNE. *Britannia's Pastorals*, II, 1616.	281
Shall I, wasting in despair .... G. WITHER. The privately printed Edition of *Fidelia*, 1615; in the Bodleian Library.	272

304

First Lines and Notes.

	PAGE
Shepherd, what is Love? I pray ..	152

Sir W. RALEGH. In J. BODENHAM's *England's Helicon*, 1600.

She, whose fair flowers no 290
W. DRUMMOND. *Poems*, Edin., 1616.

Shoot, false Love! I care not! 252
ANON. In T. MORLEY's *Balletts*, 1595. (M.)

Shun delays! They breed 59
Rev. R. SOUTHWELL, S.J. *St. Peter's Complaint*, 1595.

Sigh no more, Ladies! sigh no 11
W. SHAKESPEARE. *Much Ado about Nothing*, 1600.

Silly boy, 'tis full moon yet! Thy 244
T. CAMPION, M.D. *Airs*, III [1616]. (M.)

Since first I saw your face, I 223
ANON. In T. FORD's *Music*, &c., 1607. (M.)

Since there 's no help; come, let .. 260
M. DRAYTON. [Sixty-first Sonnet in] *Idæa*, in *Poems* [1619].

Since true penance hath suspended 124
F. DAVISON. *Poetical Rhapsody*, 1602.

Sing his praises, that doth keep .. 213
J. FLETCHER. *Faithful Shepherdess* [1610].

Sir Eglamore, that worthy knight 284
S. ROWLANDS. *Melancholy Knight*, 1615.

'Sir Painter! Are thy colours 24
ANON. In R. S.'s *Phœnix Nest*, 1593.

Sister, awake! Close not your .. 265
ANON. In T. BATESON's *Madrigals*, I, 1604. (M.)

Sleep! Silence's child! Sweet 289
W. DRUMMOND. *Poems*, Edin., 1616.

Slow, slow, fresh fount! Keep time 215
B. JONSON. *Cynthia's Revels*, in *Works*, I, 1616.

So many Loves have I neglected 248
T. CAMPION, M.D. *Airs*, II [1613]. (M.)

Some there are as fair to see too.. 121
F. DAVISON. *Poetical Rhapsody*, 1602.

So saith my fair and beautiful 265
ANON. In N. YONGE's *Musica Transalpina*, II, 1597. (M.)

Steer hither! steer your wingèd .. 276
W. BROWNE. *Inner Temple Masque*, 1615.

Still to be neat! Still to be drest .. 217
B. JONSON. *Epicœne* (1609), in *Works*, I, 1616.

Sweet! I do not pardon crave 122
F. DAVISON. *Poetical Rhapsody*, 1602.

Sweet Love, mine only treasure! 171
A. W. In F. DAVISON's *Poetical Rhapsody*, 1602.

'Sweet Phillis! if a silly Swain 78
N. BRETON. *Bower of Delights*, 1597; and in J. BODENHAM's *England's Helicon*, 1600.

Sweet Smile, the Daughter of the.. 44
E. SPENSER. *Amoretti*, &c., 1595.

Sweet Spring! thou turn'st, with .. 288
W. DRUMMOND. *Poems*, Edin., 1616.

	PAGE
Sweet Violets! Love's Paradise!	139

IGNOTO. In R. S.'s *Phœnix Nest*, 1593.

Take, O, take those lips away 16
W. SHAKESPEARE. *Measure for Measure*, in *Comedies*, &c., 1623. From C. C. GALLUS.

Tell me, dearest! What is Love? 209
J. FLETCHER. *The Captain*, in BEAUMONT and FLETCHER's *Comedies*, &c., 1647.

Tell me, Where is Fancy bred? .. 3
W. SHAKESPEARE. *Merchant of Venice*, 16xx.

That time of year, thou mayst in 12
W. SHAKESPEARE. *Sonnets*, 1609.

The fire seven times tried this! .. 5
W. SHAKESPEARE. *Merchant of Venice*, 16xx.

The forward Violet thus did I 8
W. SHAKESPEARE. *Sonnets*, 1609.

The Gentry to the 'King's Head'.. 296
T. HEYWOOD. *Rape of Lucrece*, 1608.

The Grecians used to offer up 93
R. TOFTE. *Laura*, 1597.

The lopped tree, in time, may grow 51
Rev. R. SOUTHWELL, S.J. *St. Peter's Complaint*, 1595.

The man upright of life, whose.... 247
T. CAMPION, M.D. In R. ALISON's *An Hour's Recreation*, &c., 1606. (M.)

The Poets feign, that, when the .. 268
J. SYLVESTER. In F. DAVISON's *Poetical Rhapsody*, 1602.

Therefore, above the rest.......... 291
G. FLETCHER the Younger, B.D. *Christ's Victory*, &c., Camb., 1610.

There is a garden in her face 238
T. CAMPION, M.D. *Airs*, IV [1616].

There is a jewel, which no Indian 252
ANON. In J. WILBYE's *Madrigals*, II, 1609. (M.)

There is a Lady sweet and kind .. 223
ANON. In T. FORD's *Music*, &c., 1607. (M.)

There is none, O, none but you! .. 85
R. DEVEREUX, Earl of ESSEX. Printed at page 246 of *Fasti Oxon.*, in Dr. P. BLISS's Ed. of A. à WOOD's *Ath. Oxon.* ii. 1815.

There lay this pretty perdue, safe 17
Sir J. SUCKLING. *Fragmenta Aurea*, 1646.

The sun (which doth the greatest.. 201
F. BEAUMONT. In BEAUMONT and FLETCHER's *Comedies*, &c., 1647.

Think'st thou to seduce me then .. 236
T. CAMPION, M.D. *Airs*, IV [1616].

This morning, timely rapt with.... 222
B. JONSON. *Epigrams*, in *Works*, I, 1616.

This night is my departing night .. 188
T. ARMSTRONG. This text is from Sir W. SCOTT's *Minstrelsy*, &c., I, Kelso, 1802.

First Lines and Notes.

	PAGE
Thou art not fair! for all thy red	250
T. CAMPION, M.D. In P. ROSSETER's *Airs*, 1601. (M.)	
Though late, my heart! yet turn	177
A. W. In F. DAVISON's *Poetical Rhapsody*, 3rd Ed., 1611.	
Thou more than most sweet Glove	221
B. JONSON. *Cynthia's Revels*, in *Works*, I, 1616.	
Thrice, toss these oaken ashes in	251
T. CAMPION, M.D. *Airs*, III [1616]. (M.)	
Through a fair forest, as I went	181
SHEPHERD TONY. In J. BODENHAM's *England's Helicon*, 1600.	
To shine in silk, and glister all in	271
J. SYLVESTER. *Works*, 1641.	
Truth shews herself in secret of	80
N. BRETON. *Bower of Delights*, 1597.	
Tune on, my pipe! the praises of	166
J. WOOTTON. In J. BODENHAM's *England's Helicon*, 1600.	
Turn all thy thoughts to eyes!	233
T. CAMPION, M.D. *Airs*, IV [1616]. (M.)	
Under the greenwood tree	14
W. SHAKESPEARE. *As You Like It*, in *Comedies*, &c., 1623.	
Upon a bank, with roses set about	261
M. DRAYTON. *Poems* [1606].	
Upon my lap, my Sovereign sits	103
R. VERSTEGAN. *Odes*, [Antwerp,] 1601.	
Venus, by Adonis' side	282
W. BROWNE. *Britannia's Pastorals*, II, 1616.	
Venus fair did ride!	111
H. CONSTABLE. In J. BODENHAM's *England's Helicon*, 1600.	
Weep with me, all you that read	216
B. JONSON. *Epigrams*, in *Works*, I, 1616.	
Weep you no more, sad fountains!	47
ANON. In J. DOWLAND's *Songs*, III, 1603. (M.)	
Welcome! Welcome! do I sing!	277
W. BROWNE. *Lansdowne MS. 777*.	
Were I as base as is the lowly plain	268
J. SYLVESTER. In F. DAVISON's *Poetical Rhapsody*, 1602.	
What if a day, or a month, or a	247
T. CAMPION, M.D. In R. ALISON's *An Hour's Recreation*, &c., 1606. (M.)	
What is it all, that men possess	238
T. CAMPION, M.D. *Airs*, III [1616]. (M.)	
What is our Life? A Play of	149
Sir W. RALEGH. In O. GIBBONS' *Madrigals*, 1612. (M.)	
What Shepherd can express	48
E. DE VERE, Earl of OXFORD. In J. BODENHAM's *England's Helicon*, 1600.	

	PAGE
When daisies pied, and violets blue	2
W. SHAKESPEARE. *Love's Labour Lost*, 1598.	
When day is gone, and darkness..	82
ANON. In R. S.'s *Phœnix Nest*, 1593.	
When icicles hang by the wall	2
W. SHAKESPEARE. *Love's Labour Lost*, 1598.	
When She was born, whom I	83
W. SMITH. *Chloris*, 1596.	
When thou must home, to shades	237
T. CAMPION, M.D. In P. ROSSETER's *Airs*, 1601. (M.)	
When to her lute Corinna sings	241
T. CAMPION, M.D. In P. ROSSETER's *Airs*, 1601. (M.)	
When Venus saw Desire must die	175
A. W. In F. DAVISON's *Poetical Rhapsody*, 1602.	
Where the bee sucks, there suck I!	3
W. SHAKESPEARE. *Tempest*, in *Comedies*, &c., 1623.	
Where wards are weak, and foes	63
Rev. R. SOUTHWELL, S.J. *St. Peter's Complaint*, 1595.	
Whether men do laugh, or weep	235
T. CAMPION, M.D. In P. ROSSETER's *Airs*, 1601. (M.)	
Who can live in heart so glad	72
N. BRETON. *Passionate Shepherd*, 1604.	
Who is Silvia? What is she	10
W. SHAKESPEARE. *Two Gentlemen of Verona*, in *Comedies*, &c., 1623.	
Who taught thee first to sigh	48
E. DE VERE, Earl of OXFORD. *MS. Rawl. Poet. 85*, in Bodleian Library.	
Widow, well met! Whither go	27
Sir J. DAVIES. In F. DAVISON's *Poetical Rhapsody*, 3rd Ed., 1611.	
Will you hear a Spanish Lady	108
[? T. DELONEY.] Text as reprinted by Rev. J. W. EBSWORTH, in *Roxburghe Ballads*, vi. 655, 1889.	
Willy, prithee, go to bed!	192
ANON. In T. RAVENSCROFT's *Deuteromelia*, 1609. (M.)	
Ye Highlands, and ye Lawlands!	179
ANON. In *Scots Songs*, Ed. by D. HERD. Edin., 1769.	
Ye little birds, that sit and sing	295
T. HEYWOOD. *Fair Maid of the Exchange*, 1607.	
You, brave heroic minds	262
M. DRAYTON. *Poems* [1606].	
You spotted snakes with double	10
W. SHAKESPEARE. *Midsummer Night's Dream*, 1600.	
You that choose not by the view..	6
W. SHAKESPEARE. *Merchant of Venice*, 1600.	
You, that embrace enchanting	83
W. SMITH. *Chloris*, 1596.	

GLOSSARY AND INDEX.

A', 188, all.
Acold, 80, chilled.
Adam, 271.
Adonis, 25, 111-115, 140, 245, 282.
Adown, 256, down.
A-dry, 159, thirsty.
Affection (in Sir W. Ralegh's sense), 151, feeling opposed to reason.
Afield, 142, in the field.
After-wits, 59, being wise after the event, and too late.
Aglaia (N. Breton), 73, 74.
Piped a-good, 256, vigorously, heartily.
Ajmere, 203.
Alexander the Great, 62.
All-a-pieces shiver, 45, broken all to pieces.
All too pitiless, 75, altogether.
Aman, 63, Haman.
Amaryllis (H. Constable), 118-120.
And, 141, if you.
Angel-gold, 162, standard gold used in making angels, coins valued at different times, from 6s. 8d. to 10s. Here likened to golden hair.
Angels, 160, a pun on the word; meaning the coin, which was a lawyer's fee, and also spirits in Heaven.
Anomos (the poetical name of A. W.), 168-178.
'Anon, Sir!', 198, the answer of a waiter in a tavern.
Antimachus (T. Lodge), 86.
Antique stories, 253, ancient.
Apelles, 24, 26.
Lead apes in hell, 31, 38, the fancied consequence of dying an old maid.
Arcadia, 99.
Arden, 253.
Ariel (W. Shakespeare), 1.
Armstrong, T., 188.
Arrant, 156, errand.
Strange array, 181, dress.
Art, 89, human skill, as opposed to Nature.
Arts, 158, the Liberal Arts.

Arviragus (W. Shakespeare), 7.
Aspire, 89, 292, breathe forth.
Assay, 43, attempt.
Astra (W. Browne), 279, 280.
Astrea [= Queen Elizabeth] (Sir J. Davies), 27-35.

The ba', 179, the ball.
Look babies in your eyes, 186, the small image of oneself, reflected in the pupil of another's eye.
Green balk, 72, a ridge, or mound, on the ground.
Ballating, 204, writing Ballads.
Some bare! 169, bare place.
Barginet = bargeret, 86, a pastoral song and dance.
Barnes, B., 66-69.
Barnfield, R., 18-23, 135.
Bauble, 220, a stick with a carved head with ass's ears, carried by Fools.
Bauzen's skin, 255, a badger's skin.
Beaumont, F., 196-208, 214.
Bebathèd, 143, bathed.
Bedecked, 108, adorned.
Bedlam Tamberlaine, 255, furious. The reference is to Marlow's Play.
Beechen-tree, 185, beech-tree.
Beforne, 22, before.
Berycinth (B. Barnes), 66.
Unswept stone, besmeared, 12, soiled through neglect.
Bewray, 37, 77, reveal.
Bide, 89, abide, endure.
My judgement blear, 126, beguile, blind, impose upon.
The box, 72, a garden shrub.

His breech, 255, breeches.
Breton, N., 70-80.
Bride-House, 211, the house where a wedding is held.
Britans, 262, Britons.
Browne, W., 276-282.

Cœlia, (Sir D. Murray), 228.
Cæsar, C. J., 62, 143.
Cain, 271.
Campion, M.D.; T., 229-251.
Can't, 85, cannot.
Carr, Earl of Somerset; R., 300.
Cassamen (M. Drayton), 253.
Catched, 195, caught.
Celia (B. Jonson), 219, 220.
Chalk-hill, J., 266, 267.
Chaucer, G., 22.
Chequered plain, 185, variegated.
'Cherry-ripe!' 238, a street cry; here applied to a lady's lips.
Chloris (W. Smith), 83.
Chop-church, 36, a trafficker in church livings.
Clora (J. Fletcher), 209.
Cockers, 255, leggings, or gaiters.
Cockle hat, 9, a hat with a scallop-shell in it.
Co'entry blue, 255, a blue thread made at Coventry.
Colin, 257.
Articles of the Conclusion, 76, Treaty.
Black-haired coney, 72, ? a rabbit.
Constable, H., 111-120.
Cordiwin = Cordwain = Cordovan, 255, Spanish leather.
Coridon (R. Barnfield), 19.

307

Glossary and Index.

Coridon (N. Breton), 70, 75, 76, 78, 79.
Coridon (Ignoto), 137-139.
Corin (the poetical name of W. Smith), 83.
Corinna (T. Campion), 241.
Corse, 16, a dead body.
Coryate, T., 203.
Courtesied, 13, curtsied.
Couth she, 253, knew she.
She coys, 81, becomes distant in manner.
Crabs, 3, 239, wild apples.
Cresseid = Cressida, 244.
One silly cross, 18, one simple adverse circumstance.
He crowèd crank, 254, lustily.
Curtail = curtal dog, 18, one that had his tail cut short.
Cynthia (Anon), 26.
Cytheron = Cythera (Cerigo), 172.

Daffadillies, 212, daffodils.
Daffadowndilly, 117, a daffodil.
Damelus (H. Constable), 117.
Damœtas (J. Wootton), 164-167.
Daniel, S., 23, 95-101.
Danubius, 24, the river Danube.
Daphne (H. Constable), 119.
Daphnis (J. Wootton), 164-167.
No date, 136, no end.
Davies, Sir J., 27-38.
Davison, F., 121-127.
Davison, W., 128, 129.
Decker, T., 189, 190.
[? Deloney, T.], 108-110.
Demurs, 59, delays.
Depaint, 25, paint.
Desire, 150, 151, &c., love longings.
Desire, 150, 151, &c., the same personified.
Devereux, Earl of Essex; R., 84, 85.
Diaphenia (H. Constable), 117.
Dick the Shepherd (W. Shakespeare), 2.
Ding, dong, bell! 1, 3, an imitation of the sound of a bell.

Dives, 63, the rich man in Luke xvi.
Music of Division, 149. In Music, a florid melodic passage, a run.
Dole, 228, grief, sorrow.
Dorus (Anon)., 225.
By Dove, 254, the Derbyshire river.
Dowland, J., 21.
Castle Down, 180.
Dowsabell, 253-257.
Drayton, M., 23, 253-264.
Drummond, W., of Hawthornden, 288-290.
Drybobs, 204, smart sayings.
Sing...of dumps, 11, melancholy tunes.
Go to Dunmow, 31, Little Dunmow in Essex.

Eden, 278.
E'en, 194, even.
E'en, 47, evening.
E'er, 281, &c., ever.
Eftsoons, 69, immediately.
Sir Eglamore, 284, 285.
Elves, 297. This name here applied to birds.
Endymion, 139, 206.
Estate, 156, State.

Fall of Leaf, 51, 135, 244, autumn.
Fancy, 75, 84, &c., another name for Love.
Fantasy, 24, imagination.
Faustus (Sir W. Ralegh), 152, 153.
Full featously, 253, very handsomely.
Field, 25, 75, &c., the battle-field.
Give them the fig, 145, to make a contemptuous gesture.
Fletcher, J., 16, 201, 203, 205-213.
Fletcher the Elder, LL.D.; G., 39-41.
Fletcher the Younger, B.D.; G., 291-294.
Fligg, 60, fled away.

Fond, 181, 256, &c., foolish.
Fondlings, 141, foolish persons.
Forestall, 37, to rig the market; to make a 'corner' of any article, by buying up all the available supplies, and so raising the price.
Fore-wit, 59, foresight.
Sweetly were forsworn, 16, perjured, faithless.
France, 274.
Francke (J. Fletcher), 209.
Frettished, 69, benumbed.
Frolic, 189, 253, &c., joyous, gay.
Is froward, 260, perverse, refractory.
Go full bare, 74, very scantily clothed.
Fuller, D.D.; T., 202.

Gallus, C. C., 16.
Gan, 181, began.
Gascoigne, G., 22.
Glass, 94, a looking-glass.
The gluve, 179, the glove.
God wot! 18, 70, &c., God knows!
Goodwin Sands, 246.
Gordon, Earl of Huntley; G., 179, 180.
Gower, J., 22.
Grace is said, 55, grace after meat.
Greville, Lord Brooke; F., 135.
Grovy hills, 232, hills with groves of trees on them.
Guiderius (W. Shakespeare), 7.
Gyves, 274, fetters.

Hakluyt, the Cosmographer; R., 264.
Sent them out halting, 68, limping.
Handkercher, 93, pocket-handkerchief.
Harbinger, 211, forerunner.
Harpalus (Sir D. Murray), 226-228.
Helen, 233, 237.

Glossary and Index.

Henry Frederick, Prince of Wales, 191.
Hent the stile a 1 9, seize, grasp.
Heywood, T., 295-297.
To hie, 47, 132, 168, to haste.
Hollen, 228, holly.
Holp me, 181, helped me.

I', 14, &c., in.
I! 141, Aye!
I! I! 131, Aye! Aye!
In Ida plain, 139.
Idæa of her sex, 231, the Ideal, paragon.
Ignoto, 135-146.
I'll, 246, I will.
Indifferent host, 289, impartial.
Ingross, 37, to monopolise the supply of an article. See forestall.
Fatal shafts, to death inured, 90, accustomed.
Invassal, 288, enslave.
Iope, 237.
Isembras = Isumbras, 253, a Hero of the Charlemagne Romances.
I' th', 14, &c., in the.
Iwis, 6, certainly.
Iwus = iwis, 144, certainly.

Jack (T. Campion), 239, 240.
A jack, 197, 198, a roasting jack.
James I, King, 22, 191.
Jig, 164, 165, a rapid, irregular dance.
Merry Jigs, 18, irregular dances.
Joan (T. Campion), 239, 240.
Greasy Joan (W. Shakespeare), 2.

Jonson, B., 201-204, 214-222.
Joseph, the husband of the Blessed Virgin Mary, 107.

The bees their ... King, 117, the Queen bee.
King of Scots, 22, James VI; afterwards I of England.
Three Kings, 106, the Magi.
Kirk, 253, Church.
Kirtle, 134, petticoat.
Knots, 231, flower beds.

Langer, 188, longer.
Larded, 9, garnished.
Lash out, 239, spend lavishly.
On Latmus' top, 207.
Laura (R. Tofte), 93, 94.
Lawlands, 179, the Lowlands of Scotland.
The Lazar, 63, Lazarus.
He leared, 254, taught.
Claret Lees, 201, dregs, sediment.
Leese, 77, lose.
Make legs, 201, bowing.
Leir, 253, the knowledge, manners.
Lemster, 254, Leominster.
Lesbia (T. Campion; from Catullus), 229.
Lewd brother slaw, 255, Cain.
Licia (G. Fletcher the Elder), 39.
Can ye liken it, 44, resemble it.
Lingel, 255, thread.
List, 181, listen.
When he list, 148, pleases.
Chequered Lists, 200, borders.
Lithe, 254, pliant, flexible.
I have my livery sued, 28, obtained possession of my property.
'Loth to depart,' 132, a well-known song.

Lodge, M.D.; T., 86-92, 135.
Louted, 46, flouted, mocked.
LOVE = CUPID.
Love, the affection between individuals of the opposite sexes that are capable of intermarriage. Fair House of Joy and Bliss, 130.
In love.
My Love, the Lady, or Gentleman, I love.
My love, the love I have for that person.
Lover, a man who loves a woman. Also called, Servant, True Love.
So many Loves, 248, Lovers.
Whose Loves are dead, 208, Lovers.
The old Loves, 234, the Beauties of ancient Times.
Keep our loves, 139, preserve our mutual affection.
Lucrece, 23, 32.
Lazy luskings, 67, idlers.
A lute, 21, 197, 198, a musical instrument like a guitar, or a mandolin.
Luve, 179, Lover.
Lycoris (Anon.), 225.
Lycoris (Anon.), 265.

With his main house-jest, 202, with his stock joke.
The Man in the Moon, 199.
The fine marchpine = marchpane, 253, a kind of almond cake.
Mardocheus, 63, Mordecai.
Marian (W. Shakespeare), 3.
Marlow, C., 133, 134.
Mary-buds, 9, Marigolds.
Mary, The Blessed Virgin, 103-107.
May, 68, 70, May games.
A Maying, 45, 265, gathering, especially on May Day, the hawthorn; called May, because it blooms in that month.
A Mean, 56, a medium, as the Golden Mean.
Melibœus (Sir W. Ralegh), 152, 153.

309

Glossary and Index.

Old **Melibœus** (Anon.), 81.
Memnon's rock, 39, on the Nile.
'Mends, 180, amends.
Love is merchandised! 8, bartered. .
Mermaid Tavern, in Bread Street, London, 201-203.
Feathers he meweth, 258, dries.
Mickle, 253, great.
Midas, 269.
Milken hill, 159, one feeding cows.
Milton, J., 203.
Miniver, 255, a mixed fur.
Minos, 166.
Mistress, always, in this Series, in a good sense; with its many equivalents, such as, sweet Heart! dear Joy! Saint! dearest Shepherdling! sweet Shepherdling! Sovereign! fair Sweet! pretty Sweeting! sweet Virgin! &c., &c.
Molten, 160, melted.
Round **Morrises dance**, 66, Morris-dances.
Moulted, 45, melted.
Murray, Earl of—see Stewart, J.
Murray, Sir D., 226-228.
Mushrumpts, 63, mushrooms.
Musket eglantine, 290.
Myrrha, 113, 114.

Nae, 188, no.
Nap, 168, a short sleep.
Nappy ale, 239, strong, heady ale.
Narcissus, 215.
Nectar, 44, 159, 160, the wine of the Olympian Gods.
Ne'er, 124, 197, &c , never.
Nice, 145, coy, reserved.
Niceness, 157, fastidiousness.
Nisus, 166.

O', 7, 188, &c., of.
Old Law, 180, the Mosaic Law.
Orient pearl, 64, brilliant, pellucid, lustrous.
An **orpèd** swine, 115, stout, strong.
Orpheus, 14.
O' th', 7, of the.
Outlandish spirits, 37, men who have travelled.
Owe, 207, own.
Owe also means, not to own, to be indebted.

P., S.—see Pavy, S.
Palinode, 122, a poetical recantation, or retractation.
Palmer, 159, 161, a pilgrim who had returned from the Holy Land, with a palm-branch.
Paly, 139, pale.
King **Pandion**, 20.
Panglory the Enchantress, 291-294.
Paphos, 111, in Cyprus.
Paramour, 257, Lover.
Parcel of his pomp, 64, a portion.
Parnassus, 25.
Parson's saw, 3, his sermon.
Parthenope (B. Barnes), 67, 68.
Passion, predilection, habitude. 'The ruling Passion strong in death.'
Passion, emotion, not necessarily of love. It might also be of anger, grief, zeal, &c.
Passion, Passions, 47, 54, &c., anxieties of mind and agonies of soul through love for one of the opposite sex.

Pavy, S., 216.
Peakish hill, 254, in the Peak district of Derbyshire.
In **peascod** (= peacod) time, 142, when the pea crop is ripe.
Peers the Piper (B. Barnes), 66.
Peg, and Peggie (T. Decker), 189, 190.
Penelope, 32, 38.
Perdue, 17, lost, or concealed, one.
Philena (Sir D. Murray), 227, 228.
Phillida (N. Breton), 70, 77-79.
Phillida (Ignoto), 137-139.
Phillis (N. Breton), 75, 76.
Phillis = **Phillida** (N. Breton), 78, 79.
Phillis (H. Constable), 118-120.
Phillis (T. Heywood), 295, 296.
Phillis (T. Lodge), 91, 92.
Daisies pied, 2, party-coloured.
Pierian spring, 50, a spring in Pieria, haunted by the Muses.
A **pile of steel**, 69, 261, a point.
Plaguy hide, 285, vexatious, troublesome, annoying.
Plaint, 48, complaint.
His plate, 64. Silver plate is intended.
Did plate = plait, 94, to interweave gold with golden hair.
Play-feres, 145, playmates.

PLAYS—
 Bloody Brother, 16, by J. Fletcher.
 Merchant of Venice, 5, 6, by W. Shakespeare.
A melting **pleasance**, 44, delight, enjoyment, pleasure.
Plies the box, 72, creeps close by the side of that shrub.

POEMS, BALLADS, ETC.
 Epistles, 23, M. Drayton's *England's Heroical Epistles*.
 Fairy Queen, 23, by E. Spenser.
 Furies, 22, King James' translation from G. de Saluste du Bartas.
 Iliads, 201, of Homer.
 Lepanto, 22, King James' Poem.
 Lucrece, 23, W. Shakespeare's *Rape of Lucrece*.

Glossary and Index.

Psalms, 201; by which is here intended Sternhold and Hopkins' metrical version of 1549.
Rosamond, 23, by S. Daniel.
Satires, 275, G. Wither's *Abuses stript and whipt*.
Venus, 23, W. Shakespeare's *Venus and Adonis*.
White Rose and the Red, 23, S. Daniel's *Civil Wars*.
Poopen, 67, piped.
Popinjay, 255, parrot.
'Pothecary's bill, 37, the apothecary's prescription.
Old Priam's town, 46, Troy.
Prick the path, 193, trace, track.
Prune = preen, 297, to trim, dress.

Doth quail, 182, slacken.
Quaint and gent, 181, elegant and refined.
Quat, 228, quitted.
Queen's Love, 179, Lover of Anne (of Denmark), Queen of Scotland.
Quicksedge = quickset, 93, living plants set to grow as a hedge.
Quires, 12, Choirs.

An old wife's rail, 183.
Ralegh, Sir W., 135, 147-161.
Raught, 68, reached, seized.
'Re = are, as in Ye're.
'Reave, 167, bereave.
Dost such religion use, 214, dost offer such homage.
Hearts renying, 18, renouncing.
A rest held up at tennis, 202, the quick return of the ball.
Rome, 274.
Rosalind, 257.
Rosamond, 23, 233.
Roundelay, 120, a song.
Roundelays, 26. This word is here applied to the music of birds.
The Rounds, 228, the Spheres.
Rowlands, S., 283-285.
Russell, Countess of Bedford; L., 222.
Grey russet (= a reddishbrown colour), 266, a homespun gown.

'S, 4, 84, &c., is.
Did you sae, 170, so.
Saint—see Mistress.
Samson, 62.
Sauncing (= sanctus = saint's) bell, 152.
Scallop shell, 159, the escallop-shell, the universal badge of a Palmer.
'Scape, 62, escape.
Scenes, 201, 204, entire Plays; in this case, Comedies.
Schools, 158, departments of human knowledge; as Schools of Divinity, Law, and Music.

Scouping, 67, running, scampering, skipping.
Scyll. = Scylla, 166.
Scylla, 166.
Sendall shoon, 9, sandalled shoes.
Servant—see Lover.
She set her by, 290, she sat herself down by.
Setywall = setwall, 254, the valerian root.
Shadow, 26, portrait.
Shakespeare, W., 1-17, 23, 202-203.
She, the emphatic feminine Personal Pronoun, used where the poetical name of the Lady does not occur.
Shepherd Tony, 181-187.
My shoe did wring, 38, I had family discomforts.
Shoon, 9, shoes.
The veriest shrew, 37, scold, termagant.
Shroud, 64, to cover.
Sidney, Sir P., 22.
Silly beasts, 64, harmless.
A silly point, 247, a simple slight point.
Silly Swain, 240, simplehearted, guileless.
Silvia (W. Shakespeare), 10.
Fraternity of Sirenaical Gentlemen, 203.
Noble Sirenaicks! 203.
Slaw, 255, slew.
Sleights, 118, crafts, stratagems, deceit.
Slipp'ry, 246, slippery.
Smith, W., 83.
To sell ... smoke, 36, to give, for money, mere words and no deeds; when an affair *ends in smoke*.
Solomon, King, 62.
Came sounding, 180, thundering.
Southwell, S.J.; Rev. R., 51-65.
Spain, 274.
Spenser, E., 21, 23, 42-44.
Almost starved, 69, perished from cold.
My stayless thoughts, 45, ceaseless.
In stead, 182, of any service.
Stellified, 32, made a star.
Stench, 292, stanch.
Stewart, Earl of Murray; J., 179, 180.
Stoures, 87, occasions.
Strephon (F. Davison), 122-125.
Nectar suckets, 160, sweetmeats.
Suckling, Sir J., 17.
Suppone, 226, suppose.

311

Glossary and Index.

Sutcliff, —, 201.
Swound, 115, a swoon.
Swounded, 87, swooned.
Sylvester, J., 268–271.

T', 97, to.
'T, 206, it.
White **Table**, 31, ivory tablets for making notes upon.
Ta'en, 26, taken.
Come, **take away**, 55, come, clear the table!
Tantal's, 269, Tantalus.
Tempe, 166.
Temper colours, 26, mix.
Tennis, 202.
A Tent, 198, probe.
Th', 7, 14, &c., the.
The **Thames**, 246.
Tho, 145, then.
Thrall, 171, bond slave.
Thralled, 228, enslaved.
Three-Men's Songs, 189, 190; afterwards corrupted into *Freemen's* Songs.
The Threstlecock, 186, the male thrush.
Thro', 188, through.
Thunderstone, 7, an aerolite.
Thyrsis (W. Browne), 279, 280.
Tib (T. Campion), 239.
In tickle points, 157, nice, delicate, critical.
Tihee again, 80, a scoffing exclamation.
Time, 211, Thyme.
Tiring Houses, 149, the dressing-rooms in a theatre.
'Tis, 196, 244, &c., it is.
Tofte, R., 93, 94.
Tom (T. Campion), 239.
Tom (W. Shakespeare), 2.
A league is took, 4, taken.
Sir Topas, 253.
Her old train, 193, tricks, device.
His trains, 89, 90, treachery, deceit.
Will tread a dance, 207, in a round, 213, a slow movement in dancing.

In Trent, 254, the Lincolnshire river.
Troilus, 244.
Turkey, 274.
And tutties make, 240, nosegays, posies.
'Twas, 243, it was.
Twindring arms, 133, embracing.

Ulysses, 95–97.
Ghost unlaid, 7, not exorcized.
Unmeddled joys, 51, unmixed joys.
Unrecured, 91, incurable.
Urania (F. Davison), 122–125.
Use, 37, interest: *any* rate of which was formerly considered immoral.

Costly valance, 133, a short curtain over a bedstead.
Vere, Earl of Oxford; E. de, 48–50.
Golden verges, 291, sceptres.
Verstegan, R., 103–107.
Virginia, Earth's only Paradise, 262.
The Virginian Voyage, 262–264.
Volley of light Angels, 294, a flight, or company of swift Angels.

W., A., 135, 168–178.
Wae, 179, woe.
Clothes made out of wax, 287, ? well-fitting.
Walsingham, 147, in Norfolk.
Wards, 28, Wards in Chancery.
Wards, 63, defences.
The waters warp, 15, move, ruffle.
Ways, 2, roads and paths.
My weal, 181, being well off.
Webster, J., 275.
Simple weed, 64, clothes.
Weeds of woe, 175, mourning garments.
Wend thee, 113, turn thee.
Westminster Abbey, London, 200.
What-call Hill, 192, Wood, 193, such and such a Hill, Wood.
To whet, 90, sharpen.
His White, 259. In Archery, the white centre of the target.
Whooped, 257, shouted.
Wi', 179, with.
Wight, 51, a human being.
Wisdom, R., 201.
Wiselier, 17, the more wisely.
Wither, G., 272–275.
Woned, 253, dwelt.
Wootton, J., 164–167.
Wotton, Sir H., 298–300.

Yconed, 253, taught.
Ycured, 88, cured.
Yeaffe a yaffe! 193, a representation of the cry of the Harriers.
Ye're, 188, ye are.
Yond, 185, yonder.
Ywrought, 253, made.

In Crown 8vo Volumes, Cloth extra, 2s. 6d. each; and in various leather bindings.
Each Volume is complete in itself, and may be obtained separately.

BRITISH ANTHOLOGIES.

Vol.
- I. The Dunbar Anthology. 1401–1508 A.D.
- II. The Surrey & Wyatt Anthology. 1509–1547 A.D.
- III. The Spenser Anthology. 1548–1591 A.D.
- IV. The Shakespeare Anthology. 1592–1616 A.D.
- V. The Jonson Anthology. 1617–1637 A.D.
- VI. The Milton Anthology. 1638–1674 A.D.
- VII. The Dryden Anthology. 1675–1700 A.D.
- VIII. The Pope Anthology. 1701–1744 A.D.
- IX. The Goldsmith Anthology. 1745–1774 A.D.
- X. The Cowper Anthology. 1775–1800 A.D.

EDITED BY

Professor EDWARD ARBER, F.S.A.

FELLOW OF KING'S COLLEGE, LONDON, ETC.

THIS is the first adequate attempt that has ever been made towards an historical national Anthology at popular prices.

The Series will contain about 2,500 entire Poems and Songs, written by some Three Hundred Poets.

As each Volume represents a definite period of our literary history, some Poets will, of necessity, appear in more than one Volume. Nearly every form of English Versification will be represented in the Series. Each Volume will be complete in itself; and will contain a Glossary of such words, &c. in it, as have changed their meanings since its Poems were written.

British Anthologies will therefore contain those Poems and Songs with which every one ought to be acquainted.

HENRY FROWDE: LONDON, EDINBURGH, GLASGOW, BELFAST, AND NEW YORK.

THE 'OXFORD' POETS.

'These delightful reissues.'—Athenaeum.

BURNS. The Complete Poetical Works of Robert Burns. With Notes, Glossary, Index of First Lines, and Chronological List. Edited by J. LOGIE ROBERTSON, M.A. Crown 8vo, 3s. 6d.; on Oxford India Paper, from 8s.; Miniature Edition, 3 vols. in case, from 10s. 6d.

BYRON. The Poetical Works of Lord Byron. *Oxford Copyright Edition.* Crown 8vo, 3s. 6d.; on Oxford India Paper, from 8s.; Miniature Edition, 4 vols. in case, from 14s. 6d.

LONGFELLOW. The Complete Poetical Works of Henry Wadsworth Longfellow, including the copyright poems. Crown 8vo, 3s. 6d.; on Oxford India Paper, from 8s.; Miniature Edition, 6 vols. in case, from 15s.

MILTON. The Complete Poetical Works of John Milton. With Notes, Glossary, Index of First Lines, &c. Edited by H. C. BEECHING, M.A. [*Shortly.*

SCOTT. The Complete Poetical Works of Sir Walter Scott, with the author's Introductions and

SCOTT (*continued*). Notes. Edited by J. LOGIE ROBERTSON, M.A. Crown 8vo, cloth, 3s. 6d.; on Oxford India Paper, from 8s.; Miniature Edition, 5 vols. in case, from 15s.

SHAKESPEARE. The Complete Works of William Shakespeare. Edited, with a Glossary, by W. J. CRAIG, M.A. Crown 8vo, cloth, 3s. 6d.; on Oxford India Paper, from 8s.; Miniature Edition, 6 vols. in case, from 16s.

WHITTIER. The Complete Poetical Works of John Greenleaf Whittier. With Notes, Index of First Lines, and Chronological List. Edited by W. GARRETT HORDER, M.A. Crown 8vo, cloth, 3s. 6d.; on Oxford India Paper, from 8s.; Miniature Edition, 4 vols. in case, from 14s. 6d.

WORDSWORTH. The Poetical Works of William Wordsworth. With Introductions and Notes. Edited by T. HUTCHINSON, M.A. Crown 8vo, cloth, 3s. 6d.; on Oxford India Paper, from 8s.; Miniature Edition, 5 vols. in case, from 16s.

HENRY FROWDE: LONDON, EDINBURGH, GLASGOW, BELFAST, AND NEW YORK.

HENRY FROWDE'S PUBLICATIONS.

BROWNING. St. John in the Desert. An Introduction and Notes to BROWNING'S 'A Death in the Desert.' By the Rev. G. U. POPE, M.A., D.D. Fcap. 8vo, stiff boards, 2s. net.

GELL (The Hon. Mrs. Lyttelton). The Cloud of Witness. A Daily Sequence of Great Thoughts from many Minds, following the Christian Seasons. By the Hon. Mrs. LYTTELTON GELL, with a Prefatory Note by the late Archbishop of Canterbury. With a Frontispiece and special pages prepared to form a family record of anniversaries. Demy 18mo, from 3s. 6d. Large type edition, crown 8vo, cloth, from 7s. 6d. *Eightieth Thousand.*

—— **The More Excellent Way.** Words of the Wise on The Life of Love. Compiled by the same Authoress. Printed in colours. Cloth, 3s. 6d.; and in leather bindings.

HORDER. The Treasury of American Sacred Song. Selected and Edited by W. GARRETT HORDER. Limited Edition, £1 1s. net. Crown 8vo, vellum and cloth, 10s. 6d.

À KEMPIS. Of the Imitation of Christ. By THOMAS À KEMPIS. A Revised Translation from the Original Latin. Royal 32mo, from 9d.; Oxford India Paper Editions, from 1s.; The Oxford 'Thumb' Edition, 128mo, from 1s. Also in leather bindings and illustrated.

KEBLE. The Christian Year. By JOHN KEBLE. Royal 32mo, from 9d.; Oxford India Paper Editions, from 1s.; The Oxford 'Thumb' Edition, 128mo, from 1s. Also in leather bindings and illustrated.

Sacrament in Song, The. Extracts from English poets on the Holy Communion, arranged for the Sundays and Holydays of the Christian Year. By E. A. D. 18mo, cloth, 2s. 6d.

GOLDSMITH. The Vicar of Wakefield. By OLIVER GOLDSMITH. With a Collotype. Printed on the Oxford India Paper, measuring 2⅛ × 1⅜ × ⅜ inches, and issued in various bindings, from 1s.

BUNYAN. The Pilgrim's Progress. Edited by E. VENABLES, M.A. Two parts in one volume. Complete Edition, 860 pp., from 1s. 6d.

CLARENDON PRESS, OXFORD.

SELECT LIST OF BOOKS.

BURNS. Selected Poems. Edited, with Introduction, Notes, and a Glossary, by J. LOGIE ROBERTSON, M.A. Crown 8vo, 6s.

BYRON. Childe Harold. Edited, with Introduction and Notes, by H. F. TOZER, M.A. *Third Edition.* Extra fcap. 8vo, 3s. 6d.; in Parchment, 5s.

HENRY FROWDE: LONDON, EDINBURGH, GLASGOW, BELFAST, AND NEW YORK.

CAMPBELL. Gertrude of Wyoming. Edited, with Introduction and Notes, by H. MACAULAY FITZGIBBON, M.A. *Second Edition.* Extra fcap. 8vo, 1s.

COWPER. Edited, with Life, Introductions, and Notes, by the late H. T. GRIFFITH, B.A.

I. The Didactic Poems of 1782, with Selections from the Minor Pieces, A.D. 1779-1783. Extra fcap. 8vo, 3s.

II. The Task, with Tirocinium, and Selections from the Minor Poems, A.D. 1784-1799. *Third Edition.* Extra fcap. 8vo, 3s.

DRYDEN. Select Poems. (Stanzas on the Death of Oliver Cromwell; Astraea Redux; Annus Mirabilis; Absalom and Achitophel; Religio Laici; The Hind and the Panther.) Edited by W. D. CHRISTIE, M.A. *Fifth Edition.* Revised by C. H. FIRTH, M.A. Extra fcap. 8vo, 3s. 6d.

GOLDSMITH. Selected Poems. Edited, with Introduction and Notes, by AUSTIN DOBSON. Extra fcap. 8vo, 3s. 6d.

GRAY. Selected Poems. Edited by EDMUND GOSSE, M.A. Extra fcap. 8vo, in Parchment, 3s.

KEATS. The Odes of Keats. Edited, with Notes, Analyses, and a Memoir, by ARTHUR C. DOWNER, M.A. With Four Illustrations. Extra fcap. 8vo, 3s. 6d. net.

MILTON. Poems. Edited by R. C. BROWNE, M.A. In two Volumes. *New Edition, Revised.* Extra fcap. 8vo, 6s. 6d. Sold separately, Vol. I, 4s.; Vol. II, 3s.

MILTON'S Prosody. By ROBERT BRIDGES. Extra fcap. 8vo, stiff covers, 1s. 6d.

POPE. Select Works. Edited, with Introduction and Notes. By MARK PATTISON, B.D.

Essay on Man. *Sixth Edition.* Extra fcap. 8vo, 1s. 6d.

Satires and Epistles. *Fourth Edition.* Extra fcap. 8vo, 2s.

SCOTT. Lady of the Lake. Edited, with Preface and Notes, by W. MINTO, M.A. Extra fcap. 8vo, 3s. 6d.

—— **Lay of the Last Minstrel.** By the same Editor. With Map. *Second Edition.* Extra fcap. 8vo, 2s.; in Parchment, 3s. 6d.

—— **Lord of the Isles.** Edited, with Introduction and Notes, by THOMAS BAYNE. Extra fcap. 8vo, stiff covers, 2s.; cloth, 2s. 6d.

—— **Marmion.** Edited, with Introduction and Notes, by THOMAS BAYNE. Extra fcap. 8vo, 3s. 6d.

SHAKESPEARE. Select Plays. Extra fcap. 8vo, stiff covers. Edited by W. G. CLARK, M.A., and W. ALDIS WRIGHT, D.C.L.

Hamlet. 2s.
Macbeth. 1s. 6d.
Merchant of Venice. 1s.
Richard the Second. 1s. 6d.

HENRY FROWDE: LONDON, EDINBURGH, GLASGOW, BELFAST, AND NEW YORK.

Select List. 5

SHAKESPEARE. Select Plays. Extra fcap. 8vo, stiff covers. Edited by W. ALDIS WRIGHT, D.C.L.
As You Like It. 1s. 6d.
Coriolanus. 2s. 6d.
Henry the Eighth. 2s.
Henry the Fifth. 2s.
Henry the Fourth, First Part of. 2s.
Julius Caesar. 2s.
King John. 1s. 6d.
King Lear. 1s. 6d.
Midsummer Night's Dream. 1s. 6d.
Much Ado about Nothing. 1s. 6d.
Richard the Third. 2s. 6d.
Tempest. 1s. 6d.
Twelfth Night. 1s. 6d.

SHAKESPEARE as a Dramatic Artist; a popular Illustration of the Principles of Scientific Criticism. By R. G. MOULTON, M.A. *Third Edition, Enlarged.* Crown 8vo, 7s. 6d.

SHELLEY. Adonais. Edited, with Introduction and Notes, by W. M. ROSSETTI. Crown 8vo, 5s.

THOMSON. The Seasons, and The Castle of Indolence. Edited by J. LOGIE ROBERTSON, M.A. Extra fcap. 8vo, 4s. 6d.

WORDSWORTH. The White Doe of Rylstone, &c. Edited by WILLIAM KNIGHT, LL.D. Extra fcap. 8vo, 2s. 6d.

ALFRED. King Alfred's Old English Version of Boethius de Consolatione Philosophiae. Edited from the MSS., with Introduction, Critical Notes, and Glossary, by W. J. SEDGEFIELD, M.A. Crown 8vo, 10s. 6d.

BEOWULF. The Deeds of Beowulf. An English Epic of the Eighth Century done into Modern Prose. With an Introduction and Notes, by JOHN EARLE, M.A. Crown 8vo, 8s. 6d.

CHAUCER. The Complete Works of Geoffrey Chaucer. Edited from numerous MSS. by W. W. SKEAT, Litt.D. In Six Volumes, demy 8vo, with Portrait and Facsimiles. £4 16s., or 16s. each volume.

CHAUCER. Chaucerian and other Pieces, being a Supplementary Volume to the Above. Edited from numerous MSS. by W. W. SKEAT, Litt.D. 8vo, 18s.

—— **The Student's Chaucer.** Being a Complete Edition of his Works, edited from numerous MSS., with Introduction and Glossary, by W. W. SKEAT, Litt.D. In one vol., crown 8vo, cloth, 7s. 6d.; on Oxford India Paper, cloth extra, 9s. 6d.

GAMELYN, The Tale of. Edited, with Notes, Glossary, &c., by W. W. SKEAT, Litt.D. *Second Edition, Revised.* Extra fcap. 8vo, stiff covers, 1s. 6d.

HENRY FROWDE: LONDON, EDINBURGH, GLASGOW, BELFAST, AND NEW YORK.

Select List.

LANGLAND. The Vision of William concerning Piers the Plowman, by WILLIAM LANGLAND. Edited, with Notes, by W. W. SKEAT, Litt.D. *Sixth Edition*. Extra fcap. 8vo, 4s. 6d.

MINOT (Laurence). Poems. Edited, with Introduction and Notes, by JOSEPH HALL, M.A. Extra fcap. 8vo, 4s. 6d.

OLD ENGLISH DRAMA. York Plays. The Plays performed by the Crafts or Mysteries of York, on the day of Corpus Christi, in the 14th, 15th, and 16th centuries: now first printed from the unique MS. in the library of Lord Ashburnham. Edited, with Introduction and Glossary, by LUCY TOULMIN SMITH. 8vo, £1 1s.

—— **English Miracle Plays, Moralities, and Interludes.** Specimens of the Pre-Elizabethan Drama. Edited, with an Introduction, Notes, and Glossary, by ALFRED W. POLLARD, M.A. *Third Edition, Revised.* Crown 8vo, 7s. 6d.

—— **The Pilgrimage to Parnassus, with the Two Parts of the Return from Parnassus.** Three Comedies performed in St. John's College, Cambridge, A.D. MDXCVII-MDCI. Edited from MSS. by W. D. MACRAY, M.A., F.S.A. Medium 8vo, bevelled boards, gilt top, 8s. 6d.

—— **Marlowe's Edward II.** With Introduction, Notes, &c. By O. W. TANCOCK, M.A. *Second Edition.* Extra fcap. 8vo, stiff covers, 2s.; cloth, 3s.

OLD ENGLISH DRAMA (*cont.*).
—— **Marlowe and Greene.** Marlowe's Tragical History of Dr. Faustus, and Greene's Honourable History of Friar Bacon and Friar Bungay. Edited by A. W. WARD, Litt.D. *New and Enlarged Edition.* Crown 8vo, 6s. 6d.

SWEET. Old English Reading Primers:
   I. Selected Homilies of Ælfric. *Second Edition.* 2s.
   II. Extracts from Alfred's Orosius. *Second Edition.* 2s.

Specimens of Early English. A New and Revised Edition. With Introduction, Notes, and Glossarial Index.
   Part I. From Old English Homilies to King Horn (A.D. 1150 to A.D. 1300). By R. MORRIS, LL.D. *Second Edition.* Extra fcap. 8vo, 9s.
   Part II. From Robert of Gloucester to Gower (A.D. 1298 to A.D. 1393). By R. MORRIS, LL.D., and W. W. SKEAT, Litt.D. *Third Edition, Revised.* Extra fcap. 8vo, 7s. 6d.

Specimens of English Literature, from the 'Ploughman's Crede' to the 'Shepheardes Calender' (A.D. 1394 to A.D. 1579). With Introduction, Notes, and Glossarial Index. By W. W. SKEAT, Litt.D. *Fifth Edition.* Extra fcap. 8vo, 7s. 6d.

Typical Selections from the best English Writers, with Introductory Notices. In 2 vols. *Second Edition.* Extra fcap. 8vo, 3s. 6d. each.
   Vol. I. Latimer to Berkeley.
   Vol. II. Pope to Macaulay.

Select List.

ADDISON. Selections from Papers in *The Spectator*. With Notes. By T. ARNOLD, M.A. Extra fcap. 8vo, 4s. 6d.

AUBREY. 'Brief Lives,' chiefly of Contemporaries, set down by John Aubrey, between the Years 1669 and 1696. Edited from the Author's MSS. by ANDREW CLARK, M.A., LL.D. 2 vols. 8vo, 25s.

BACON. I. Advancement of Learning. Edited by W. ALDIS WRIGHT, D.C.L. *Third Edition*. Extra fcap. 8vo, 4s. 6d.

—— II. The Essays. Edited, with Introduction and Illustrative Notes, by S. H. REYNOLDS, M.A. 8vo, half-bound, 12s. 6d.

BEAUCHAMP. Hindu Manners, Customs, and Ceremonies. By the ABBÉ J. A. DUBOIS. Translated from the Author's later French MS. and Edited with Notes, Corrections, and Biography, by HENRY K. BEAUCHAMP. With a Prefatory Note by the Right Hon. F. MAX MÜLLER, and a Portrait. *Second Edition*. 8vo, 15s. net.

BOSWELL'S Life of Samuel Johnson, LL.D.; including BOSWELL'S Journal of a Tour to the Hebrides, and JOHNSON'S Diary of a Journey into North Wales. Edited by G. BIRKBECK HILL, D.C.L. In six vols., 8vo. With Portraits and Facsimiles. Half-bound, £3 3s.

BUNYAN. I. The Pilgrim's Progress, Grace Abounding, Relation of the Imprisonment of Mr. John Bunyan. Edited, with Biographical Introduction and Notes, by E. VENABLES, M.A. Extra fcap. 8vo, cloth, 3s. 6d.

BUNYAN. II. The Holy War, and The Heavenly Footman. Edited by MABEL PEACOCK. Extra fcap. 8vo, 3s. 6d.

BURKE. Select Works. Edited, with Introduction and Notes, by E. J. PAYNE, M.A.
I. Thoughts on the Present Discontents; the two Speeches on America. *Second Edition*. Extra fcap. 8vo. 4s. 6d.
II. Reflections on the French Revolution. *Second Edition*. Extra fcap. 8vo, 5s.
III. Four Letters on the Proposals for Peace with the Regicide Directory of France. *Second Edition*. Extra fcap. 8vo, 5s.

CHESTERFIELD. Lord Chesterfield's Worldly Wisdom. Selections from his Letters and Characters. Edited by G. BIRKBECK HILL, D.C.L. Crown 8vo, 6s.

CLARENDON. Characters and Episodes of the Great Rebellion. Selections from Clarendon. Edited by G. BOYLE, M.A., Dean of Salisbury. Crown 8vo, gilt top, 7s. 6d.

FULLER. Wise Words and Quaint Counsels of Thomas Fuller. Selected by AUGUSTUS JESSOPP, D.D. Crown 8vo, 6s.

HEWINS. The Whitefoord Papers. Being the Correspondence and other MSS. of Colonel CHARLES WHITEFOORD and CALEB WHITEFOORD, from 1739 to 1810. Edited, with Introduction and Notes, by W. A. S. HEWINS, M.A. 8vo, 12s. 6d.

Select List.

JOHNSON. Wit and Wisdom of Samuel Johnson. Edited by G. BIRKBECK HILL, D.C.L. Crown 8vo, 7s. 6d.

—— **Letters of Samuel Johnson, LL.D.** Collected and Edited by G. BIRKBECK HILL, D.C.L., LL.D. 2 vols. Medium 8vo, half-roan (uniform with Boswell's Life of Johnson), 28s.

—— **Johnsonian Miscellanies.** Arranged and Edited by G. BIRKBECK HILL, D.C.L., LL.D. 2 vols. Medium 8vo, half-roan, 28s.

MORE. The Utopia of Sir Thomas More. Edited by J. H. LUPTON, B.D. 8vo, half-bound, 10s. 6d. net.

HOMER. Homeri Opera et Reliquiae. Recensuit D. B. MONRO, A.M. Crown 8vo. On Oxford India Paper, 10s. 6d. net.

PLATO. A Selection of Passages from Plato for English Readers; from the Translation by B. JOWETT, M.A. Edited, with Introductions, by M. J. KNIGHT. 2 vols. Crown 8vo, gilt top, 12s.

VIRGIL. The Complete Works of Virgil. Edited by T. L. PAPILLON, M.A., and A. E. HAIGH, M.A. Including the Minor Works, with numerous Emendations by Professor ROBINSON ELLIS. 32mo. On Writing Paper for MS. Notes, 3s. 6d.; on Oxford India Paper, Paste grain, 5s.

PALGRAVE. The Treasury of Sacred Song. With Notes Explanatory and Biographical. By F. T. PALGRAVE, M.A. *Sixteenth Thousand.* Extra fcap. 8vo, 4s. 6d.

SELDEN. The Table Talk of John Selden. Edited, with an Introduction and Notes, by S. H. REYNOLDS, M.A. 8vo, half-roan, 8s. 6d.

STEELE. Selections from *The Tatler, Spectator,* and *Guardian.* Edited by AUSTIN DOBSON. *Second Edition.* Crown 8vo, 7s. 6d.

SWIFT. Selections from his Works. Edited, with Life, Introductions, and Notes, by Sir HENRY CRAIK, K.C.B., M.A. 2 vols. Crown 8vo, cloth extra, 15s. *Each volume may be had separately, price 7s. 6d.*

Uniform with the Virgil.

HORACE. The Complete Works of Horace. Edited by the Very Rev. E. C. WICKHAM, D.D. 32mo. On Writing Paper for MS. Notes, 3s. 6d.; on Oxford India Paper, paste grain, 5s.

DANTE. Tutte Le Opere di Dante Alighieri, nuovamente rivedute nel testo dal Dr. E. MOORE. Crown 8vo, 7s. 6d.; on Oxford India Paper, cloth extra, 9s. 6a.; and Miniature edition, 3 vols. in case, 10s. 6d.

MOLIÈRE. Les œuvres complètes de Molière. Crown 8vo, on Oxford India paper, cloth extra; and Miniature edition, 3 vols. in case. [*Shortly.*

LONDON: HENRY FROWDE,
OXFORD UNIVERSITY PRESS WAREHOUSE, AMEN CORNER, E.C.
EDINBURGH: 12 FREDERICK STREET. GLASGOW: 104 WEST GEORGE STREET.
NEW YORK: 91 & 93 FIFTH AVENUE.

www.ingramcontent.com/pod-product-compliance
Lightning Source LLC
Chambersburg PA
CBHW030743230426
43667CB00007B/817